Palgrave Studies in Oral History

Series Editors: Linda Shopes and Bruce M. Stave

The Order Has Been Carried Out: History, Memory, and Meaning of a Nazi Massacre in Rome, by Alessandro Portelli (2003)

Sticking to the Union: An Oral History of the Life and Times of Julia Ruuttila, by Sandy Polishuk (2003)

To Wear the Dust of War: From Bialystok to Shanghai to the Promised Land, an Oral History, by Samuel Iwry, edited by L. J. H. Kelley (2004)

Education as My Agenda: Gertrude Williams, Race, and the Baltimore Public Schools, by Jo Ann Robinson (2005)

Remembering: Oral History Performance, edited by Della Pollock (2005)

Postmemories of Terror: A New Generation Copes with the Legacy of the "Dirty War," by Susana Kaiser (2005)

Growing Up in the People's Republic: Conversations between Two Daughters of China's Revolution, by Ye Weili and Ma Xiaodong (2005)

Life and Death in the Delta: African American Narratives of Violence, Resilience, and Social Change, by Kim Lacy Rogers (2006)

Creating Choice: A Community Responds to the Need for Abortion and Birth Control, 1961–1973, by David P. Cline (2006)

Voices from This Long Brown Land: Oral Recollections of Owens Valley Lives and Manzanar Pasts, by Jane Wehrey (2006)

Radicals, Rhetoric, and the War: The University of Nevada in the Wake of Kent State, by Brad Lucas (2006)

The Unquiet Nisei: An Oral History of the Life of Sue Kunitomi Embrey, by Diana Meyers Bahr (2007)

Sisters in the Brotherhoods: Working Women Organizing for Equality in New York City, by Jane LaTour (2008)

Iraq's Last Jews: Stories of Daily Life, Upheaval, and Escape from Modern Babylon, edited by Tamar Morad, Dennis Shasha, and Robert Shasha (2008)

Soldiers and Citizens: An Oral History of Operation Iraqi Freedom from the Battlefield to the Pentagon, by Carl Mirra (2008)

Overcoming Katrina: African American Voices from the Crescent City and Beyond, edited by D'Ann Penner and Keith Ferdinand; Preface by Jimmy Carter (2009)

Worker Narratives of Plant Closings and Job Loss, by Tracy K'Meyer and Joy Hart (2009)

Women Survivors of the Bhopal Disaster, by Suroopa Mukherjee (2009)

Bringing Desegregation Home, by Kate Willink (2009)

Speaking History: The American Past through Oral Histories, 1865–Present, by Susan Armitage and Laurie Mercier (2009)

Stories from the Gulag, by Jehanne Gheith and Katherine Jolluck (2010)

Iraq's Last Jews

Stories of Daily Life, Upheaval, and Escape from Modern Babylon

Edited by
Tamar Morad,
Dennis Shasha,
and
Robert Shasha

IRAQ'S LAST JEWS
Copyright © Tamar Morad, Dennis Shasha, and Robert Shasha, 2008.
Softcover reprint of the hardcover 1st edition 2008 978-0-230-60810-8

All rights reserved.

First published in 2008 by
PALGRAVE MACMILLAN®
in the United States—a division of St. Martin's Press LLC,
175 Fifth Avenue, New York, NY 10010.

Where this book is distributed in the UK, Europe and the rest of the world, this is by Palgrave Macmillan, a division of Macmillan Publishers Limited, registered in England, company number 785998, of Houndmills, Basingstoke, Hampshire RG21 6XS.

Palgrave Macmillan is the global academic imprint of the above companies and has companies and representatives throughout the world.

Palgrave® and Macmillan® are registered trademarks in the United States, the United Kingdom, Europe and other countries.

ISBN 978-0-230-61800-8   ISBN 978-0-230-61623-3 (eBook)
DOI 10.1057/9780230616233

Cover by Karen Shasha ©2008. This design is a composite of several images digitally collaged together. They include an antique map of Iraq, an old image of the banks of the Tigris-Euphrates as well as a 1996 photo of the artist's father, Dr. Victor E. Shashoua, with her son, Tyler E. Shasha, both of whom are of Iraqi Jewish descent.

Library of Congress Cataloging-in-Publication Data

    Iraq's last Jews : stories of daily life, upheaval, and escape from modern Babylon / edited by Tamar Morad, Dennis Shasha, and Robert Shasha.
      p. cm.—(Palgrave studies in oral history)
    Includes bibliographical references and index.

    1. Jews—Iraq—Interviews. 2. Jews—Iraq—Social life and customs—20th century. 3. Jews—Iraq—Social conditions—20th century. 4. Jews—Cultural assimilation—Iraq. 5. Jews, Iraqi—Israel—Interviews. 6. Jews, Iraqi—United States—Interviews. 7. Iraq—Biography. I. Morad, Tamar. II. Shasha, Dennis Elliott. III. Shasha, Robert.

DS135.I713A15 2008
305.892'405670922—dc22   2008015081

A catalogue record of the book is available from the British Library.

Design by Newgen Imaging Systems (P) Ltd., Chennai, India.

First edition: November 2008

*To the members and decendants of the proud and
productive community of Iraqi Jews.
Their heritage gives them valuable support
as they contribute to the lives of their adopted nations.*

Contents

Series Editors' Foreword	ix
Foreword	xi
Preface	xiii
Acknowledgments	xv
Introduction: The Historical Context Shmuel Moreh	1
Section One: Iraq, Our Country	11
Introduction	13
Shlomo el-Kevity	14
Ezra Zilkha	25
Salim Sassoon	33
Salim Fattal	41
Oded Halahmy	49
Alfred and Hanina Shasha	57
Sami Michael	63
Section Two: An Audacious Plan	77
Introduction	79
Shlomo Hillel	80
Ilana Marcus	94
Shlomo Sehayek	100
Mordechai Ben Porat	110
Section Three: Our Country No More	125
Introduction	127
Saeed Herdoon	128
Oddil Dallall	138
Zuhair Sassoon	146
Ronit Dangour	151

Linda Masri Hakim	158
Aida Zelouf	168
Richard Obadiah	176
Section Four: On the Outside	189
Introduction	191
Eli Amir	193
Dhiaa Kasim Kashi	199
Conclusion	209
Bibliography	213
Index	217

Series Editors' Foreword

In another book in the Palgrave Studies in Oral History series, *Soldiers and Citizens*, an Assyrian Christian explains how his group in the Iraqi town of Dora was threatened with death if they didn't convert to Islam or pay a special tax or abandon their homes and leave within 24 hours. He remarked, "I heard there was talk of doing to the Christians what they did to the Jewish in the 1940s."[1] The year 1941 witnessed the Farhoud, a Nazi-inspired pogrom, which began a series of events that propelled a Jewish exodus from Iraq. Of the approximately 137,000 who resided in Iraq during the early 1940s, 124,000 had fled, most to Israel, by 1952. The relatively few left behind suffered as a result of the Six Day War in 1967 when Iraq restricted their movement, jobs, and opportunity to communicate in and outside of the country. Some suffered imprisonment and torture. Hence, the once vital and vibrant Iraqi Jewish community had all but disappeared from its homeland by the 1970s.

Oral histories have widely documented the Holocaust, but the stories recounted in this volume are less well-known and serve to expand our knowledge of Middle Eastern Jews outside of Israel. Oral history is particularly well suited to capture the drama and trials of this historical experience and to humanize the past condition of a community that exists in exile. With American attention focused upon Iraq as a consequence of two recent wars, public curiosity about that nation will benefit from these accounts.

Iraq's Last Jews joins a number of other volumes in this series that consider issues of world-historical significance. Whether it be the contemporary Iraq War or the decades-past Chinese Cultural Revolution, or any number of other topics, the series encourages the employment of oral history to investigate the memories of ordinary and extraordinary people in order to make sense of past and present.

BRUCE M. STAVE
University of Connecticut

LINDA SHOPES
Carlisle, Pennsylvania

Foreword

The American Sephardi Federation (ASF) is proud to sponsor the publication of this important book, a historic series of firsthand recollections from some of the last members of the now-vanished Babylonian Jewish community in Iraq—the oldest and longest-ever continuous community in the Jewish Diaspora. The Babylonian Jewish Diaspora was instrumental, through the writing of the Babylonian Talmud, in the development of Judaism as we know it today. Given all the important contributions of the Iraqi Jews throughout history, it is remarkable that the community is not even mentioned in conjunction with the remaking of Iraq today. These facts have not received the attention they deserve in the Jewish and general media. This book, together with the efforts of the ASF, is an attempt to rectify this.

Now the community is no more. But there are still strong bonds and organized community life within Iraqi Jewish circles in Israel, England, Canada, and the United States. Arabic and Judeo-Arabic are still spoken among the older emigrant parent generation and their delicious cuisine is preserved. But as fewer and fewer Iraqi-born Jews remain, the risk is great that these strong bonds and the knowledge of the traditions will disappear. This book is therefore an essential memory bank preserving the experience, traditions, and anecdotes in firsthand form from the last generation of Iraqi-born Jews.

As part of its effort to educate the public about the Jewish communities in the Arab world, the ASF, in 2006, announced a major new program series under the title *Historic Jewish Communities in the World of Islam* to present lectures, writings, and exhibitions and to secure records about the history, culture, and significant contributions of the old Jewish communities in the Islamic world. The first program, *Back to Babylon: 2,600 years of Jewish life in Iraq,* a four-day scholarly conference, took place in November, 2006, at the Center for Jewish History in New York. The ASF is very proud of this major new initiative in line with its mission to support all Sephardic communities and organizations in the United States, and to promote and preserve the rich spiritual, historical, cultural, and social traditions of all Sephardic communities as an integral part of Jewish heritage. This book is a vital part of these efforts.

DAVID E. R. DANGOOR
President

Note

1. Dr. Donny George Roukhanna in Carl Mirra, *Soldiers and Citizens: An Oral History of Operation Iraqi Freedom from the Battlefield to the Pentagon* (New York: Palgrave Macmillan, 2008).

Preface

Some 2,500 years after the first Jews established roots in Babylon, the once-vibrant and prosperous Jewish community of Iraq has disappeared. A community that numbered close to 140,000 in the late 1940s—and comprised fully one-third of Baghdad's population—consisted of a mere 20 when U.S. tanks rolled into the Iraqi capital in 2003. Today, fewer than ten Jews remain in Iraq.

Yet as late as the 1920s and 1930s, Iraqi Jews felt the heady potential of full equality in a secular society for the first time in their long history of subordination to Muslim rulers. From music to politics to commerce, Jews played a major role in Iraqi society and culture. For centuries after the destruction of the Second Temple in Jerusalem, Babylon was the world's epicenter of Jewish life and religion—the place where the Babylonian Talmud was written and where rabbis from across the region and Europe came to learn from the most scholarly sages. But the community dissolved in the middle of the 20th century when pro-Nazi forces, Arab nationalism, and the formation of Israel led to violence against and a general sense of insecurity among Iraqi Jews, causing them to flee, mostly over the course of about a year and a half.

This book tells the story of that last generation, people who in many cases grew up with strong patriotic feelings but were always prepared for a future beyond Iraq's borders—just in case. The storytellers of these first-person accounts vary as widely as any group of Jews does, reflecting the breadth and texture of the community: wealthy businessmen and Communists, popular musicians and reformist writers, Iraqi patriots and early Zionists. Many had close friends among the Muslims and Christians of Iraq of whom they speak warmly. They tell the tales of a people with a love for their birth country that persisted even as they were forced to leave their homes.

The story of the final decades of the Jewish community in Iraq divides into three periods. First is the period before 1939 when the Jews in Iraq saw themselves as part of the Iraqi national fiber in government, commerce, and the arts. That ended verbally with the rise of Nazi influences and violently with the Farhoud, a pogrom against the Jews, in 1941. Second is the period between then and 1953 when Arab hostility toward the new state of Israel turned most Jews into Zionists and the vast majority of the community left. The final period records an Iraq that drifted towards increasingly autocratic leadership, culminating in the sadistic dictatorship of Saddam Hussein, with the Jews often playing the role of scapegoat. Finally, the book closes with several moving retrospectives of the community.

These stories are sometimes funny, often tragic, touching, and insightful. Readers will find that the editors, in addition to recording descriptions of daily life, have also uncovered acts of heroism, adventure, and intrigue: from the undercover Israeli agents who helped orchestrate the mass emigration of Iraqi Jews to the young Jewish state at mid-century, to those who argued for the lives of their loved ones in the brutal prisons of Saddam Hussein. What has been compiled here, ultimately, is a book about quiet bravery in times of distress and a celebration of the possibility of peace.

Acknowledgments

Many people have helped us with this book. Judy Weinstein and Ariana Green conducted several interviews in addition to the interviews we did. Anat Rotem translated and transcribed the Hebrew interviews and transcribed many of the English ones as well, all with intelligence, alacrity, and precision. Elyse Seener and Pamela Giambalvo also transcribed some of the interviews. Nick Pikoulis and Gene Singer helped us greatly with the index. We are grateful also to Charles Jacobs, Jennifer Monsky, and Paula Blumenfeld-Gantz.

We would like to express our profound gratitude to Professor Shmuel Moreh of Hebrew University who wrote the introduction and suggested many important written sources to use. He possesses a deep well of knowledge about the Jews of Iraq and was ready and willing for us to draw from it whenever necessary. Likewise, Nissim Rejwan was a forthcoming source of information about the history of the community.

Mordechai Ben Porat, the director of the Babylonian Jewry Heritage Center (whose account appears in these pages), was of tremendous help in identifying interviewees, tracking them down, assisting us with basic historical facts and figures, and supplying us with photographs for the collection. Dedicated to the cause of disseminating the history of the Jews of Iraq, Ben Porat and his colleagues at the museum, most notably Einat Roth and Tami Avni-Huber, responded with care and accuracy to our numerous e-mails, phone calls, and faxes. Edwin Shuker in London put together a brilliant list of recommended interviewees in that city, and several others in Israel as well.

To be sure, this book could not have come to fruition without the willingness of dozens of Iraqi Jews to sit down and tell their stories patiently and in a forthcoming way—and then spend many additional hours with us via phone and e-mail editing their accounts for smoothness and cohesion. That gratitude applies not only to the 20 subjects who appear in the collection but also the 44 others in the United States, Canada, England, and Israel whose stories—all of them wonderful and often emotive—we were forced to omit due to lack of space.

Those storytellers include Mayer Attar, Carole Basri, Yvonne Cohen, Yair Dallal, Doreen Dangoor, Jack Dunnous, Nabil Fattal, Abraham Gabbay, Shoua Gigi, Herzl and Balfour Hakak, Benjamin Hayeem, Abraham Halima, Elias Hawa, Latif Hoory, Moshe Kahtan, Jamil Khazoom, Yeheskel Kojaman, David Khalastchy,

Eileen Khalastchy, David Lavipour, Susan Lawi and her father Saleh Masri, Yigal Loshi, Edmund Masri, Sara Menasseh, Linda Menuhin, Raya and Violet Moalem, Aziza Mowlem, Victor Moche, Meir Murad, Albert Nissim, Yitzhak Saieg, Sammy Salem, Sammy Samuels, Isaac Sassoon, David Shohet, Maurice Shohet, Joyce Sopher, Sasson Somekh, Sami Sourani, Aodi Zilkha, and Maurice Zilkha.

And finally, we owe great thanks to our editor at Palgrave, Christopher Chappell, who worked tirelessly with us to make this book happen. He believed in our project from the very start, thus providing us with invaluable moral support. Erin Ivy at Palgrave and the production staff at Newgen Imaging Systems did a tremendous job copyediting and packaging the book.

Introduction: The Historical Context

Shmuel Moreh

Over its 2,500 years of existence, the Iraqi Jewish community formed a homogeneous group and was able to maintain communal identity, culture, and traditions throughout the centuries—all despite multiple conquests and political upheaval, war, and plagues. They were distinguished from their Iraqi brethren by their old Arabic dialect, Judeo-Arabic, which is replete with biblical Hebrew, biblical references, and words from Persian, Turkish, and Aramaic. They were set apart by their dress, their observation of Shabbat, holy days, and Kashrut, their unique cuisine, and, among many other things, a deep yearning for their spiritual Jerusalem and Zion. They purchased land and established yeshivot, religious houses of study, in Jerusalem and Hebron. Their social and religious life was based upon Talmudic and biblical rites, and they led an independent communal life headed by the Chief Rabbi (Hakham Bashi), who oversaw the community's educational system, religious court, and tax imposed upon Kosher meat.[1]

At the same time, they were well-integrated into the country in all aspects—politically, socially, and economically—and thoroughly Arabized in that their language, social traditions, and ways of life that were in many ways indistinguishable from those of their Arab compatriots.

For this reason, the disappearance of the Jewish community of Iraq is a particularly compelling story, and is distinguished from the Jewish exodus from other Arab lands by its precipitous nature.[2] The exodus also offers us a unique opportunity to understand the many political forces sweeping the Middle East in the twentieth century, including colonialism, Nazism, Arab nationalism, Communism, and Zionism, the history of all of which led to the disappearance of the Iraqi Jewish community.

Iraq, as it is called today, was the home of the ancient civilizations of Sumer, Assyria, and Babylonia. It was known by the Greeks as Mesopotamia—meaning, "the land between two rivers," the Tigris and Euphrates—and by the Jews as Babylonia. In 597 BC, Nebuchadnezzar II, King of Babylonia (605–562 BC) invaded the Kingdom of Judah and brought back its Jewish king, Jehoiachin, with 10,000 of his subjects to Babylon. Eleven years later, after Nebuchadnezzar's destruction of the First Temple, he brought forty thousand Jewish captives to his capital in Babylon, ninety kilometers south of modern-day Baghdad.[3] The Jewish captivity ended when the Persian King Cyrus II occupied Babylon in 538 BC and allowed the Jews to return back to their land. Some returned, but many stayed.[4]

Following the destruction of the Second Temple by the Romans in 70 CE, waves of exiled Jews traveled west and were assimilated among other tribes and nations. The Babylonian Jews—and those who migrated east from Eretz Yisrael—became the keepers of the Bible. Jewish culture flourished in Babylonia during the Persian regime (331–638). Jewish scholars compiled the Babylonian Talmud starting in 474 as the spiritual codex of Judaism, transforming Judaism into a spiritual and moral movement. Starting in the year 219, the academies of Sura and Nehardea were founded in Babylon. The heads of these academies were referred to later on as "Gaons" and were considered the highest authorities on religious matters in the Jewish world.[5]

In 570, Muhammad was born in Mecca and later on he emigrated in 622 to Medina, where Jews were active in commerce and industry. Shortly thereafter, Muslim armies conquered the regional armies and defeated the Persian Empire. The building of Baghdad during the Caliphate of al-Mansur in 762 established the most important center of culture, commerce, science, and arts in the western world. The Jews settled there, built new yeshivas, and attained important status, especially the Jewish Exilarch who was widely recognized as the descendant of King David and was the faith's highest authority.[6] The Exhilarch administered Jewish affairs for the community, deciding disputes and collecting taxes, and could impose bans, fines, imprisonment or flogging for punishment on religious matters.[7]

After the destruction of Baghdad by the Mongols in 1258, centuries of chaos followed. As late as the beginning of the sixteenth century, the conflicts between the Sunni Ottomans and the Shi'i Safawis of Persia, in addition to repeated plagues, floods, and Bedouin invasions, devastated Iraq. Baghdad was diminished to the point that it became a marginal settlement of no political or commercial importance.[8]

The Ottoman rule (1534–1917) brought recovery and a degree of tolerance. Jews enjoyed relative freedom of religion, administrating their own affairs, especially in education. The Jews appointed a Nasi [prince] as their head, following the end of the institution of the Exilarch in 1401, by which time the heads of the yeshivot, or academies, wielded greater religious power. The Ottoman Sultan Murad IV was reputed to have had 10,000 Jewish officers in his government. During this time, wealthy Jewish men such as Heskel Ben Yusuf Gabbay in Baghdad and Istanbul and Sassoon Saleh

David in Baghdad served as treasurers for the Ottoman rulers.[9] Tolerance depended on local rulers. For example, Sultan's governor in Baghdad, Daoud Pasha (1817–1831), was considered one of the cruelest to the Jews and many Jews left the city during his rule. The Jewish population also declined after epidemics of cholera and typhoid.

After Pasha's death, the Jews began to build up influence in commerce and government. The position of Nasi was replaced by the Hakham Bashi in 1849. The prominent chief rabbis of the twentieth century were Hakham Ezra Dangoor, who had been the first rabbi of Burma and began one of the first printing presses in Iraq, and Hakham Sasson Khedouri.[10] The chief rabbi was also president of the community and was assisted by a lay council, a religious court, and a schools committee.[11]

The revolution of the Young Turks in 1908 adopted the slogan of *hurriya, 'adala, and musawat* (freedom, justice, and equality). Liberal Arab writers and politicians supported these principles. The common people, however, rejected those concepts as infringing upon the sovereignty of Islam and the benefits of the *dhimmi*—a status to which Christians and Jews had to conform in exchange for protection of their lives and property. *Dhimmi* status forbade Christians and Jews from testifying against Muslims, riding horses, owning a home whose building height was greater than those of Muslims, holding high office over Muslims, bearing arms, or drinking wine in public, and during the rule of strict and fanatic rulers they were required to wear a special emblem on their clothes—blue for Christians and yellow for Jews. The *dhimma* also entailed a special tax that, in some communities, constituted the majority of the tax revenue.[12]

In the nineteenth century, new opportunities for Jews in international commerce, banking, and administration arose as a result of a handful of important events: the establishment of the Alliance Israelite Universelle school in 1864, one in a network of Alliance schools across the Middle East after their founding in Paris in 1860; the opening of the Suez Canal in 1869; the reforms of Midhat Pasha who was appointed a *wali* (governor) of Baghdad and Basra; the atmosphere of physical safety that prevailed in Iraq after Midhat Pasha defeated a Bedouin uprising and made it practical for the Jews to settle in cities in southern Iraq; the construction of the first railways in Iraq in 1903; and the declaration of equal rights for non-Muslim minorities in the Ottoman Constitution of 1908. Jews flourished financially and socially, and many left for India, China, and England to engage in international trade, as the Suez Canal and railroads facilitated trade across the vast British Empire.[13] Among those adventurers were Sir Elie Kadoorie (1865–1944), who went to Shanghai, and Sir Albert David Sassoon (1818–1896), who settled in India. Both established Jewish schools in Baghdad to help educate the wider Jewish population, and they were highly philanthropic in the countries in which they settled. Thousands of other Iraqi Jews followed them to their new outposts, and, as a result, prosperous Iraqi Jewish trading communities developed across Asia, from Calcutta and Bombay to Rangoon, Shanghai, and Kobe, Japan.[14]

The British alliance in 1916 with Sharif Hussein of Mecca and his Arab nationalist sons Faisal (1885–1933) and 'Abd Al-'Allah (1882–1951), against the Ottomans resulted in the creation of Iraq as a state following World War I. When the British entered Baghdad in 1917, Jews were the largest single group in the city's population, about 80,000 out of a total population of 202,000, or about one-third.[15] In 1921 Iraq was placed under the British mandate. Iraqis immediately revolted against their new occupiers so the British allowed them to form a self-governing kingdom under British advisory administration. After the expulsion of King Faisal bin Hussein from Damascus in 1920 by the French, a Jewish former member of the Ottoman Parliament, Sir Sassoon Hezkel, joined the Cairo Conference on the Middle East, headed by Winston Churchill. Hezkel backed the recommendation of crowning Faisal King of Iraq. As an acknowledgment of his abilities and loyalty, Heskel was appointed minister of finance in the first Iraqi government of King Faisal I, where he served for five years and continued to serve the country as a member of parliament until his death in 1932. Heskel greatly benefited the Iraqi economy by insisting on payment in gold rather than banknotes for Iraqi petrol in negotiations with the British Petroleum Company.[16] Faisal, who was educated in Istanbul and was influenced by the Young Turks' liberal ideology, genuinely seemed to believe in religious equality, even coining the dictum: "Religion is for God, the Fatherland is for everyone,"[17] giving priority to patriotism over Pan-Arab and Pan-Islamic sentiments.

The 1920s and 1930s were considered a golden age for the Jews of Iraq, thanks in large part to the modernizing influence of the British and Faisal's friendly policies.[18] In 1919, he signed the Faisal-Weizmann agreement, declaring sympathy for the national aspirations of the Jews to create a homeland in Palestine. In that decade, Iraq was a small country of less than three and a half million (compared to 25 million today).[19] Two-thirds of the Jews lived in Baghdad; Basra had the second-largest concentration of Jews in the country and there were also Jewish communities in Mosul in the north, Kirkuk, Arbil, Sulaymaniyah, Khanaqin, Ba'qubah, Al Kut, Al Amarah, Al Hllah, and An Nasiriyah.[20] In this period, many Jews felt secure in Iraq and actively participated in the country's development.[21]

They built social clubs where they met often to listen to music, talk, and play cards, including in places such as the Laura Kadoorie Club, the Zawra' Club, and the Rashid.[22] Meir Elias founded the Meir Elias Jewish Hospital in 1910 and Sir Elie Kadoorie founded the Rimah Kadoorie Hospital for ophthalmology, named for his mother.[23] They contributed to the political system as representatives of parliament and as civil servants, to education and culture as writers and journalists and musicians, and to the commercial, industrial, and financial prosperity of the country as merchants and government officials. The most prominent Jews had good relations with the monarchy; for instance, when Sir Elie Kadoorie visited Baghdad from Shanghai, he was received by Faisal I, and when Faisal I visited London, he was a guest at Kadoorie's mansion. The community built dozens of schools with high educational standards and an emphasis on foreign language, many of which were attended by Muslim and Christian pupils, though the majority of students were Jewish.[24] Half of the Iraqi students who received government scholarships to study abroad were Jewish.[25]

But the Jews' command of European languages and their international outlook also caused the Iraqi populace to identify them with Britain and France, the European occupying powers in the region.[26] And even during this peaceful period, other Iraqis decried the Jews' apparent control of the economy, generally superior social status, and the fact that they were disproportionately represented in government offices.[27]

In 1930, the Anglo-Iraqi Treaty between the UK and British-controlled Iraq set out the basic terms of Iraq's nominal independence two years later at the termination of the British mandate and paved the way for Iraq's admittance to the League of Nations in 1932.[28] When Iraq gained its independence that year, many Iraqi ex-Ottoman officers considered the establishment of an Iraqi state a first step to a larger Pan-Arab state promised to the Hashemite dynasty for joining the British against the Ottomans during World War I. In addition, many Iraqi nationalists sought to restore the Caliphate to Arabs. Together, these groups formed an obstacle to a Western, secular political world order in Iraq and opposed any non-Arab or non-Muslim religious or ethnic activities.[29]

The secularists held the upper hand as long as Faisal I was king. Among them was the former military attaché to the Ottomans, the Jewish journalist and MP Salman Shinah who established the first Jewish magazine published in literary Arabic, *Al-Misbah-Ha 'Menorah* (The Lamp as a symbol of the Jewish people) (1924–1927), which had a strong Zionist orientation. Its co-editor, Anwar Shaul, also published the weekly magazine *Al-Hasid* (The Harvestman), between 1928 and 1939. Although Shinah became one of the defenders of Iraqi patriotism and Pan-Arab policy, his magazine was closed on the eve of World War II under pressure from Iraqi and Palestinian pro-Nazi nationalists.[30]

Many of these Jewish writers joined forces with liberal and leftist groups and wrote patriotic poems and short stories in praise of Iraq and in support of social and cultural reforms such as the liberation of women and inter-religious harmony. The Jewish headmaster of Mesouda Shemtob primary school, Shaul Haddad published the journal *Al-Burhan* (The Proof) to defend the Jewish minority against escalating Nazi activities. The poet Abraham Obadia wrote in praise of the Iraqi royal family. The economist Meir Basri, who joined the Iraqi Foreign Office, published articles on the Iraqi economy as well as poems and short stories on Iraq's social problems. Both Basri and the Jewish writer Ya'qub Balbul (Lev) edited the magazine *Al-Tijara* (The Commerce) (successively, 1938–1945, 1945–1951), published by the Chamber of Commerce in Baghdad.[31]

The Jews' success at unifying religious Zionism and Iraqi patriotism ended with the death of King Faisal I in 1933. The Iraqi government began to employ Sunni Palestinian teachers who had taken refuge in Iraq since the riots of 1929 in

Palestine and the massacre of the Jews of Hebron, and then after the revolt of 1936 in Palestine. Iraqi and Palestinian nationalists increased their pro-Nazi activities, forming the quasi-military organization Al-Futuwwa and the nationalist Al-Muthanna Club that incited violence against Jews.[32]

The resulting anti-Jewish, Pan-Arabic sentiment put an end to the government's tolerance of Jewish preeminence in commerce and influence in the political sphere, but especially of Zionist activities. Hebrew language lessons at Jewish schools were abolished in 1936 and quotas were imposed on Jews in institutions of higher learning. Jewish teachers from Palestine were expelled.[33]

Palestinian leaders were given hospitality, support, and the freedom of political activity in Iraq. They included the Mufti of Jerusalem, Hajj Amin al-Husayni, who had been expelled from Jerusalem by the British; Jamal al-Husayni, head of the Arab Party; Abd al-Qadir al-Husayni, a Nazi supporter who studied in Germany; Musa al-'Alami (1897–1984) who because of his involvement with the Arab rebellion, was dismissed from his position of the Palestine Government Advocate; and the Palestinian nationalist activist and poet Buhan al Din Al-Abbushi, who called for the people and the government of Iraq to expel or massacre the Iraq's Jews.[34]

The activities of these Palestinian nationalists and of Dr. Fritz Grobba, Germany's consul in Baghdad, led to the establishment of the pro-Nazi government headed by Rashid 'Aali al-Gilani in April, 1941. At the encouragement of the Mufti of Jerusalem and his entourage, Gilani instigated war with the British. The war was short. The British reoccupied Iraq to protect the flow of oil to the allies and out of fear of a broader German invasion to the Middle and Far East. The British victory over the Iraqi army at the end of May, 1941, created a brief vacuum of leadership and security in Iraq that led to the pogrom against the Jews of Baghdad known as the Farhoud (June 1–2, 1941) in which 130 Jews in Baghdad and 9 Jews outside Baghdad were killed and some 2,500 injured. During the Farhoud, the British army was camped outside Baghdad, abstaining from interfering under the pretext that the violence was an internal matter. Jews' houses and shops were looted, women and children were raped, and others were kidnapped and brutally killed. The Palestinians took active part in the incitements against the Jews.[35]

The Farhoud was a pivotal event in the history of the Jews in Iraq. It divided the Jewish community into three factions. First was the patriotic faction, which consisted of intellectuals, professionals, and wealthy merchants. They believed that their future lay in Iraq as loyal citizens. Their intellectual leaders included Anwar Shaul, Meir Basri, and Dr. Salman Darwish. Second were the Jewish Communists. They were convinced that the only solution to the problems faced by minorities in Iraq was a Communist revolution, which would bring freedom and equality to all. This group was well organized and enjoyed solidarity with and the appreciation of much of the Muslim Shiite majority and various ethnic and religious minorities throughout Iraq. Among their intellectual leaders were Yusuf Zilkha, Masroor Qatan, Yehezkel Kojman, Eliahir Hourie Sami Michael and Shimon Balas. Last were the Zionists. Some of them, as reported in the narratives of Mordechai Ben Porat and Shlomo Hillel, already had relatives in the Holy Land at the time and were convinced that the only solution for the Jewish minority was the establishment of a national home in Eretz Yisrael [the biblical land of Israel] where they could live in security and equality.

After the establishment of the State of Israel in 1948, and especially after the humiliating defeat of the Arab armies, Arab nationalists in Iraq (and throughout the region) came to identify Jews with Zionism.[36] In July, two months after the outbreak of the War of Independence, Zionist affiliation was made a criminal offense in Iraq.[37] Later that year came the hanging of Shafiq 'Adas, a wealthy Jewish merchant from Basra accused of selling arms to the Zionists in Palestine. The event was another pivotal one for the community, as many Jews viewed his brutal death as a sign that the Jews had no future in Iraq. The government issued edicts removing Jews from many aspects of public life, cancelled the operating licenses of Jewish bankers, forced wealthy Jews to subsidize the Iraqi war effort in Palestine, and imposed restrictions on travel and the buying or selling of property.[38] For Jews, the Farhoud, the ongoing daily assaults and persecutions against them, and 'Adas' stunning murder gave rise to the spread of the Zionist underground movement in Iraq and its attempts to help Iraqi Jews escape to Israel as discussed in the narrative of Shlomo Sehayek.

In the 1940s, Jews began escaping from Iraq, first in small numbers via Syria and Lebanon to Palestine, then in large and growing numbers to Iran at the end of the decade, aided by Zionist emissaries who soon set their sights on transferring increasingly large numbers of Iraqi Jews to Israel. Frustrated and embarrassed by the illegal escapes, the Iraqi government issued the Citizenship Revocation Law in March, 1950, enabling Jews to revoke their citizenship and leave the country legally and permanently.[39] Virtually the entire Jewish community of some 140,000[40] (most of whom lived in Baghdad) on the eve of the exodus later named Operation Ezra and Nehemiah registered for this right, among them nearly all of Iraq's 20,000 Kurdish Jews, who lived in the north and were mostly poor, uneducated rural farmers.[41] After the registration process, the government enacted a second law in 1951 in which the properties of those who renounced their Iraqi nationality to leave Iraq had their assets frozen, rendering them penniless refugees in Israel. Most other Arab countries followed suit and expelled or persecuted their Jewish citizens.[42]

By the end of the period of the mass exodus, only about 6,000 Jews remained in Iraq. Those who stayed behind in those years—in many cases, wealthy Jews or those with great stature in Iraqi society—initially prospered once again, especially between 1958 and 1963, under the liberal government of Abd al-Karim Qassem (1914–1963), which overthrew the royal family, executing many of them including the young king Faisal II and the Crown Prince Abd al-Ilah.[43]

During Qassem's 1958 coup, Jews were falsely charged with having committed arson to petrol tanks on the outskirts of Russafa in Baghdad and anti-Semitic elements seeking revenge destroyed the Laura Kadoorie School for Girls, then occupied by Palestinian refugees. But life returned to normal for Jews about two months after the coup, and Qassem gave complete freedom and equal rights to the Jews throughout his regime.[44] In 1961, however, he destroyed the Jewish cemetery in Baghdad to make room to build a tower in imitation of 'Abdul-Nasir's tower in Cairo.[45]

After Qassem's overthrow in 1963 by the Baath Party under Hasan al-Bakr (1914?–1982) the Jewish community began to suffer again. Al-Bakr's coup lasted 10 months, until the government of Abd al-Salam 'Aref (1920–1966) took over. Aref confiscated the remainder of the Jewish cemetery, denied Jews passports, and enacted a series of other discriminatory measures against Jews including exclusion from colleges and stripping any Jew of his or her citizenship if he or she were out of the country for more than three months. After his death in 1966—when his helicopter exploded in an apparent assassination efforts of political opponents—Abd al-Salam 'Aref's brother, 'Abd al-Rahman 'Aref (1963–1968), took over but the conditions of the Jews remained similar to those during his brother's reign.[46]

In 1968, a year after the defeat of the Arab armies by Israel in the Six Day War of June, 1967, the Ba'ath Party came into power again under al-Bakr. Backlash from the war, and the brutal regime led by al-Bakr but largely controlled by his nephew, Saddam Hussein (1937–2006), led to what became the last chapter in the history of the Iraqi Jewish community. At the end of the Six Day War, only about 3,350 Jews remained in Iraq—but that number diminished to just a few hundred Jews by the middle of the 1970s.[47] In 1969, the regime, humiliated and frustrated by the Arab defeat in the Six Day War with Israel, terrorized the community with a wave of arrests and hangings of innocent Jews, most notably the January 27 hanging of nine Jews whose bodies were showcased in Baghdad's central square. Jews were thrown out of public and private sector jobs, intermittently denied passports, suffered restrictions on travel inside Iraq, had their bank accounts frozen and business licenses revoked, and had their telephone lines disconnected, among other discriminatory measures. Many Jews escaped between 1970 and 1973 with the help of Kurdish smugglers in northern Iraq. By the middle of the decade, the community was virtually extinguished, ending 2,500 years of Jewish Babylonian exile.[48] As this book is being written, fewer than a dozen Jews associated with the community live in Iraq today, mostly the elderly.[49]

Debate continues to this day about the reasons for the demise of Iraq's Jewish community. Burgeoning anti-Semitism, the result of the Nazi influence in the 1930s and 1940s, however, is only a partial explanation for the impetus behind the emigration of 1950–1952. Others put more emphasis on Arab nationalism and the creation of the State of Israel as the impetus for the upheaval; yet others emphasize the work of Zionist activists and emissaries from Israel. This version is popular in the Arab world.

What story do the interviews in this collection tell? Even for the well-off, Jews within Iraq were second-class citizens, evidenced in many ways, starting with the pole tax they were forced to pay as *dhimma* during the Ottoman regime (when Zionism was a negligible issue) to the common need among Jews to bribe officials and police in order to conduct business and get on with daily life, to assure the protection of their neighbors or influential officials, and to intermittent restrictions on travel and commerce. For the Jews, escaping to a Western country or to Israel would mean they could breathe freely. The Farhoud put this all in sharp focus: being a second-class citizen might be tolerable, but being the target of arbitrary physical violence was not. Other Jews were pulled by the Zionist dream of a country where they could live freely. For many, Israel and the West offered a chance for prosperity, at least for their children.

Notes

1. Ben-Jacob, *The Jewish Annual Cycle in Babylon*; Rejwan, pp. 185–224, Kazzaz, pp. 245–258; Twena.
2. Moreh and Yehuda, pp. 7–11.
3. Speiser; Roth; Raphael, pp. 15–39; Rejwan, pp. 3–16.
4. Raphael, p. 26; Rejwan, pp. 11–16.
5. Goitein, pp. 19–45; Rejwan, pp. 94–109, 140–103, 151–152.
6. Goitein, pp. 33–45; Rejwan, pp. 85–103; Stillman, *Jews of Arab Lands* and *Jews of Arab Lands in Modern Times*.
7. Benjamin of Tudela, pp. 131–139, 196–205; cf. Adler, pp. 39–42.
8. Ben-Jacob, *A History of the Jews*; Goitein, 120–124.
9. Ben-Jacob, *A History of the Jews*, pp. Quf-Quf-Het (100–108); cf. Rejwan, pp. 166–168.
10. On E. Dangoor, see Twena, pp. 22–24; Ben-Jacob, *A History of the Jews*, pp. 172–174.; cf. Rejwan, pp. 166–168; Moreh and Kazzaz from *A Leader and His Community* by Sassoon; Bekhor, p. 76.
11. Saadoun, pp. 50–76.
12. Bat Ye'or, *Dhimmi, Jews and Christians under Islam* and *Islam and Dhimmitude, Where Civilizations Collide*; Rejwan, pp. 85–93; Stillman, *Jew of Arab Lands*, pp. 157–162.
13. Ben-Jacob, *Babylonian Jewry in Diaspora*; Rejwan, pp. 26, 182–184.
14. Elias and Cooper; Kranzler; Ben-Jacob, *Babylonian Jewry in Diaspora*; Cernea.
15. Rejwan, pp. 210–216; Saadoun, pp. 31–38; Eppel, pp. 27–32. The best biography of Sassoon Hezkel is written by Meir Basri, Vol. 1, pp. 28–37.
16. Rejwan, pp. 215–216.
17. Basri, *Eminent Jewish Men of Modern Iraq*, Vol. 2, p. 9.
18. Kazzaz; Shiblak, p. 50.
19. Saadoun, pp. 31–38; Longrigg, pp. 1–27.
20. Kazzaz, pp. 29–32.
21. Rejwan, pp. 214–215.
22. Yosef Meir, *Socio-Cultural Development*, pp. 232, 314, 332.
23. Longrigg, pp. 53, 170, 391; Darwish, pp. 49, 199; Yosef Meir, *Socio-Cultural Development*, pp. 6–8, 81–82; Bekhor, p. 20 and 62.

24. Y. Meir, *Socio-Cultural Development*, pp. 105–253; Bekhor, pp. 37–60.
25. Shiblak, p. 42.
26. Moreh in *Zion & Zionism* by Misgav Yerushalayim, pp. 419–441.
27. Rejwan, p. 214.
28. Louis, p. 322.
29. Darwish, pp. 100–107.
30. Moreh in *Zion and Zionism* by *Misgav Yerushalaim*, pp. 419–441; Moreh in *Misgav Yerushalayim Studies in Jewish Literature*, pp. 143–151; Kazzaz, pp. 149–157; Moreh, *Arabic Works by Jewish Writers*, p. 103.
31. Dabby-Joury, pp. iv–vi; Moreh in *Ya'acov Lev (Balbul): The First Ember & A Mind's Plight*, pp. 9–16 (Hebrew), pp. 17–21 (Arabic).
32. Rejwan, pp. 217–224; Kazzaz, pp. 217–221.
33. Cohen; Moreh and Yehuda, pp. 189–210.
34. On these Palestinians activists, see Shimoni, *Biographical Dictionary of the Middle East* and *Political Dictionary of the Arab World*; Moreh in *Zion and Zionism* by Misgav Yerushalaim.
35. According to a recent list of names prepared by Dr. Zvi Yehuda and read during a ceremony in memory of the Farhoud on June 4, 2007, at the Babylonian Jewry Heritage Center in Or-Yehuda. Cf. also note 29 above. See also Kazzaz, pp. 206–209.
36. Kazzaz, pp. 270–286; Esther Meir, pp. 1–8; Moreh and Yehuda, pp. 187–193.
37. Shiblak, p. 24.
38. Cohen; Kadoorie; Kazzaz, pp. 275–293, see especially pp. 287–293.
39. Hillel.
40. Figure from Babylonian Jewry Heritage Center.
41. Raphael, pp. 226–227; According to the Babylonian Jewry Heritage Center, 95 percent of the 20,000 Jewish Kurds in Iraq immigrated to Israel during Operation Ezra and Nehemiah.
42. Gilbert, *Jews from Arab Countries*, pp. 1–15.
43. Kazzaz, pp. 15–21. A description of Princess Badi'a, an eye-witness of the massacre, see Al-Sheakh-Ali, pp. 307–347.
44. Shaul, pp. 291–293, Darwish, p. 90.
45. Sassoon, pp. 307–309; Babylonian Jewry Heritage Center.
46. Kazzaz, pp. 20–22; Bekhor, pp. 141–142.
47. Kazzaz, p. 183.
48. Ibid.; Carole Basri; interviews conducted for this book.
49. Babylonian Jewry Heritage Center.

SECTION ONE

Iraq, Our Country

Introduction

We begin this book with oral accounts from Jews who recall the final days of the Ottoman Empire in Iraq—then Mesopotamia—and the start of the British mandate in the newly formed Iraq. They mostly describe daily life during those relatively calm times for the Jewish community and Iraq at large.

We start with the account of Shlomo el-Kevity, whose father was one of Iraq's all-time most popular musicians. His story as well as that of the husband and wife duo of Alfred and Hanina Shasha describe what is commonly referred to as the "golden age" of Iraq's Jews—the 1920s and 1930s. The way of life of the most prosperous is exemplified in the account of Ezra Zilkha, who gives us a taste of Old World business conducted in the Middle East in his description of his father's banking mini-empire that originated in Baghdad at the turn of the century.

Salim Sassoon takes us back a few years with a jarring portrait of a backwater country that the Ottoman Empire left behind when it ceded the territory to the British, and an Iraq that fails to catch up with modernity even during its period under the British mandate. Artist Oded Halahmy, by contrast, recalls sweet, rich memories of his youth a few decades later, bringing to life the tastes, smells, and sights of the Baghdad he recalls fondly to this day.

The relative tranquility of the 1920s and early 1930s ended with King Faisal's death and his son Ghazi's rise to the throne that year, 1933, which coincided with the rise to power of Nazism in Germany. Ghazi's pro-Nazi stance enabled the infusion of Nazism into Iraq, and many minorities in Iraq felt the effect, particularly Jews. When World War II began, Iraqi Jews could be forgiven to believe the war was a faraway problem. Sure, German agents had linked anticolonial feeling with anti-Semitism, but the community had known such experiences before. So, when a pro-Nazi, anti-British government took over in 1941, the Jewish community knew well enough not to make waves. The British then woke up to the fact that the Germans filled the vacuum that was created as a result of their departure nine years earlier, and they especially didn't like the idea that Iraqi oil would begin flowing to the Nazis. Iraqi forces attacked British outposts in Baghdad, and the British retaliated by attacking Iraqi positions, beginning the Anglo-Iraqi War in May, 1941. The Iraqi forces were soon defeated and the pro-Nazi leadership left—but not before it vented its frustration. The army couldn't fight successfully against the British, but they could take on unarmed Jews. So in the vacuum of governance on June 1 and 2, that's what they did, often joined by ordinary civilians whipped into a frenzy of random violence. Jewish families barricaded themselves inside their homes and hoped for the best as they waited to see whether their Muslim neighbors would protect them or join the rioting mobs.

The pogrom on those two days known as the Farhoud became a major turning point for the Jews of Iraq. As they buried their dead (those they could find) and tended the thousands who were wounded, the Jews of Iraq began searching for alternatives: for many middle- and upper-class Jews, the solution became Zionism, the creation of a new Eretz Yisrael to which they could move. Until then, the Iraqi Jews had had an altogether different conception of Zionism—as a religious yearning for the restoration of Israel—than the European Jews, for whom Zionism was a secular concept that they were prepared to actualize through political acts. For others, including many of Iraq's poorer Jews, the solution was Communism—changing Iraq from within. In their accounts, filmmaker and writer Salim Fattal and novelist Sami Michael remind us of this all-but-forgotten narrative. Jailed, persecuted, and tortured, the Jewish Communists finally resigned to the hopelessness of creating a utopian Iraq and set off for Palestine.

* * *

Shlomo el-Kevity is the son of Salah el-Kuwaity who with his partner and brother Daoud, comprised the "Kuwaity Brothers," perhaps the most popular music troupe in Iraq and known throughout the Arab world. The Kuwaity Brothers enjoyed their greatest popularity in the 1920s, 1930s, and 1940s, but their songs are popular still today, particularly in Iraq and Kuwait. Born in Kuwait to an Iraqi family from Basra, the family moved back to Iraq after the duo achieved early fame. Shlomo, who was born and grew up in Israel (and Hebracized his last name) describes the Kuwaity Brothers' passion for and innovations to Iraqi maqam music,[1] and how they were courted by emirs and kings who gave them gifts and invited them to their palaces. Their story also has a political side: when they left for Israel in 1950, their music continued to be taught and played but without attribution. Only recently are their identities gradually being rediscovered in the Arab world.

My father was a composer and violin player, my uncle a singer and oud player [a classic Iraqi instrument that is similar to a guitar]. But above all else, my father was an innovator. He took the existing *maqam* music and gave the traditional songs that everyone knew another dimension, a fresh style. And the audience loved it.

In the Arab countries, there were only two musicians who did that—my father in Iraq and Mohammed Abdul Wahab, one of the most famous musicians in Egypt. They were two composers who created new songs out of music that had been frozen in time for 200 or 300 years. The *maqam* is a kind of musical singing, and the singers are called *kari*, which came from the Hebrew verb, *li'kroh*, to read. *Maqam* has lyrics that follow a story line and a very sharp, clear pattern that must be maintained. Until these men came along, nobody ever tried to change or renew the *maqam* songs, of which there are 52, and there were great musicians who played *maqam* beautifully but they never broke outside these existing boundaries.

Of course you cannot come to a nation that is used to hearing *maqam* for hundreds of years and suddenly play the tango. No one would get that. One of my father's great successes was that he introduced small changes a little bit at a time, and his changes took place over the course of 20 years. He did this in addition to composing over 1,200 entirely original songs. The music played and composed until today in Iraq imitates the musical patterns my father created.

At a concert, the *maqam* singer used to sing and my father led the orchestra. What Abdul Wahab did in Egypt and what Salah did in Iraq was to tell the singer: the orchestra will lead you, not the other way around—which is how it used to be. As a result of that innovation, today in Iraq and in other Arab countries the singer follows the orchestra. Essentially, they adopted a Western approach. My father was very familiar with Western music and got this idea from it. He also introduced Western instruments into the Iraqi music: the cello, accordion, and violin.

Salah was born in 1908 and Daoud in 1910, in Kuwait, to the Arzouni family. Their names became el-Kuwaity [from Kuwait] only after they left Kuwait for Iraq. They were the only boys in the family and they had nine sisters. Their father told them: "You can get married only after all of your sisters get married, because I have to pay out nine dowries." He needed his sons to help him financially until the girls were out of the house. So the brothers married late in life. My father married at the age of 36, and my mother, who was his cousin, was 16.

When Salah and Daoud were children, their uncle—my mother's father—who was a merchant, brought them an oud and a violin from India, and as children they started listening to records from Hijaz [in Saudi Arabia], Yemen, and Egypt. They loved listening to this music and played it by ear themselves, without notes—there wasn't such a thing as notes then. When their father saw that they were enjoying themselves and played well, he sent them to a Muslim music teacher. They learned quickly and were very successful. Their great talent as young children was obvious. By the age of 10 they began performing at weddings and before sheikhs in Kuwait, together with their teacher. They became very famous in Kuwait as wonder children and they were invited to play concerts and *haflot* [smaller performances]. There were no concert halls. Instead, they played in people's homes. For instance, a sheikh would get married and pay my father and uncle to perform at the wedding in the sheikh's palace.

The family was originally from Basra. At some point, my grandfather, who was a fabric merchant, went to Kuwait to trade and had his children there. There were only 40 Jewish families in Kuwait at the time, all of whom were involved in commerce. Today there is no community to speak of—only Jews who are stationed there as diplomats or American Army personnel, of course.

At some point the brothers began making records. A record company called Baidaphone, from Basra, came to Kuwait and made records of the two. But in 1928 the company stopped coming to Kuwait, so the brothers had to travel to Basra frequently to make records. And then someone who owned a club in Basra heard them perform and asked them to perform in his club. One of the greatest Iraqi *maqam* singers, Mohammed al Gubanji, also came to perform there. The owner told Al Gubanji, "Listen, you no longer have to bring musicians from Baghdad to accompany you. I have two musicians here who can perform with you." Al Gubanji listened to my father and his brother and he really enjoyed himself. And then he decided he wanted to work only with them. The Basra club owner told the brothers, "I don't want you to return to Kuwait. Bring your family to Basra. I'll take care of housing for them." So the entire family moved back to Basra.

When the emir of Kuwait heard that the family was leaving the country, he offered them Kuwaiti passports—which they didn't have, as Jews—in order to persuade them to stay. Even after the family left, the Kuwaiti people continued to admire Salah and Daoud not only because of the music—there were almost no other musicians in Kuwait at the time—but also because the brothers began using the name el-Kuwaity. For the Kuwaiti people it was an honor to be associated with the family.

The brothers performed in Basra for nearly two years with al Gubanji and other singers who came from Baghdad, and on their own. At the end of 1929, the family decided to move to Baghdad because it was more cosmopolitan and was a center of music in the region. The new environment in Baghdad suited them and in the first week alone, my father composed 10 songs. They began working in a famous nightclub where a Jewish singer named Salima Pasha Murad performed frequently. She was very enthusiastic about Salah and Daoud. She asked my father to compose songs for her and she gave him lyrics by a famous poet in Iraq named Abdul Karim Alach. Using the lyrics, my father wrote music for a song, called "Galbak Sachar Jalmud," which means, "Your Heart is Hard as a Rock." It became a huge hit.

In that song, my father made his first innovation to *maqam*: he built this song from several *maqam* styles. He took a bit from one *maqam*, a bit from another *maqam*, and added some of his own features. People loved it. Then Salima asked him to compose all her songs, and he began composing several songs each week. Between the end of the 1930s and the end of the 1940s, he got to the point that he was composing for all the female singers in Iraq.

In Iraq, the Kuwaity Brothers' creativity blossomed. For instance, before my father came along, there was no such thing in the Arabic music world as a song without a singer. But he made instrumental-only songs part of Arab music. He replaced the singer with his violin. Another innovation he made was adapting the music to the lyrics so that the lyrics were appropriate for the music and vice versa. Before he did that, the lyrics often didn't match the music—for instance, the melody might be joyful when a man was singing about his mother getting run over! Each Arab country has its own *maqam* style, and he integrated elements of Egyptian and Lebanese *maqam* into his music.

So the brothers established new rules and abolished old ones, and the *maqam* had very strict rules. Initially, the *maqam* was comprised of five groups, called *fasl*, with four intervals in between for the musicians to rest. If musicians performed at a wedding, they would perform from the evening until the morning—an average of 10 hours. The time between the evening and the morning were divided into five parts. My father came along and broke the existing pattern: instead of five *fasl*, he did seven.

My father didn't come from a background of Western music, so he didn't integrate it into his music to the extent that Abdul Wahab did, but my father did listen to waltzes and so on, on records, and he did make use of some of those Western elements. And he did it in a way that the Arab ear would appreciate. He also integrated Western rhythms and tones and half tones. Middle Eastern music has quarter tones and eighth tones, so this was an addition that made the music richer. This usage of Western tones continues among young Iraqi composers today. In short, he paved the way, creating new freedom to experiment.

When I speak today with Iraqi artists who live in Iraq, all have heard about the Kuwaity Brothers, even if they're young. And although mentioning their names was forbidden on the radio, television, and in public settings all these years because they were Jewish, they were whispered about in secret. I have an Iraqi TV show on tape that reviews the history of Iraqi music with a panel of three experts. When they get to the period of 1930 they play my father's songs, exclusively. The panel analyzes the songs, and then at a certain stage, the interviewer asks the panel: "We've heard a lot of songs by Salah el-Kuwaity. Who was Salah el-Kuwaity?" And then you see how the fear of Saddam still grips the Iraqi people. No one answered for an entire minute. Total silence. And then she asked again, "Is someone willing to answer this?" The panel was silent. Eventually, they all pushed their fears aside and answered.

Salah made good money, a name for himself, and achieved great fame. His name became famous throughout all of Iraq to such an extent that in 1933, the Egyptian singer Umm Kulthum, the most popular singer in the Arab world, arrived in Iraq to perform and when she heard the song "Galbak Sachar Jalmud," she loved it. Umm Kulthum had rules: she never sang songs that weren't written for her, and she never sang non-Egyptian songs. But she asked to sing this song. So my father, together with Salima Murad, sat with her and taught her not only how to sing it, but also the language, because the Arabic spoken in Iraq was different than that spoken in Egypt. At a certain stage my father proposed that she accompany herself by playing the oud, which she did while performing in Iraq. This was the first time she played an instrument to accompany her singing. She didn't continue to perform his songs—only that song. But the experience continued to influence her indirectly, I believe.

That influence was a result of my father's relationship with Abdul Wahab, who also came to perform in Iraq. One day Abdul Wahab went to the club where Salima, Salah, and Daoud performed and heard the brothers play. He asked to meet the two of them, and when they met they made a fantastic connection both musically and personally. Abdul Wahab would perform and then my father would perform, separately, and after the show they would sit until the wee hours of the morning talking about music. They did this virtually every day for an entire month.

My father taught him a *maqam* called *maqam lami*, which is a *maqam* of a Bedouin tribe named Lam in Iraq—it was their *maqam* style. Abdul Wahab taught my father an Egyptian *maqam* called *zanjaran,* and my father took the *zanjaran* and planted it in the Iraqi *maqam*. Today the *zanjaran* is now part of the Iraqi *maqam*. When Abdul Wahab went back to Egypt, he began composing songs in the *maqam lami* style. One was called *Al Zarat al Portucal,* meaning, "You Planted the Orange Plant," which was sung by the famous Egyptian singer Laila Murad, and another song about the Nile. Abdul Wahab also wrote music for Umm Kulthum, so somehow indirectly she was, perhaps, influenced by what Abdul Wahab picked up in Iraq. All these singers loved and respected each other. My father and Abdul Wahab in particular continued to keep in touch from afar.

There is a term in Arabic that doesn't exist in Western music called *tarab*. *Tarab* is a kind of ecstasy. In other words, when I experience *tarab* it's as if I am under the influence of a drug. I absorb the music to such an extent that I begin to be a part of it. I cry with it, really cry, I feel it flowing in my veins, I feel it in my blood. It's a kind of mood that my body is in, like a kind of hypnosis. One of the reasons that Arab songs are very long is that a person cannot experience a state of *tarab* from a three-minute song. It has to be 20-minutes long so that he can enter this process of *tarab*. When you talk to someone who understands and loves Arab music he will tell you: this song made me experience *tarab*. Or, "I listened to it, but it's not for *tarab*." The Kuwaity Brothers' songs made people experience *tarab*.

One of Umm Kulthum's greatnesses was that she repeated the same verse over and over but her voice had nuances. Someone who is inside this *tarab* she creates identifies the nuance. When she sang, "My life is hard," the audience whistled and wanted to hug her because it felt this hardship. It was the same when my father composed a song and my uncle sang it. When they played a sad song, anyone listening in *tarab* would cry because he would remember his dead aunt, or his suffering mother, or his forgotten love.

Royal Audiences, Radio Fame

My father was so admired that he was asked to write the music for the crowning of King Faisal I for his funeral, and for the crowning of his son, King Ghazi. Ghazi loved the brothers' music very much. He frequently invited my father and uncle to have lunch with him at *Kaser Zrur*, the "Golden Palace." In 1936, Ghazi established the Iraqi public radio broadcasting station, Radio Baghdad, and invited the brothers to play live for it, broadcast from his palace. The only station preceding that was a short-wave radio station, which was located at the palace and used mainly to broadcast propaganda. The radio was a major factor that contributed to their widespread popularity because it enabled the middle and poor classes, who didn't attend the parties and the clubs where the Kuwaity Brothers performed, to listen to their music. Ghazi gave my father a gold watch that I have at home. It's large, with the king's insignia on the back and an inscription. A king giving a watch to a Jew! A Muslim king!

In many cases, Jews who needed favors, including helping relatives in mortal danger in jail or sentenced to death, came to the brothers to ask for their help because of their friendship with the royal family. One time a family came to my father asking for assistance to release a loved one from jail who had been sentenced to death, and my father called Ghazi. The following day the man was released. The brothers were completely immersed in the musical experience but they never forgot their Jewish origins.

Every four to six weeks, the ruling Sheikh of Kuwait at the time, Ahmed Al-Jaber Al-Sabah[2] came to Iraq with some of his ministers and they showed up at my father's house in fancy cars. Carpets and cushions were placed on the floor for them and they would get a special performance that went on for hours and hours, until the morning. Jaber was a very good friend and a big fan of my father and uncle. This man wouldn't fall asleep at night if he didn't listen first to my father's violin. When my eldest brother was born my father named him after this Sheikh: he called him Sabah.

Most of the musicians in Iraq at the time were Jews. Out of about 250 musicians in Baghdad then, only 3 were Muslims. There was a reason for that: in the eighteenth century there was a Turkish regime in Iraq and its ruler, or *wali*, in Baghdad, was a pious, fanatic Muslim. He issued a religious decree, a *fatwa*, that Muslims were not allowed to play music. He declared music a non-Muslim profession, a contemptible profession. Muslims were allowed only to play the drum because it accompanied religious ceremonies, and to sing.

So a vacuum was created, and Jews entered this vacuum. Music fit the Jews like a glove because it requires patience, the will to learn, and a willingness to work very hard—it's a classic Jewish profession in my mind. A father would teach his son how to play, and in that way the expertise would be passed down through the generations. The Jews didn't have music schools or any formal training and they even built musical instruments themselves because there was no other way to acquire them in Iraq. So certain families, for example, specialized in a certain instrument. The Fataw family specialized in the *santur* [a rectangular string instrument]. The Basun family specialized in the *joza* and the *kamana*. The Shutas specialized in drums, and so on. In the same way, my father and uncle received their instruments from their uncle. That teaching method meant that even once Muslims were allowed to play music after the decree was nullified—with the British occupation in 1918—they didn't know how and had no way of learning.

Many Jewish musicians happened to be blind because the Jewish community built a school for the blind to enable them to have an occupation. They were taught how to make chairs from bamboo, for instance, and other things that would enable them to make a living for themselves. Eventually the school introduced musical studies into the curriculum because it was discovered that some of the blind were very musically talented. My father and uncle encouraged the players and integrated them into their own shows.

In 1936, the royal family asked Salah and Daoud to establish the Iraqi Broadcasting Authority Orchestra. Except for one person, the orchestra was entirely Jewish—not because my father deliberately selected Jews but because most musicians were Jews. The orchestra played three times a week live for the new Radio Baghdad. It was comprised of four musicians who accompanied a *maqam* singer. Its name, Chalghy Baghdad, was taken from the word *char* in Persian, which means four. Daoud was one of them. Then my father formed a more modern orchestra for the Iraqi Broadcasting Authority which also played on the radio and was a little bigger and played more modern music, which he composed. But this entire affair lasted only four years. Why did it end? One day, in 1942, the prime minister, Nuri el-Said—who treasured Iraqi music and was said to have loved their broadcasts—turned on the radio and there was no music. He called the Broadcasting Authority and asked, "Why is there no music?" They told him, "It's Yom Kippur. Jews don't work today." "What?!" he exclaimed. "Jews don't work so there is no radio today?! No music?!" He was infuriated and kicked out the orchestras my father had created. Then el-Said created a new orchestra headed by a Christian named Jamil Bashir, and Chalghy Baghdad continued to operate privately.

Then my father and his brother opened a nightclub called *Malhat abu Nawas* [Nightclub of the Abu Nawas (neighborhood)]. They essentially relocated the orchestra there, and Salah and Daoud continued to compose and sing. The brothers discovered several singers at that club who became quite famous. One of them, Hzeri Abu Aziz, was a policeman and my father discovered him as a singer and promoted him. He also composed songs for the first Iraqi movie, *Alya Wa'lssam*, in 1948.

I have in my possession most of the Kuwaity Brothers' songs. I keep collecting more and more. It's not easy because they also composed for other singers and because the Arab world turned against Israel and the Jews after the formation of Israel. After the brothers emigrated to Israel in 1951, the Arabs erased the Kuwaity Brothers altogether from their collective memory—denied that the songs they were listening to belonged to the Kuwaity Brothers, because they were Jewish. For decades, when their songs were played on the radio or by other troupes, the Kuwaity Brothers' names were not mentioned. So it's hard to know which songs are theirs in some cases. In addition, musicians in the Arab world taught their songs and young people learned these songs without knowing who wrote them—an absurd situation which is hard to fathom in the West.

In Kuwait in recent months, there has been an outcry about the fact that the identity of the Kuwaity Brothers was suppressed by the Kuwaiti government for years. Within progressive, intellectual circles in Kuwait, people have asked the government: "Why didn't you say that all the music that we have heard from childhood—our heritage—was composed and played by Jews? We thought it was Kuwaiti folk music all along. Why did you conceal this information all these years?" This story was in the press and I was interviewed for it.[3] In response to the article, a Kuwaiti history professor wrote that, in essence, "First of all, we expelled the Jews. They didn't leave of their own free will. We expelled them because they traded in alcohol." Intellectuals and other historians were outraged by this claim and wrote back, saying, "You're talking nonsense. They left of their own free will, and we wanted them to come back."

Today the young generation in Iraq is discovering that they have been kept in the dark about the makers of some of their favorite music and they are beginning to ask questions. This is creating controversy because people are coming out and saying the truth, which not everyone wants to hear. "How could so much of the body of popular Iraqi music have been created by a set of Jewish brothers?" they ask. "How could this be?"

The End of an Era

When my father submitted a request to make aliyah in 1950, he was asked not to make it public because it was an embarrassment to the government. That's why, for example, he didn't go to the Interior Ministry to retrieve the necessary travel documents. Instead, the interior minister personally delivered them to his house. The minister signed the documents and told my father: "You know, for hundreds of years we have dealt with the Jews. We blamed you for everything. Now that there won't be Jews in Iraq, we'll start having to deal with each other. There will no longer be any factor to unite the Muslims once the Jews are gone and there won't be anyone to blame anymore." And look at what's happening today. The Sunnis are killing the Shiites, the Shiites are killing the Sunnis, the Kurds are killing both—and they still manage to blame the Jews when they can.

The brothers' families honored the government's request to keep quiet their decision to go but when the brothers and their families were at the airport boarding the plane the story broke out. The Kuwaity ambassador in Baghdad heard and got into his car and drove to the airport. He boarded the plane and begged Salah and Daoud to stay. He told them, "Don't go to Palestine. Don't go. You want to leave Iraq, fine. So come to Kuwait. In Kuwait, they'll make a statue of you. It's your country." My father told him, "I'm going." The man begged him with tears in his eyes, but my father wasn't moved. My mother and our entire family wanted to make aliyah, and it was clear to him that with the establishment of a Jewish state, things wouldn't be so good in Iraq anymore. So he felt he had no choice but to leave.

The authorities didn't let Salah and Daoud take their musical scores with them—the guards took all the scores out of their suitcases. When they got to Israel, they had to reproduce everything from scratch.

It suddenly dawned on the government that Iraq's entire musical tradition would disappear with the departure of the Jews. So it detained two families during Operation Ezra and Nehemiah until they taught two Muslims how to play their two instruments: the Pataws, who knew the *santur*, and the Basuns, who knew the *joza* [a small instrument made of a coconut]. Only after the two Muslims learned how to play the instruments were the Jewish families allowed to leave. To me, that is one of the most outrageous stories about the demise of the community: it was like the government said, "We hate you because you're Jewish and we've done everything to drive you out of the country but before you go, we want your talent."

In leaving Iraq, my father's sacrifice was very substantial, though he never complained about life in Israel. Whatever thoughts he had he kept to himself. He once told me why Salima Murad, who was also Jewish, didn't leave. She had told my father, "Who will I sing to in Israel? My life is singing, and in Iraq people know me. No one knows me in Israel."[4] My father knew that too about himself: that his musical career ended when he boarded that plane. After all, the most important thing for any artist is his audience. In Iraq he had an audience of millions while in Israel there were just 100,000 Iraqi Jews, all of whom were too busy starting their lives from scratch to have time for luxuries such as music anymore.

After my father made aliyah his exchanges with Abdul Wahab ended. Even after there was peace with Egypt [in 1978], Egyptian intellectuals boycotted Israel, so it was still difficult to communicate with his old friend. But Abdul Wahab sent his regards to father through the Israeli embassy in Cairo, and asked how he was doing. He asked my father not to come to Egypt to meet him, however, because he—Abdul Wahab—would be boycotted in all the Arab countries as a result. Yet throughout the years he continued to check up on my father and uncle in Israel and he expressed great sorrow to us when my father died. Abdul Wahab died five years later.

Meanwhile, in Israel the ruling doctrine was to westernize the Jews from the east in every way, which meant that the Kuwaity Brothers' music wasn't appreciated except by the small Iraqi immigrant population. Only the Israeli Broadcasting Authority's Arabic station gave the brothers a chance to play. At that time the station only played Egyptian and Lebanese songs. But the managers said to the brothers, "We've heard about you. We know that you are great artists." So the station gave them a half-hour segment every week. When the radio played their music, entire families in the transit camps and in Schunat Hatikva [Tel Aviv's Iraqi neighborhood] would gather around the radio to listen, just as they had in Iraq. Men would sit next to a table where a radio stood and which was filled with drinks—cognac and coffee—and olives and other snacks, and children were not allowed to speak during the broadcast.

But the brothers couldn't support themselves on that, so they had to find a new source of livelihood, and one that didn't suit them as music had. One person who recalls the juxtaposition of the brothers' careers in Iraq versus Israel is Yehezkel Kojaman [a leading expert on *maqam*, though not a professional musician himself]. The incident that led him to write his book, *The Maqam Music Tradition of Iraq*, was that in 1960 his sister told him to come to Schunat Hatikva, where we lived, to meet the Kuwaity Brothers, whom he wanted to see very much. Deep inside the marketplace Kojaman saw the brothers sitting in the simple houseware[s] store where they worked—and he just stood there and cried. He didn't even go up to speak to them. Kojaman later explained to me: "In Iraq, in order to meet with your father and uncle you had to go through a government minister who would arrange a meeting. And you got one only if you were lucky."

I was born in 1956 in Israel. My father was already over 50. I didn't have many years with him. But my great advantage was that because I was his youngest boy and therefore had plenty of time on my hands as compared to my siblings, I accompanied him to all his performances and spent a lot of time with him. He told me all sorts of stories about his compositions. He never discussed his former fame. In Israel he had to write lyrics as well, because he couldn't find good poets like the ones in Iraq who would write for him. But he had to send the lyrics for approval to the Israeli Broadcasting Authority if he planned to play the song on air because he was from Iraq and therefore he wasn't understood.

The heartache that my father experienced as a result of losing his career was one of the reasons he didn't allow any of his children to learn music. I begged him to teach me, but he wouldn't. He still played and composed a lot at home and eventually began to do small performances for the Iraqi community. For the Iraqi Jewish community as a whole, music was ingrained in their religious life—through the Torah, the liturgies, and the Shabbat songs. Iraqi Jews had songs for circumcision ceremonies, for weddings, for Rosh Hodesh [the first day of the Jewish month], Hanukah, Passover, and Sukkot. The community had integrated local music and *maqams* and applied them to words from the Bible. They sang when they visited the tomb of Ezra the Prophet and the tomb of Yehezkel the Prophet and all the way there they sang songs of pilgrimage, then special songs for visiting the grave, and songs for the way back from the grave. Because of this appreciation for music, Iraqis in Israel invited the brothers to perform at holidays and events.

Eventually, the store in the Hativka market evolved into an office of sorts where people came to book performances for weddings and bar mitzvahs. The brothers agreed to perform at small events and do things that they would never have had to agree to in Iraq, just to make money, and I'm sure that hurt them. For instance, people asked them to play songs that were not even close to their genre because people were ignorant of their expertise. But what mainly hurt my father—perhaps my uncle too—was the fact that he was no longer even mentioned in Iraq. He would hear his songs on Iraqi radio and the announcers said they were folk songs and never identified the Kuwaity Brothers. The BBC [British Broadcasting Corporation] played their music on its Arabic channel and did the same thing. It was like their names were erased from history.

I grew up on this music and loved it all my life. But I only learned about my father's stardom later in life from other people, and only in the last few years have I really understood the extent of what he achieved as I began to research his career. Part of the reason I've delved so deeply into this research on my father and uncle was in order to educate my children about who their grandfather was.

I discover new stories about them all the time. For instance, in 1964, the Baghdad Symphony Orchestra was established with a resident conductor, a German named Hans Gunter Womar. When he arrived in Baghdad, he began listening to local music. He was crazy for my father's music. He composed an entire composition for a symphony orchestra, which was 20-minutes long, and called it "Tunes of Iraq." It was based on five of my father's songs. The thing that is most painful is that Womar didn't know then that they were my father's, according to Womar's widow, who lives in Australia and with whom I recently spoke. She was so excited to speak to me. I told her that I wanted this composition to be performed in Israel and she gave me her consent. In this composition, every instrument in the orchestra has separate notes. She told me, "Your father was huge. I don't want money for this. I don't want the rights. Take it. Play it. Do what you want with it."

Academics from the Fine Arts Academy in Baghdad and the Baghdad Philharmonic Orchestra write to me about my father and uncle. They also talk about them on TV interviews today—they are no longer afraid. They say that Salah el-Kuwaity was the greatest composer in Iraq, ever. They don't mention that he was a Jew but at least they say my father's name and they say that he was a reformer and an innovator. Still, many don't know who composed and originally played the songs Iraqis sing today. In addition to the song "Galbak Sachar Jalmud," which Salima Murad sang, some of the Kuwaity Brothers' other popular songs were "El Hagir Muada Gariba" [Neglect Isn't a Foreign Custom], and "Hadri Chai" [Make Tea], which Iraqi and Lebanese still sing today. "Hadri Chai" was sung by Samira Tawfiq, a famous Bedouin singer living in Lebanon.

The largest collection of the Kuwaity Brothers' recordings in Israel is at my home, although in Iraq and Kuwait there are larger collections than mine. Academics and musicians that I have connected with in those places send me copies of recordings in their collections—that's how I've built my collection. Young people in Iraq send me a lot of requests via e-mail requesting books and recordings, and I have a setup where I send it to them via London.

I'm not angry about how Israel and its culture didn't appreciate my father and the music and culture of Iraq. Let bygones be bygones. But let's fix it now. Let's give back to those Mizrachi artists—not just my father, but also those who were great artists in their countries of origin in the Arab world, and who greatly influenced the culture there, yet here in Israel were totally forgotten. Let's talk about the traditions, learn about them, celebrate them.

One of those artists is a woman from Morocco named Zohara, who was very famous there. A Jewish Moroccan poet named Ezra Biton wrote a poem about her. He wrote that when Zohara sang, the Muslim soldiers would use their knives to make their way to the front of the crowd to hear her. She was that popular. She sang for the king. Biton writes in his poem, "Do you want to know where Zohara is today? Go to the Ashkelon *shuk* [market], find a small house, and you'll find a woman living in one room with one bed wearing a robe because she has no money to buy clothes. That's Zohara, the woman for whom men would literally kill each other for a space to watch her perform."

Daoud el-Kuwaity died in 1976 at age 66 and Salah died in 1986 at age 78. Shlomo released a CD of the Kuwaity Brothers' biggest hits in 2006, and is compiling a short biography of the troupe. Both are features of celebrations in Tel Aviv and London that Shlomo planned for fall, 2008, the year that would have been his father's hundredth birthday. The event will include performances of the Kuwaity Brothers' music and other music by contemporary Iraqi artists. Israeli musician Yair Dallal, of Iraqi descent, has led a small renaissance of Jewish Iraqi music. His music draws specifically from the Kuwaity Brothers' music, as well as from Arabic, Israeli, and jazz influences in general.

* * *

Ezra Zilkha is the son of Khedouri Abdoudi Zilkha, who started the first branch banking system in the Arab world, K.A. Zilkha, Maison de Banque, commonly known as Bank Zilkha. Ezra Zilkha left Iraq at age two with his family, bound for Beirut, where Khedouri opened his head office and later on, with the help of Ezra, three other sons, and a brother-in-law, continued to build his banking empire across the region, and a network of partners and clients that stretched to Europe and eventually the United States. The family moved to the U.S. in 1941, and by 1955, the "House of Zilkha" comprised nine foreign exchange and banking houses linking five continents. It was the largest private bank in the Middle East. In his personal account, Ezra Zilkha describes his father's ventures, the old-fashioned business ethics that were the foundation of Khedouri's successful enterprise, and, eventually, the bank's disappearance, the result of the political upheaval caused by World War II, the creation of Israel, and growing Arab anti-Semitism.

My father was born in 1884 in Baghdad. In 1899, at age 15, father had had enough of going to school and wanted to get out in the world and be productive. I recall him telling me and my other siblings a funny story about the day he decided to quit school, a small Hebrew school where the education was very limited. In Iraqi Arabic, the word *fasad* means "rot." One day, his French teacher was talking about *façade de l'ecole*, the façade of the school. He came home and told his mother that his teacher said the school is rotten and he didn't want to attend anymore. He was a rather spoiled boy, and his mother agreed without a second thought. At that point, he already had his sights set on becoming a banker.

Father founded his bank that same year with 250 gold Turkish Pounds—a lot of money in those days—which his father, a wealthy merchant, gave him. He made up for his lack of schooling with his natural intelligence and agility, and read the newspaper thoroughly every day to keep himself informed. When he began his bank there were few banks in the country, which was still ruled by the Ottoman Empire. My father learned about balance sheets and, later, even hired an outside auditor, an English firm which established itself in Baghdad because of the entry of three British banks into Iraq: the Imperial Bank of Persia, the Ottoman Bank, and Eastern Bank. At the time, virtually no businesses hired outside auditors.

Business entailed lending money on promissory notes and taking deposits. All business in the bank was settled on Fridays because on Saturdays all commerce was stopped for the Sabbath. His dream was that each one of his sons would manage one of his banks in a different city. In Baghdad, he began working on realizing his vision of going beyond Iraq's borders to create a network of foreign exchange: one of his earliest voyages, in 1902, was to Istanbul, then the capital of the Ottoman Empire, where he stayed for two years. There, he forged a correspondent relationship with Banque de Salonique, which was run by Sephardi Jews from Turkish-ruled Salonika, and the Menache Cousins Bank, another private bank owned by a Jewish family from Aleppo [in Syria] that later opened a bank in Cairo as well. He traveled to Istanbul with his uncle, Joseph Shasha. It took them 20 days to get to Aleppo by caravan—that was the safest way to travel, to protect oneself from thieves—and from Aleppo they took the railroad to Istanbul. Bedouin tribes had carved up the desert among themselves, and if you drank from the wrong tribe's oasis, you were in trouble, so you had to travel with someone familiar with the terrain. Camels and mules carried the group's food and tents and father brought along a jester to entertain him and his fellow travelers with stories.

He then began his gold arbitrage business between Istanbul and Baghdad. Because gold was cheaper in Turkey than in Mesopitamia at the time, he bought the gold in Turkey and sold it for a profit in Baghdad. The gold was physically carried to Baghdad by couriers and caravan. Father devised an insurance system by telling the courier that the subsequent shipment would be larger and in that way compelled the courier, if he were a thief, to wait for the next shipment. He continued shipping gold this way until the market shifted and there was no longer a margin for profit. Years later, when we paid so much to insure gold shipments, I thought about how father's insurance scheme was very clever: it cost nothing and it worked.

He returned to Baghdad when his father died and resumed his business, taking deposits on which he paid interest, discounting merchants' bills, trading in precious metals, and conducting foreign exchange through Istanbul. These were the days before oil was discovered in the Middle East. It was a different Middle East: a backwater of the Ottoman Empire. There were no real industries, and the Iraqi economy relied simply on dates and wheat, imported textiles, exported wool, and other ordinary things that people needed for subsistence. My father lent money to businesses and advanced it to merchants and farmers against their future crops. The only important economic feature in the region was the Suez Canal because it was the passage from Europe to India and the Far East.

At the end of World War I, before the Turks left Baghdad, they killed about 25 merchants and bankers by tying rocks around their necks and throwing them into the Tigris. Most of the victims were Jewish, though it wasn't as much an act of anti-Semitism as it was greed and vindictiveness, as the Turks wanted to loot Baghdad before they had to leave. Father was on this list of targets but was able to buy himself out of this situation.

By the time my father married my mother, Louise Bashi, in 1912, he was already so well off that he requested not to receive a dowry as was the custom. At the time, there were about two or three hundred affluent Jewish families in Baghdad, and most of them were either closely or distantly related. We were among the first families in Baghdad to eat with knives and forks—most people ate only with spoons. World War I made father an even richer man. Shortages of goods drove up prices, and his strength was that he always had a lot of liquidity so he was able to take advantage of the many financial opportunities the war created.

Father was delighted when the British arrived in 1917 because he was sick and tired of dealing with the corruption pervasive in the Ottoman Empire and was relieved that he would now be able to operate under the rule of law. The Ottoman provincial governors, or *walis*, extorted whatever they felt like whenever they could, and the only way to do business in that world was to use bribery every step of the way. Bribery didn't disappear with the entry of the British, but it greatly diminished. My uncle Saleh, my mother's brother who later played an important role in running the bank, once told me, "Ezra, you know how we pay taxes in Europe and the U.S. and so on. The way we used to pay our 'taxes' in the Middle East, when there were no taxes, was by paying protection money to the government."

The discovery of oil in Mosul in the 1920s had a tremendous effect on father's business because it enriched some Iraqis and set off a flurry of business activity in the region. Banking activity also rose after the railroad was built in Iraq during that decade. In addition, after World War I, the Nairn brothers, who had come from New Zealand as soldiers, started a transportation company that managed the transport of goods from Baghdad to Damascus and beyond. When we left Iraq for Lebanon, my parents must have taken us in a car that was owned by the Nairn brothers. And in fact, a few years later, one of the Nairn brothers came to our bank in Beirut and made an offer to buy our bank, which enraged my father because as its creator he found the suggestion offensive.

An International Childhood

I don't remember the neighborhood I lived in when I was born, as I left Iraq when I was less than two years old. My mother gave birth to 10 children. Seven survived: Abdulla, Helene, Maurice, Hanina, Berthie, myself, and Selim. I was one of the youngest—number three out of four sons, and the sixth child. In 1925, my parents were expecting a baby after having two girls and went on a pilgrimage to the tomb of Ezra the Scribe in Basra in order to wish for another boy. I was born and they named me Ezra.

In 1927 a group called the Black Hand Society began to extort money from a number of important merchants and bankers in Iraq, mostly Jews, and father was among them. The Society was a criminal gang made up of Muslims and Jews, and there was nothing particularly anti-Semitic about them—their targets were mostly Jews because Jews were among the wealthiest Iraqis. Father even recognized some of the names of its members. The group demanded a certain sum from him. He feared that this group or others like it would try to harm the family or continue to steal from us, so that's when he decided to leave Iraq for Beirut. He left the bank to be run by the managers who had worked with him and my father moved the family to Beirut, but he kept our home in Baghdad which was sold many years later. I never returned to Iraq.

We left by car to Damascus over western Iraq's and eastern Syria's desert terrain, as there were no roads yet in those areas. From Damascus to Beirut, we drove on proper roads. There, in 1927, he opened his second branch, which became the head office both because our family was there and because Beirut was then the most important economic center in the region and the region's gateway to Europe. That was his second major step in realizing his vision to open branches throughout the Arab world, and ours became the most prominent private commercial bank in Beirut. In 1931 we bought the Beirut business of the Anglo-Palestine Bank, now Israel's Bank Leumi, when it wanted to close that branch, and a few years later we bought the business and the premises of Banque Francaise de Syrie, located on the city's Allenby Street, the main thoroughfare going from the center of Beirut to the harbor.

In time, my father had 50 employees in that office. What my father's bank offered was better service and more connections to overseas banks than other banks, and he was known for his expertise in gold trading and foreign exchange. While Baghdad did little international commerce, Beirut, because it had a port, had a thriving foreign exchange market and was a way station for goods. A large part of his business was financing car importers—General Motors and Chrysler. Because father spoke Arabic, Turkish, French, and a bit of Hebrew, he was able to communicate with people throughout the Middle East and Europe, which helped him create his vast network of clients and colleagues, and, ultimately, what became a multinational corporation. Later, his branch system was copied by the Arab Bank and the Rafidain Bank, the largest state-owned bank in Iraq.

Most local banks were sole proprietorships and bankers were personally liable for all deposits. I recall that during the Depression, father once had a run on his bank. He sat down at a table which he piled high with bank notes and money. Anyone with accounts at the bank who wanted to withdraw money could come and ask for it. After a day, the panic subsided. Years later, in 1946, when he came back from America to visit the region, many of his clients to whom he had lent money during the Depression came back to him and kissed his hands and thanked him for helping them make it through that difficult period.

In Beirut, we lived in Ras Beirut, a Muslim district, and had a summer house in the mountains. Ours was one of the first private homes in Beirut to have a telephone: our number was, simply, 121, as there were so few of us with telephones. Life was generally peaceful, though there were sometimes riots in the city as Zionism became more and more of a force and came closer to achieving its goal, a national homeland for the Jews. Thus father cleverly made friends with several prominent Muslims in key political positions. One of them was Riad al-Solh, who later became the first prime minister of independent Lebanon. He had his own private army and when a disturbance occurred, he would send his soldiers to stand guard in front of our bank.

Our table conversation at dinner was always about banking: selling francs against sterling, buying dollars, foreign exchange, et cetera. Banking was in our blood. I was always very close to my father and because of that special relationship I learned the banking business from him. When father bought a building for his new bank in Damascus in 1935—a decision he made after his Damascus agent began charging him higher fees—he took me with him from Beirut by car. I was 10 years old. He took me on trips often, which is why I was never a very good student. The closing took place in a coffee house along the Barada River and the building cost father 4,000 Turkish gold pounds. Two messengers came, each carrying two bags. They opened one bag, counted a thousand pounds and put them back in the bag. Using a scale, they weighed each of the other three bags against that one, which meant they didn't have to count the contents of all of the bags because gold value was based on its weight. It was a beautiful building that had previously belonged to the Ottoman Bank. The purchase was a natural extension of his bank, as Damascus was situated along the trade route between Baghdad and Beirut.

While I learned about finance from him, I also learned about important human values like compassion. For instance, after the purchase that day, we went to our hotel, Hotel Omayyad. And as we walked through the lobby, a man was sitting hunched over and looking downtrodden. Father touched his shoulder and shook his hand. As we continued on to our room, he told me about this man, a Christian-Syrian banker. He said, "This man is suffering a fate worse than death. He's a banker who went bankrupt and I shook his hand because one must have compassion for the fallen."

Father conducted his business based on a strict code of traditional business ethics: loyalty and trust. He instilled this ethic into all his banks. He was always reliable and true to his word. He could just look at somebody and figure out almost immediately whether he was trustworthy, and he made many of his business decisions according to that sense. He knew that a good banker should know the history of his clients' families, and he had an extensive knowledge of Baghdad families of all creeds. And if there were moral or bankruptcy issues even five generations back in a family, he would not conduct business with them. He had the whole genealogy of Jewish and other merchants mapped out in his head. He also did not lend money on collateral, as the best collateral, he believed, was integrity and the financial capability to repay. For him, human value—the quality of the people themselves—was the most important way to judge whether to enter into a business relationship. He also warned me never do business with any religious fanatic, no matter what religion, because if such a person wanted to cheat, he would find an excuse to cheat in some religious text.

Father wasn't a tall man but if he walked into any room filled with people, they immediately knew he was there. He had a fantastic presence, and he dressed elegantly. He hired the best tailors from all over the world, and always wore a white shirt and a suit, and in summer a perfectly ironed white linen suit. When outdoors, he wore a fez. He was very fashionable, very proper, and maniacal about his cleanliness.

Although an earlier generation of the family had founded one of Baghdad's most important religious schools, Midrash Beit Zilkha, father was not very observant, and none of his sons except for Abdulla were bar mitzvahed. He went to synagogue only on the high holidays. Still, he said his prayers every day in the car on the way to work, and if I were with him then, I couldn't talk to him for three minutes.

In the summer in Lebanon his Arab customers—merchants, sheiks, landowners, farmers, even prime ministers, many dressed in traditional Arab garb—would bring their bags of gold to deposit with their Jewish banker, my father. They would stay for hours afterwards and smoke their water pipes and drink coffee. Father's desk was large and wooden and he had four armchairs on each side so his customers would all sit in them to do their business, as though in a club or a coffee house. They would talk with each other and with father, and interrupt each other and father while he was on the phone. People would come in and out throughout the day like this. A man employed as a coffee maker in the bank was constantly busy making Turkish coffee and preparing the water pipe for anyone who requested one, including my father.

According to father's principles, a third of the employees he hired were Muslim, a third Christian and a third Jewish—his own little affirmative action policy before it came into style! He employed Italians, English, and French, because they helped recruit customers from many countries.

In Beirut, it was discovered that Selim, my younger brother, had asthma, so my parents sent him to a British boarding school in Cairo, where the weather was drier. After that, they sent me to join him. Then, in 1937, father came to Cairo to open a new branch. He opened another in Alexandria in 1939 to take advantage of the cotton trade there. After the Japanese entered the war in 1941, the Japanese closed the Yokahama Specie Bank in Alexandria, and we took over that business and premises.

Maurice and Abdulla and my uncle Saleh all assisted my father in running the bank. In particular, Uncle Saleh was a very important figure in our family and in the business. He ran the Beirut branch and was a wonderfully highly principled man—a good businessman, not a visionary like my father but very intelligent and very honest. Later, when my father died, he held the family together like a second father. We, all the siblings, had all become little spoiled princes—there is a saying in Arabic "I'm a prince. You're a prince. Who will drive the donkeys?"—and that's how we were, spoiled. We always lived well, always had servants, a driver, and everything we wanted. We went to the best schools and wore the best clothing. And we never suffered as a result of the Great Depression. So Uncle Saleh was there to make sure we didn't have to fend for ourselves.

My father continued to run the business from Beirut while Abdulla ran the bank in Cairo and Maurice in Alexandria. Abdulla and Maurice returned to Iraq in 1938 to serve in the army, as we all held Iraqi citizenship and passports until after the war. They each served only 90 days which made me realize what a poorly managed army Iraq's was.

At that point, in effect, we had fully expanded our business and were bankers in the traditional sense: financing trade, providing the equity part of the capital necessary to launch or expand a business, and finding other sources of additional funds. Before World War II, the Beirut branch aided European Jews by buying and selling a currency called Register Marks. In 1933, the Nazis negotiated an agreement with the Jewish community whereby German Jews could deposit marks in blocked accounts and a year later receive an equivalent in Palestinian pounds. These Register Marks could be used only to buy German goods, and thus a bizarre situation occurred in which money belonging to Jews from Nazi Germany was helping to build Palestine. In those prewar years we were also active in buying promissory notes from the Jewish Agency which was buying land from Arab landowners in Palestine. Because the agency lacked cash, we paid the landowners in cash and made a profit when the notes came due.

The Tide Turns

In 1938, when the war scare took place, I was with my parents in Paris. We were booked on a French ship from Marseilles to Alexandria to return home but there were rumblings of war. Father said we couldn't be in the Mediterranean during war, so we waited in France for a short time until the end of the Munich Conference—which prevented a war—when we then took the next ship back to Egypt. But the war scare frightened father, so he transferred $300,000 to the U.S. in case we might have to move there in due course. But when we came to America in 1941, Beirut was under Vichy control, so that money was blocked and we couldn't access it. It was then unblocked at the rate of $3,000 a month, which is how we survived initially, and then a few months later it was freed up altogether.

My father brought my mother, two of my sisters, Hanina and Berthie, and my younger brother Selim and me to America because he believed that we younger siblings should finish our studies outside the Arab world and because Europe wasn't an option because war was ravaging the continent. He also thought we might find a place in the U.S. to cure my stuttering, which we did. He viewed this move as temporary at first. Abdulla and Maurice stayed in Egypt to run the branches there. Uncle Saleh continued to run the banks in Beirut and Damascus. But with the war on, it wasn't easy getting to America. First we went to South Africa, where we stayed a month waiting for an American cargo ship to bring us to New York, which took 18 days. We were able to travel on an American ship because the attack on Pearl Harbor hadn't occurred yet, and therefore America hadn't yet entered the war.

The bank continued to thrive during World War II despite father's absence from the region: shortages of goods and industries starting from scratch created many financial opportunities. But father was very lonely in America during the war. He had an office but he was far away from his business. I went to boarding school and then to university, but I used to come back every weekend to be with him to help assuage his loneliness and because I enjoyed being with him. During those years our relationship blossomed. I absolutely loved my father and he loved me. We would play game after game of backgammon while he recounted stories about his business. I was learning and learning—about the principles of life, and about banking.

After the war, in 1946, father returned to the Middle East. Our Egyptian business had suffered reverses at the end of the war but our bank in Beirut was prospering. Then, in 1948, the Arab-Israeli War and the resulting tensions and anti-Semitism in the Arab world put an end to his business and his dreams for each of his sons to manage a branch. But father had anticipated that the problems in the region would affect us and had planned accordingly. During his trip, he realized that after the British mandate in Palestine ended and Israel declared its statehood, the Arabs would attack Israel immediately. And if that happened and the Jews won, we—our family and our business—were sunk, and if the Arabs won we were sunk as well. As a result of the Arab-Israeli War, people lost confidence in Jewish banks and enterprises in the Middle East. Muslim borrowers also felt that they didn't have to repay their loans from Jewish banks because the Jews had lost all their legal avenues even before they formally lost their rights. Luckily, we were making money in the West and we sent money back to the Middle East to pay back depositors because, for my father, the preservation of our name was most important. He returned to the U.S. and told us that our stay in the U.S. was no longer temporary. We should build new lives there, he said, and leave the Middle East behind us.

Middle Eastern Jews continued to send us funds to care for through our office in New York, which was initially located in the Empire State Building and then on Wall Street. In the U.S., father didn't succeed in learning English well. At such an age, it wasn't easy for him to remake himself. He largely functioned thanks to his business manager, a man named Joseph Sassoon who wrote him a letter every day in Arabic describing what he needed to know about his business. Mr. Sassoon used to translate for him, as would I.

Our branch in Baghdad was expropriated in 1951 and the Iraqi government extorted money from us by throwing our managers in jail. We had to ransom them: we sent a quarter of a million pounds ($700,000) to free them. Then the Syrian government expropriated the Damascus bank in 1954. Likewise in Egypt, at the time of the Suez Crisis and the start of government nationalization of private enterprise in 1956, we were expropriated. The only reason we lasted that long in Egypt was that my brother Maurice had very good connections with government officials. We then decided to bail out of the region altogether and sold the Beirut branch in 1957. By that point, Selim had already set up an office in London and Maurice then moved to Paris, where we bought a bank. Uncle Saleh went to Europe soon after and established an office in Geneva. I continued to help father in New York, where we had to start virtually from scratch, although father still had his first-class reputation and the remnants of his former network, so the banks in the U.S. gave us credit.

One day Madame [Jehan] Sadat, the wife of the president of Egypt, asked me what my feelings were after our banks were expropriated in three out of the four Middle East countries in which we had branches. I answered her, "Only sorrow, no bitterness."

After the collapse of K.A. Zilkha, Maison de Banque, Khedouri Zilkha established the American Nile Corporation in 1941, which exported goods to the Middle East. It was later renamed Zilkha & Sons in 1956 and transformed into an investment business. Ezra serves as its president. Khedouri died in Geneva in 1956 at age 72 (he is buried in New York), and his wife Louise Bashi died in 1985; Maurice, Abdulla, and Berthie also passed away. In 1999, Ezra self-published his memoirs, from which parts of this account are drawn, entitled From Baghdad to Boardrooms: My Family's Odyssey. *Ezra and his wife Cecile have three children and live in New York. The personal account of Ezra's sister, Hanina Shasha, appears in this collection.*

* * *

Salim Sassoon was born in 1909 in Baghdad. In contrast to the view voiced by many other Iraqi Jews that the 1920s and 1930s were the golden years of Iraq's Jews—and of the country itself—he paints a rather dismal picture of a poor, backwater capital, both during the last years of Ottoman rule and the British mandate. Some of his most vivid descriptions are of the dearth of adequate health care in Iraq, which caused his family great suffering on several occasions. Stabbed and beaten during the Farhoud, he also details the days he spent in a Baghdad hospital after the Farhoud, where he was surrounded by hundreds of other injured and dying Jews. Sassoon died in 2003, shortly after being interviewed for this collection. His son, Robert, an obstetrician/gynecologist whose interest in medicine was partly inspired by his father's experiences at the hands of Iraq's medical establishment, helped fill in details of his father's life.

When I was born, Baghdad was under Turkish occupation. Iraq was a very backward place far different from the West. There were no telephones, motor cars, or electricity. The houses were cheaply built and did not even have bathrooms. A toilet was more like a trench, usually dug in the fields. The accumulation of residue would be removed from time to time by special cleaners and carried away in leather bags on donkeys. There were no faucets for running water. The drinking water was bought from water sellers called *sakka*. The *sakka* would carry the water in large leather containers on donkeys and deliver it to individual homes where it would be dumped into large containers made of clay, called *hib*. Most homes had wells. Water from the wells was used for bathing, laundering, and necessities other than drinking.

The houses were built with an open interior and most were usually two stories high. On the lower level were the kitchen and another room called a *nim*. This room was used during summer days for socializing since it was a cooler spot. Sleeping quarters were on the second floor, though roofs were flat and the entire family used to sleep on them in the summers, which in Baghdad were extremely hot. The climate of Baghdad ranged from freezing during the winter to 120 degrees (F) during the summer, and one can hardly imagine living in such extremes of weather without the comforts of heating or air conditioning. Fortunately, the climate was very dry, which is why we were able to sleep outside in the summer months.

There were no refrigerators, so we used to buy meats on a daily basis and hang them from a net so that bugs wouldn't crawl into them. We made *leben* which is like a thick yogurt that would keep for a couple of days without refrigeration. On Friday evenings we would make a dish called *tib'it*, which contained chicken, rice, and eggs, and it was put on a slow fire that would cook all night, because we couldn't cook on Sabbath. The eggs would then turn brown, and the dish was rather greasy so it would be a very heavy meal.

My family's life was a modest one. My father, Isaac, ran a business as a rice merchant but his income was hardly enough to make ends meet. He actually could have been well off had he been left alone to provide for his immediate family. However, he was surrounded by relatives with little or no income and he believed it was his responsibility to help. He had an older brother who never worked throughout his entire life and who lived with us in our home for many years. Another brother with many children—families then were very large—also needed help. And he had an invalid sister who had been stricken with polio and whose husband had died, and she and her son, too, became dependent on my father.

But most significantly, my father had to largely support my two married sisters, Gourjiyeh and Regina. Gourjiyeh's husband lost all his money in a robbery and although he maintained a small hardware business, he was not self-sufficient. Regina's husband stopped working as a textile merchant after they married. He ate through all their savings and everything they owned vanished, including Regina's dowry. He then began selling her jewelry and their furniture. In the meantime, they continued having children—six, in fact. And the entire family was dependent on my father.

I can hardly imagine a situation like this occurring today, but in those days the family network was tight. That had its advantages and, as in my father's case, its disadvantages. But despite all these burdens, my father did not neglect his immediate family and his home, his wife, and his children were cherished by him.

My father's rice shop was called *Bait abu Timan* (The House of Rice). In fact, our family was known for generations as *Bait abu Timan*, as it was a business handed down from father to son many times over. But neither I nor any of my brothers took over the business so it died with my father. Father was a very venerable, pious, and generous man—not only with his relatives but with strangers as well. He sported a long white beard and any time he passed his Muslim neighbors in the street they would bow in reverence to him. In his shop he used to keep a little money bag under his cushion and when anybody came to him in need he would take it out and give him some money. This bag was really his own bank—his family fortune—and he wouldn't just give away small amounts—he would literally split the full 10 dinars he had in there, for instance, and give 5 away. He was himself one of many brothers and sisters, some of whom had fallen on hard times at the decline of the Ottoman Empire, which is why, I believe, he was very sensitive to the needy. Prior to that, the very successful part of my family, the famous Sassoons, had left in the mid-1800s for Bombay and Shanghai and made a fortune there. But we had very little connection to that richer branch. For us, life was a hand-to-mouth existence.

Every morning, my father woke me up to go to synagogue, and we went together every evening as well. On the way there in the morning, my father always stopped at a café and had a cup of Turkish coffee. Normally he'd pay for it, except for on the Sabbath when we couldn't touch money, so the Muslim café owners never held him to pay on that day. Instead, he would come back to pay the next day.

We never had a house of our own. Rather, we rented houses from year to year. Some years we were able to renew the lease, but most years, for one reason or another, we would have to move. We often lived in close quarters, and our family was large: I was the eighth of nine children. The diverse types of names of my siblings were typical of an Iraqi Jewish family, which was influenced by local Arab culture, Jewish culture, and the Western, international orientation of the community. My older brother Khedoury, my sister Gourjiyeh, and I were given Arab names, as were our half-siblings Masouda and Hayawi. Masouda and Hayawi—who ended up being a very successful businessman—were the eldest. Their mother had died and my father remarried her niece, my mother, who was about 16 years old at the time. My younger brother, Heskeil, was the only sibling with a Jewish name. And my sister Regina and two other brothers, Joe and Neville, were given English names. In Iraq, we didn't use surnames. I was initially called Salim Hugi Shimon, which was my first name, my father's first name, and my grandfather's first name. Later on, when I was about 10 or 11, we added our family name, Sassoon, so I was called Salim Sassoon.

Medical care was poor, and many people suffered from illnesses that we don't even think about today. Epidemics of many kinds struck every few years. There was no medical knowledge or any means to combat such epidemics, so many victims fell prey to them.

When I was about 10 years old, in 1919—at the end of the Ottoman occupation and the start of the British one—a calamity struck my family. Heskeil, who was the baby of the family, had been the picture of health and beauty. But he had difficulty speaking and never went to school. So my father pitied him and took Heskeil with him everywhere he went. Heskeil spent most of the day sitting on father's lap in the rice shop. At the end of each day, they would go together to synagogue and then to a coffee shop before returning home. One day when he was six or seven years old, Heskeil woke up in the morning with a fever which continued to rise during the day. On the second day, a swelling appeared on his neck, and on the third day he died. No one knew the nature of his illness or how to combat it. Many people in our area were being struck down by a similar illness, which everyone simply referred to it as "the strike." After Heskeil's death, my father fell into a deep depression, and we all began to worry that another one of us would contract the strike. We decided to leave the house for the suburbs so as to escape the plagued area and recover from Heskeil's death. We later learned it was diphtheria.

Transportation was also poor. Everyone either walked or got around in horse-led buggies. The roads weren't paved and streets were muddy and unclean. After Heskeil's death we moved in with my sister Gourjiyeh who lived in a small cottage outside Baghdad, and getting to the city was an ordeal. The only way to go was to walk a mile to reach a terminal and then ride a horse-drawn carriage to another terminal, then walk for another half-mile.

The standards in public education were as low as in any other field. Most of the Muslim inhabitants were illiterate. There were Islamic religious schools called *mulla* where students studied the Koran, but little else. The standards within Jewish schools were only moderately better when I was a young child—only in the 1920s and afterwards did Jewish schools proliferate and became known for their high standards and strength in foreign language in particular. As a child, I attended a Jewish primary school where I was taught Bible and written Hebrew. It was run by a man and his wife in their house. They were the only teachers. Hundreds of Jewish students were jammed in there like sardines and the sanitation and drinking water were very poor. At age 10, I was able to leave and go to a better school. There was not much of a choice at the time—there were only two Jewish upper schools: Ta'awan, which mainly just taught Hebrew and Arabic, and the Alliance Israelite Universelle, a French school built with funds donated by David Sassoon, our distant cousin going five generations back who had made his fortune in India. I chose the Alliance, where we studied in French, Arabic, English, and Hebrew.

The Alliance was a very good school in relation to the standards at the time in Baghdad, though it would have been considered quite limited if compared to today's standards. It was not beholden to any national matriculation standards and often it would allow good students to jump two grades at a time. So by the age of 15, I had completed my high school studies. That was 1924 and I had no place further to go with my education unless I left Iraq. I had to roll up my sleeves and go to work.

A Sudden Adulthood

Jobs were hard to get, particularly in Baghdad. There were no major industries to speak of—people mainly worked in small businesses run by one or two individuals with perhaps the help of a few employees. I managed, however, to find a job in a large company that imported agricultural machinery and whose clients were large farms. The company imported diesel engines, irrigation pumps, and spare parts from England. I was hired as a clerk and was offered a salary of 100 rupees per month[5]—the equivalent of $37. This was considered a good salary, especially for a boy of 15. But starting from my very first pay, half went toward helping relieve my father of his many financial burdens.

I started out by doing simple tasks such as ensuring the hay was baled correctly. Within a few months, I had learned the jobs of everyone in the office, including the partners, and in less than a year I was placed in charge of the employees I was originally hired to assist. I often had to ride into the fields by horse to manage accounts with the farmers, which meant sleeping overnight in tents with them. They were totally illiterate. I measured accounts with them by means of small rocks. Eventually, they became used to me and put their full faith in me, so much so that they would agree to anything I told them. They used to call me *Salim el Yehoudi* (Salim the Jew).

Although I had a good job and was surrounded by friends and family, I never liked life in Baghdad. Jews were considered second-class citizens, and the government was run by fanatic nationalists who considered Jews to be at their mercy. The Muslims sometimes showed us intimacy as if we were brothers and at other times could be hateful. Even though Jews considered the 1920s and 1930s the best period for the Jews of Iraq, Muslim hatred of Jews was nevertheless obvious and deep. I would have very much liked to leave everything behind and emigrate, but I was stuck there, concerned for the welfare of my parents and relatives. By my mid-'20s my father was already quite old and was very attached to me, so to leave would have been a serious blow to him.

Resolved to stay, I decided to make the most of my life in Baghdad, and I do have some wonderful memories. In fact, my life was rather peaceful during the 1930s. I was a member of the Laura Khadourie Club, a beautiful estate located in the nicest part of the city. It was built by Eliezer Khadourie, the husband of the woman for whom it was named. It had large grounds with sweeping, green lawns with flowers, tennis courts, and large rooms for the winter season. It was the meeting place of many friends, exclusively Jews, and it became my second home as it did for many people. All my free time was spent there playing games and socializing, and I often had dinner and drinks at the club. Some nights a *chalghi* band [classic Iraqi instrumental group] would play there and we would stay into the wee hours of the night. My other pleasure in Baghdad was boating and swimming on the Tigris, picnicking on its banks, and eating *mazgouf*, the most delicious fish.

In 1933, at age 86, father died of a hernia—again, something that would have been so easily treated in the West but was often a cause of death in Iraq. He lived in pain for many years with the ailment, and like other Iraqis, was afraid of any surgery and tried to avoid it even when he knew there was no other cure. One day, it was clear that the hernia had worsened and he realized he had no choice but to go to the hospital, where he was admitted immediately to the operating room. The surgeon emerged a short while later and gave me the news that my father had died before they could complete the operation.

His death left me and my older brother Khedoury to care for my grandmother, who was about 50 years old at the time, in those days a rather old age. Shortly afterwards, my mother needed an operation on her eyes as her tear ducts were blocked—another condition that would be cleared up today with simple surgery. Doctors in Iraq suggested she go to Palestine for the surgery and we made a month-long family trip out of it. In Jerusalem, a renowned eye doctor operated on her successfully. Several years later, my mother broke her hips, but wary of the treatment she'd get in an Iraqi hospital, we brought her to one of the local healers people often called upon, called *mujabbir*, who took care of scrapes and bruises. This man told us that she had a fracture, not a bruise, and she must be operated on. However, there were no orthopedic surgeons in Baghdad at that time, and a general surgeon operated on her. When her cast was removed a month after the surgery, an x-ray showed that the bones had not been properly realigned. As a result, she walked in pain and with a limp for the rest of her life.

Father's death left Khedoury and me to deal with the liabilities of the many relatives he had been providing for. Together we began a flourishing banking business and eventually I left my other job. Khedoury, with whom I was living, was nearly twice my age, and he became my surrogate father. The burdens of the other relatives grew more and more severe. I also became the family matchmaker, which embroiled me in many feuds. At the start of World War II, Khedoury was diagnosed with a malignant tumor in his nose and traveled to Jerusalem—not a simple matter in wartime—for an operation. When his condition worsened, I went to Jerusalem to see him, and he died shortly thereafter. I suddenly found myself at age 31 largely responsible for the financial well-being of a large, extended family.

Impetus to Leave

Then came the first day of the Farhoud in 1941. I was going to visit my friend Abdulla Elias who lived nearby. He had just driven into the city and turned around to come back home when he witnessed the beginning of the pogrom. I wanted to get news from him of the events. On my way, three armed soldiers ran after me and one of them, wielding a knife, blocked my way. I fought with him and tried to get to Abdulla's door, but it was locked. The three of them knocked me down, fired shots over my head, and the man with the knife plunged it into my chest and made a deep cut in my wrist. Then a Muslim woman walking by threw bricks at me in attempt to finish me off. They left and as I lay on the ground bleeding I looked over and saw that my mother was watching helplessly from our window. A taxi passed by and the driver, who knew me, picked me up and brought me to the hospital. He sped through the streets as I hunkered down in the back seat, fearing another attack.

Outside the Majidiyeh Hospital I was laid on a stretcher and waited in the hot sun. Two Muslim workers then picked me up and as they carried me inside they decided to have a game of it by throwing me up into the air and catching me and they laughed while I writhed in pain. Two soldiers approached me. One of them put his bayonet at my throat and spat at me: "You dirty Jew." He then asked his partner, "Shall I finish him off?" His friend replied, "To hell with him. He's already finished."

I was transferred to another building where I was lined up along the corridor with about 60 other stretchers holding injured Jews. Within minutes, there were over 100 such stretchers. I began to understand that there were only a few doctors and nurses on duty to treat all these victims. A Jewish nurse named Miss Bassuss came to me and told me that she was going to assign me to a bed and told me not to ask for nor take from anyone drink or food or an alleged drug until she retuned to see me. I was taken to the bed and was still bleeding profusely. I had a terrible thirst. She reappeared a short time later with a Muslim surgeon by her side. I immediately recognized this doctor—he had held a pistol to my head at a party, breaking up the celebration, because I was dancing with a girl he was in love with. So naturally I was scared as hell to see that this was the doctor who was about to treat me. But he stitched me up and the nurse later told me that the man felt sorry for what he had done to me at the party. I then sat in a wing of the hospital with dozens of beds filled with injured people like myself, and we were all unattended to the entire day.

I had nothing to eat or drink all day and night aside from an orange that a nurse had brought me in the morning. In those hours, many patients died in indescribable misery.

The next day, I was transferred to another wing where I was the only Jew recuperating in a room full of Muslim soldiers who had been injured while fighting the British. Eight days later, feeling much better but very weak, I was discharged. But a doctor friend of mine came to visit me and discovered that I was having trouble breathing. He advised me to get an x-ray which revealed that I had an accumulation of fluid in the pleura that had gone undetected at the hospital as I had had no x-ray done. I was literally drowning in my own blood and secretions. I was told to be hospitalized immediately.

Baghdad only had two hospitals at the time, and I was not about to go back to Majidiyeh. I went to Meir Elias, a hospital founded by the Jewish philanthropist Meir Eliahu and run by the Jewish community. I was treated by a doctor named Krushkin, a Canadian and one of the few foreign doctors recruited by the government to work in Iraq. Although I was treated well there, my condition was worsening, and I told Dr. Krushkin that I had enough money to pay for the best doctors and that he should muster up a team of them to consult with him on my case. He did, but none could help me: one after the next, they trooped in and out of my room to examine me, each one leaving with a befuddled look on his face. Finally, one of them told me, "Your situation is very grave. You have internal bleeding and we have no way to stop it. No operation of this type has been done here before and consequently we are totally helpless." Since I was being left to die, I asked them, "Can I eat anything I want?" They said yes. "Can I smoke too?" I asked. They agreed. So I lived it up. In those days, because the medical care was so poor, we just lived our lives and believed in God and felt that when our time was up, it was up. We had a very fatalistic approach to life. And then, miraculously, I began to heal. It was a medical mystery to all. I spent four months in the hospital, and eventually recovered fully.

Now my first aim was to get the hell out of Iraq. The only question was, "Where to?" The war was at its peak and the only place Jews could easily get into was India. But after suffering in Iraq, I would only settle for a first world country, and I set my sights on the U.S. Yet it was virtually impossible to get a visa to the U.S. at that time. In the meantime my inventory on the Baghdad stock exchange skyrocketed and I was doing quite well. By that point, I was living in a large, beautiful home and had many servants attending to us and caring for my mother. Still, the more money I made, the more I wanted to get out of the country. In anticipation of leaving, I wired as much money as I could to my brother Joe in New York.

My U.S. visa request finally came through because I was able to prove that I was on financially sound footing. Then I began to worry about the feasibility of actually getting to America in the midst of war. A travel agent I knew gave me a ray of hope, explaining that there may be a way to travel by air via about eight countries, including several in Africa, to the U.S. However, there was no guarantee that I would actually be able to board the flights in each country. I also fretted about how my incapacitated mother would be able to handle such a trip, but I eventually decided to buy two tickets.

I knew it would not be easy to get passports enabling our entry into each of these countries, which required having them named explicitly in the passports. But with bribery, I was able to get that done within two days. I made arrangements to sell the house and liquidate my business, and then waited for the call from the travel agency that our flight was imminent. We received the call, and that afternoon, July 14, 1942, my mother and I left Iraq by seaplane from Habaniyeh Airport. As we flew over the deserts of Iraq, my feelings overwhelmed me: I was leaving the country of my birth, where I had passed my life in pleasure and turmoil, for good. A long chapter had come to a close. My mother—perhaps because this was her first experience flying, perhaps too because she was feeling the same things I was—began chanting *Shema Yisrael*,[6] over and over.

After a two-week trip with stopovers in Palestine, Egypt, Sudan, Nigeria, Ghana, Liberia, Brazil, Florida, and, finally, New York, Salim Sassoon and his mother arrived in the United States. Three months later, he was drafted into the U.S. Army and served in Europe during World War II, for which he received the Bronze Star Medal. After returning to New York, he began a business importing Persian rugs, and was engaged to Violet Shemtob, who was in Baghdad at the time, via proxy. She moved to the United States and they married. The couple had five children.

* * *

Salim Fattal was born in the poor Jewish neighborhood of Tatran in Baghdad in 1930. In his account, he describes the life of poor Jews in Iraq and Iraq's Communist Party, in which he was active—what he says are the two untold stories of the Iraqi Jews. He also recalls the two days of the Farhoud in 1941, when his uncle was attacked by an angry mob in a Muslim neighborhood and never seen again.

Two storylines that tend to be obscured in the recounting of the history of Iraq's Jews are that of the poor Jews, who comprised the vast majority of the community, and of the Jewish Communists, many of whom were Jews from the lower classes.

The aristocratic class of Iraqi Jews, which probably comprised no more than 5 percent of the community, has dominated the historical narrative. And while these Jews tried their best to describe what they saw and experienced, they were often ashamed to say that our community did indeed have many defects and instead focused on burnishing the community's image. The fate of the poorest Jews was of interest to almost no one.

Meanwhile, those involved in the Zionist underground have dedicated their memoirs and efforts to describing the activities of the Zionist underground. But that too is only a small part of the story of the Iraqi Jews. Many poor Jews turned to the Communist Party after having been neglected or overlooked by the Zionist movement. The fact is that the Zionist movement paved its ideological way mainly among rich and well-established families who could afford financing the travel expenses of their children to Eretz Yisarel and because such families invested considerably in their children's education and at the core of the Zionist movement was education about Eretz Yisrael.

The upper classes frequently referred to Iraqi Jews as highly educated and successful. Yet among the lower class, there was a great deal of illiteracy. The government had quotas for the number of Jews it admitted to universities every year, and the upper-class Jews, for the most part, were admitted. Among Jewish women, in particular, illiteracy rates were very high. Prostitution among Jewish women did exist, and in fact a Jewish woman who lived in our house—as her father worked for my grandfather in his embroidery factory—later became a prostitute. Jewish girls and women lived secluded lives inside their homes and only a few of them started going to school in the early part of the twentieth century. During the 1940s radical change took place and growing numbers of females began to go to school and even to work, but even then most poor Jewish women remained at home.

My book *In the Alleys of Baghdad* (2004) is dedicated to the poor heroes of Baghdad and to the poor neighborhood, Tatran, in which I was born and raised. In Tatran, people didn't read newspapers because they didn't know how to read, and they didn't listen to the news on the radio because they couldn't afford radios. So news simply traveled by word of mouth. Men would sit in a café and listen to the news from the café radio, and if something big was happening, they gathered there or at the homes of someone they knew who owned a radio. The Jews in Tatran worked to get through the day—they didn't have the luxury of thinking about the future. Their horizon was between home and work, no further. Sometimes men had only two days of work in a week. Some people went hungry, although the community was somewhat philanthropic and helped the poor in small ways.

My grandfather, Abraham Khlaif, was the authoritative leader of his large clan, a righteous man and very religious but not fanatic. He never missed *shaharit*, *minha*, and *a'ravit* [morning, afternoon, and evening prayers]. His wife and children, including my mother, Aliza, were religious like him, and consequently my mother ran a religious household: we kept Shabbat, kept kosher, and performed all the Jewish rituals on the holidays. My grandfather built a small factory in his house in which he embroidered special handmade cloaks for women, called *ezagh*, which were extraordinary, beautiful works of art. Hence our name was *fattal*, which means "weaver." It often took him several months of hard work to complete one, and therefore only rich women could afford them. My grandfather was known for his talent and he loved his work.

My father, Abraham Fattal, worked for my grandfather in his factory, supplying threads to tailors. It was there that he met my mother. My father died of rheumatic fever at age 36. I was six years old, and today I can hardly remember his face. That left my mother to take care of the whole family—all five of us children: myself and four brothers. She didn't look for another husband and began working days and nights in the factory. She was an incredibly self-sacrificing woman who was simply dedicated to her children and their well-being. Her story touches on the most awful wounds of economic despair. Her goal was that her children would finish their academic studies in particular fields and ultimately serve her needs in her old age. One would be a physician who would cure her when she got old and sick. The second would be an engineer who would design her grave. The third would be a poet to eulogize her after her death. That turned out to be me. The fourth, she decided, would be a lawyer, and the fifth a scientist. What a dream! Her dream eventually came true, but only shortly before her untimely death at age 50.

My mother assisted her father in his business and was so efficient and effective that he appointed her as his business manager. At the time, business in Baghdad was directed only by men: to see a woman in a business was very unusual. When clients, mostly Arabs, came to buy merchandise and saw my mother managing my grandfather's business, they were rather stunned. My grandfather insisted the clients deal only with her: "Talk to Aliza," he used to say. "She's the boss." It took people a few months to get used to the idea but then they saw that she was the best manager my grandfather could have ever found. Consequently, they began to call my grandfather "Abu Aliza" [father of Aliza]. This was highly unusual because fathers were typically identified by the names of their first-born sons.

My mother was the third child in her family. My grandfather and his wife Serah had hoped for a son, and my grandfather promised that if his hope would come true, he would make a festive celebration the likes of which Tatran had never seen before. The first five babies were girls. Then Serah gave birth to two boys who died shortly after birth. My grandfather felt desperate, and spoke to God, asking, "What sin did I commit that you refuse to give me a son? Is it a curse? Or something wrong with me? Help me! I fear that when I die, I will have no son to read Kaddish for me." As a believer, he sensed that something was wrong with him. That very night, he saw in a dream Rabbi Meir Baal Ha-nes, who is buried in Tiberias. The rabbi told him that a guest will visit him and Serah at their house. When he woke up, Abraham believed that the curse was lifted and that this time God would fulfill his wish.

Indeed, after the dream, a son was born. They named him Meir, after the rabbi, and he became the spoiled and beloved child of the family. When people called my grandfather "Abu Meir," he felt proud. Then Abraham was blessed with two more sons, Yosef and Naim. But in 1940, my grandfather died while on his way to the synagogue—before he was able to witness the tragic end of his three beloved sons.

Meir's Story

The 1930s and '40s were a turning point in my life as well as in the history of the Iraqi Jewish community. Palestine landed in Baghdad like a wild hurricane and dominated the very foundation of Iraqi society. In the name of Palestine, Iraqi nationalists formed an alliance with the Nazis in 1941 and sucked the hatred of Jews directly from the contaminated swamp of the Third Reich. In the name of Palestine they established a rigid policy of persecution against Jews and deprived us of our freedom, citizenship, identity, and sometimes our lives.

Those decades were dark with anti-Semitic hostility. The worst of it came in 1941, with the pogrom. Among the dead were my uncle, Meir, and his business partner, Nahum, who were attacked by a hostile mob in the Muslim neighborhood of Bab el-Shaikh and never seen again. The murdered were buried in a huge grave. Nobody heard their shouts—not in the Muslim Arab world, not in the West or East, and even not in Eretz Yisrael. Poets didn't eulogize them. Protest demonstrations didn't break out in the streets. Newspapers were silent.

In his 1941 coup, Rashid Ali Gilani became prime minister and banded together with the Mufti of Jerusalem who had been expelled from Palestine and came to Baghdad. Together, Gilani and the Mufti and their inner circle, guided by Fritz Groba, the Nazi ambassador to Iraq, tried their best to bring the whole Middle East under the umbrella of Nazi regime. The pro-British royal family fled to Palestine. And so a war began between England and Iraq that lasted one month. The British won the war by the end of May, 1941. Gilani and the Mufti fled to Germany, and for two days, on June 1 and 2, Baghdad was abandoned to lawlessness. The British army and the victorious Iraqi leaders waited in the suburbs of Baghdad, leaving the city to the mercy of murderers and thieves.

Meir and his business partner Nahum Kazzaz, who also lived in Tatran, owned horses that they housed in Bab el-Sheikh, about five kilometers from their house. They raced the horses and just had them to play with and take care of as a hobby. On the morning of June 1, Meir, his brother Naim, Nahum and his 11-year-old son Nissim left Tatran in a carriage and spent some time with their horses. Between 4 and 5 o'clock in the afternoon they headed back home in a minibus. There were other passengers as well and a driver's helper who collected the fees from riders. The bus was filled with Jews because it was headed toward our neighborhood. Suddenly, it was stopped by a mob as it was going through Bab el-Sheikh. The mob was also stopping other buses. Meir became a quick target because he had a typical Jewish face. How did the Arabs see that? They just knew—all Iraqis had a kind of instinct for identifying an Arab face versus a Jewish one.

The mob opened the bus door and pulled Meir out. Naim tried to grab Meir and pull him back inside, shouting, "This man is not a Jew!" They didn't listen and Naim couldn't fight them off. The Arabs beat Meir almost to the point of unconsciousness. In an attempt to save Meir, Nahum went out through the window on the opposite side of the bus: he felt he could help because he knew people in that neighborhood who worked for him. He thought it would be easy for him to find some friends and save Meir.

Nahum's son Nissim was with him on the bus and saw his father go out. Nissim was confused and scared about why his father suddenly left. He tried to follow him by jumping out of the window as well, but didn't get that far: the driver told Nissim, "If you leave, you will be killed. Stay here." Fearing more bloodshed, the driver decided to drive on without any warning, abandoning Nahum and Meir.

The bus brought the remaining passengers back to Tatran and Naim came rushing into the house. He shouted, "Meir was kidnapped. We don't know where he is." My mother said, "I'm going to Bab el-Sheikh." He said, "Are you being foolish? I came from there. People are being killed there. You are a woman, and in almost one hour it will be night." So she didn't go. To this day nobody knows what happened to Meir and Nahum. It was as if the earth opened its mouth and swallowed them up. There was no closure: no bodies, no grave, nothing.

My cousin Salima was a nurse in the Majidiyeh hospital, to which many of the murdered and injured Jews were brought. She estimated that on the second day of the Farhoud, some 300 bodies were piled up in the hospital courtyard. She went to the hospital wearing an *abaya* [Muslim headscarf], to disguise herself as a Muslim in order to search for Meir, her uncle. Together with Nahum's son, Avraham, who came to search for his father, they looked for Meir among the bodies, but found no trace of either man.

The search for them went on for years because there were rumors that people had seen them, but those rumors were probably initiated just so someone could make a profit off of us by demanding money for information. The search came to an end in 1950 when our family came to Israel. Only then could my mother say, "For the first time, here in Israel, I can talk about Meir and not cry." She was ready to start a new chapter in her life.

Yosef's Story

Several years later, after we arrived in Israel, I learned of the death of Meir's second brother, Yosef, who had been the most successful son in his family. He was a tailor and had many connections with army officers and government officials because he made their clothes. But he had a friend named Abu Sa'adia who was Jewish though in a way he was also a Muslim: he spoke the Muslim dialect of Arabic, behaved as a Muslim, and all his friends were Muslims. One day this friend told Yosef, "Let's make some money. Let's buy a flock of sheep. I have good friends who can deal with this transaction. They know everything about sheep." Yosef didn't want to get involved because he didn't know these people. He said, "Forget it, I'm not interested." But Abu Sa'adia tried again and again to convince him and finally Yosef agreed, invested his money, and they bought a flock of sheep. But Yosef still wouldn't go to inspect what he had bought. Instead, he authorized Abu Sa'adia to supervise everything and to report back to him.

It so happened that this Abu Sa'adia had a very evil plot against Yosef. He told Yosef one day, "You should come with me to see the flock. It's not far from here—it's in the desert but we can take a car. This is your money, your property. You should come with me." But Yosef said no again and again. He just had a bad feeling about it. Several Bedouin were in charge of the flock, and the general feeling among the Jews was that Bedouin were not people to deal with—that the best way to handle them was to keep a respectful distance from them and make no contact. And this is what Yosef said to his friend: "I don't want any contact with them. Do it yourself and I'm here."

But one day Abu Sa'adia succeeded in persuading him to go see the Bedouin and the flock. The two of them met in the morning in a cafe near the Tigris. They drank some coffee and headed towards the desert. Yosef never came home—he was assassinated there. The Bedouins had probably hoped that he would arrive with a lot of cash but they found only 50 pounds in his pockets and they killed him and hid his body. The police did not find the body. Abu Sa'adia was interrogated and he denied any involvement, and nobody believed him but he wasn't punished.

Underground

Out of our communal despair and grief, there emerged among the Iraqi Jewish youngsters, including myself, a strong readiness to fight for our security and freedom. We had two choices: to be indifferent and to live in Baghdad as humiliated citizens, or to fight the government. At the time there were two main political streams, Zionism and Communism. So if you decided to struggle, you could choose one of those two options—fighting to change the government, which meant joining the Communist underground, or fighting for a new alternative altogether, which meant joining the Zionist underground and escaping to Palestine. But because the Zionists did not include the poor in their activities, we never heard about them—they didn't come to our houses, schools, or synagogues. The Zionists also assumed that youth from well-established families would have achieved a higher level of education, and that's what Eretz Israel wanted from the Jews in the Diaspora: the prototype it had created for the best youth—the educated fighter, the crème de la crème. And the Zionists knew it would be difficult to find anyone to finance the escape of poor Jews to Israel.

So poor Jews chose the Communist Party. And that is what I did. The party was very strong but it was underground—the government had ruled it illegal. The

Jews of Iraq were, generally speaking, real patriots. They loved Iraq, they loved Baghdad, they loved the folklore of Baghdad, they loved the songs of Baghdad; they spoke Arabic, and they knew the literature of the Arabs and their history, even the Koran. But during the 1940s they were treated as enemies of Iraq and collaborators with the Zionists in Eretz Israel. Lower-class Jews felt especially disenchanted. The Communists among them, including me, felt like second-class citizens and eventually became persecuted both as Zionists and as Communists. Many were thrown in jail. Others were hanged. So we lived in a hell. Finally, once the Jewish Communists felt that Iraq had rejected their sincere desire to fit in and change Iraq from the inside, they joined most of the rest of the Jews of Iraq in adopting the Zionist solution. In the end, the state of Israel financed the whole operation [Ezra and Nehemiah], transferring almost all the Jews to Israel.

Jews managed to penetrate the Communist party leadership. Two of those who were hanged in 1948 and 1949 were Jewish party leaders. I saw the body of one of them, Yehuda Sadik, hanging from the gallows for public display. Over the course of two days, four Communist leaders were hanged: one Jewish—Sadik—one Christian, Yusuf Salman, and two Muslims, Zaki Basim and Muhamad Shabibi. Their hangings convinced me to join the party. Later on, Sasson Dalal, another Jewish Communist leader, was hanged. Yet the murders of the other Jews in this era have been far more highly publicized than the hangings of Sadik and Dalal.[7]

I joined the party in 1948, and it so happened that I attended a high school in which the party was very active—in fact, it was known as "the school of fighters"— and in which all the youngsters were eager to act against the government. It was called the Scientific Institute, a public school for which we paid a small fee to attend. Many of the students participated in all the antigovernment demonstrations and strikes—Muslims, Christians, and Jews together.

In the school itself there were many government spies collecting information against the Communist Party and the Zionists, and my name was on the list of Communist activists that they compiled. I worked closely with a very nice guy who went to school with me and named Al-Janabi. He was known as leftist, and he was from a very well-known Muslim family, so nobody would dare arrest him. He was also on this list. One day, I was asked to hide the library of the party in my house. I agreed and put the books under my bed, where they stayed for about a month.

One day we went to take part in a demonstration against the regime. Several of us were chased by the police. We hid in the house of a Muslim family who loved the Communist students and saw them as the party's bright future. We stayed for about half an hour until we thought the police had stopped chasing us. Then we went to meet the leader of our cell who had not met us at the protest and we wanted to find out what had happened to him. As we walked towards his house, we saw a man reading a newspaper on a street corner nearby and a second man reading a newspaper on the opposite corner. We thought our leader had probably been arrested and his house was being watched by detectives in case others who worked with him showed up. So we passed the house and didn't glance at it. Later on, we learned that he had been arrested and those men were indeed waiting to snatch anyone who came to see him.

That day, I realized that if our leader had been arrested, he probably was going to be tortured and he might disclose the fact that the library was in my house. I went to school later that day but decided that I would move the library once I got home. Then, as I was sitting in the classroom, in the middle of a lecture, the principal came into the room and asked, "Is Salim Fattal here?" I said, "Yes." He asked, "Can you come with me?" I followed him to his office where two men were waiting. "We just want to ask you a few questions," the director said to me. "Don't worry." The two men escorted me out the door and a police car was waiting there. Then I understood they were policemen. They said, "Let's go to your house." I feared they would find the books I had stashed under my bed.

When we got there, they searched for the library right away—clearly they had been tipped off. Even if our leader hadn't told them, they had enough spies to find out. One of the detectives remained with my family and the other one came to my room to look for books. He looked through my own Arabic and English books that had nothing to do with Communism. Meanwhile, the party books were under my bed in a jute sack. He spent three hours searching through my own library and found an English book by [Russian writer Anton] Chekhov. He said, "Chekhov is a Russian name. This is a proof that you are a Communist!" I tried to explain to him that Chekhov was born and wrote before the Russian Revolution. But the officer didn't know English—not a word. A third of my library was English books. And it was clear that he was a bit embarrassed as he wanted to show me that he was an intellectual.

When he got up, he kneeled down, looked underneath my bed and he saw the jute sack. He pulled it open and two or three books fell out. Luckily they were English books. He was holding in his hand *The Dialectical and Historical Materialism* written by Joseph Stalin. If he had wanted any evidence that he had the right guy, it was right there. Looking at the book, he asked, "This too is literature?" I said, "Yes, do you want me to tell you what's in it?" And he was tired by that time and said, "No, no, it's alright. But why is it down here?" I said, "I don't have enough room for all my books, so I put some down there." That was a very dramatic moment. I was lucky because there were Arabic books in the bag too and it just so happened that none of them came out. In the end, he just took a few poems I wrote and said he planned to hand them over to police headquarters and they would decide if they had something on me. And then he arrested me, despite failing to find—or at least failing to realize that he found—the evidence he was looking for.

I was in jail for four days and my uncle Yosef bribed the police to get me out. It was a horrible place, and during the night I heard people being tortured. After my arrest, my family took the bag of Marxist books and set it on fire. They knew that I was a member of the Communist Party, and they wanted no more risk. The same policeman who had searched my room kept returning to ask for me and inquire as to what I was up to. Then he went to Yosef's shop and Yosef hosted him and bribed him just to get rid of him. I felt hunted. It was very clear to me that I was being followed and that I might soon be thrown in jail again if I stayed in Baghdad. And that is when I decided to leave Iraq.

Yet I didn't have money for a smuggler. So I approached my friend, also a member of the Communist Party, David Sassoon. He met me in a coffee shop one day. I told him that I wanted to leave the country but that I had no money. He said, "I can arrange for you to leave." He explained: "There is a family named the Attars and they have an invalid son, Yehezkel. He has no chance of recovering in Iraq. He has problems with his kidney and he cannot walk. If you would take responsibility for bringing him to Israel and getting him to a hospital there, and giving him his medications and injections on the road, I can arrange for you to be smuggled out with him for free." The family agreed to the deal and financed the journey.

On February 13, 1950, we crossed the Iraqi border to Iran. We stayed in Tehran for two months before coming to Israel. I arrived in Israel at Sha'ar Ha'Aliya.[8] My four brothers and mother came in August with Operation Ezra and Nehemiah. After arriving in Israel I learned of the murder of Yosef. Naim had died earlier of complications with his kidney and liver when he was in his '30s. So my grandfather, who had wanted a boy so desperately and finally had three, lost them all in tragic circumstances.

In Israel I needed a job and wrote a letter to *Kol Yisrael* [The Voice of Israel Radio], telling them I knew Arabic. I was hired but three months later they fired me when the Shin Bet [Israeli equivalent of the FBI] learned I was a Communist and didn't want me working in such a sensitive position where I'd have access to all the country's news and information. That job, at least, saved me from having to go to the *ma'abarot*: I was able to stay at a place called the Pioneers' House. But what a jolt my firing was—I had been on the run in Iraq for being a Communist and found myself not accepted in Israel either.

Salim Fattal forged a distinguished career in broadcast journalism in Israel, initially as a member of the committee that established Israel's Channel One after the Six Day War and later head of its Arabic programming department. Fattal has worked passionately to set the record straight about the community's history through writing and film. The three-part documentary he made for Channel One about the modern history of the Jewish community in Iraq was produced between 1984 and 1988 and has been screened in Israel, Europe, and the United States. His memoir, In the Alleys of Baghdad, *describes the life of five generations of his family. He lives with his wife Lea in Tsur Hadassah, Israel. They have three children.*

* * *

Oded Halahmy is an artist whose abstract sculptures, the bulk of his work, incorporate themes and the aesthetics of the Iraq he knew. Born in Baghdad in 1938, he moved to

Israel in 1951 and now splits his time between his home in New York's SoHo district and the artist colony in the old city of Jaffa. His artwork is infused with the beauty of the Iraqi landscape that he recalls vividly here. In that landscape, too, are the tastes and the smells of Iraq; his passion for Iraqi Jewish food has made him an expert in the cuisine.

In my memories, everything about Baghdad is beautiful and colorful: the people, food, the city, and its museums and parks, its rivers and landscapes. I remember eating by the Tigris River and watching the beautiful palm trees sway in the wind. I felt like they were dancing and performing for me. Even now I can see the narrow alleyways, the beautiful houses built with ancient stones and beautiful doors sculpted by carpenters, exquisitely colored glass in circular windows in reds, blues, greens, and yellows. To me, Iraq was the most beautiful place on earth—a paradise. Its landscape is in my mind every day. When I left Iraq, I felt that I was leaving behind the Garden of Eden. Still today I feel that way.

My family lived near el-Shorjah, a fruit and vegetable market near the coffeehouse my father co-owned with a Muslim partner on Gazy Street. Sometimes he took me with him in the evenings to sit with friends and drink tea or coffee, play *shesh besh* (backgammon), and participate in the conversation of the day. He brought watermelon seeds and a pocket flask filled with arak to share with his friends around the table. I enjoyed listening to the men—it was always men—talk about politics or the events of the day, and I loved to watch people walking by in the street.

My mother, Salima, studied at the Alliance school, eventually teaching there for a year until my older brother Heskel was born. Almost every year she gave birth to a new child, until there were eight of us. I went to the Rachel Shahmoon School until 1951, the year we left Iraq. I especially loved calligraphy, drawing, painting, and crafts, as well as reading, writing, and math.

My father, Salech Haskel Chebbazah, was a goldsmith who owned his own workshop. He had a machine shop where he made bracelets and necklaces. He took gold, put it on a plate and hammered it until it became thin wire. His job became easier and more efficient when he became one of the first goldsmiths to introduce metalworking machines into Iraq, in 1932, which he and his partner had brought from Germany. Goldsmiths all over the country knew him and brought their gold bars to his workshop for processing. People nicknamed him "Saleh Abu Makaien," because *makaien* means machine. The people who knew him well also called him "Saleh Abu Heskel" [Saleh father of Heskel], because fathers were given the name of their oldest son. He made a lot of money. In the summer, when I had no school, I liked to go see my father working in his shop and sometimes I brought him a lunchbox from home. He preferred eating my mother's cooking rather than taking a chance on a restaurant or food stand. When I brought him the food, I would sit in the shop and watch him do his work and listen while he talked to his customers. He loved his craft. And he loved his family.

I grew up in a home in which three generations lived together, and it was a wonderful, loving, big family. We lived in a large, beautiful three-storey house with a spacious courtyard big enough for us to play volleyball or have a live orchestra play. As a child, I made all of my own toys and crafts, and I invited my school friends to come and play in the courtyard. We often played *belbel wahach* (stickball), using pieces of wood that I crafted, or marbles or ping-pong. Because the house was so large, we frequently had private parties for the weddings of close relatives or to celebrate the birth of a baby. For those events we invited the Chalghy Baghdad, the Iraqi orchestra made up largely of Jews, to play for our guests. The orchestra was in demand among Muslims and Christians as well as Jews for the biggest, fanciest parties. At these events, many guests stayed with us overnight or for several days.

On the ground floor we had an indoor kitchen and an outdoor kitchen, and my mother baked breads in the outdoor oven called *tannour,* often used in nice weather for large parties. Outside, we made food for the holidays: for Hanukah, Purim, Sukkot, and Passover. On hot days, we had a ground-floor parlor room that had a shaft to the roof. When we put the lead icebox in the shaft and turned on the ceiling fan, it became a cool oasis from the heat. We had several benches and couches there, and it was a wonderful place to relax with guests. Also on the ground floor was a big-open portico called a *tarar* and in it was a large wood-framed bed that would swing back and forth called a *jelalah*. Mothers would gently swing with their babies on it, and children loved to lay on it and swing, surrounded by the adults gathered on the cushioned benches.

There were bedrooms on the first and second floors, a large guest room, a room for the maid, and a large playroom where my friends and siblings and cousins played ball games. On the third floor we had more rooms for family and guests. In the attic I made arts and crafts. On the roof, I had a room to myself where I kept my pet pigeons and I used to go up there in the evening, let them fly out and then call them back. In the summer we ate our light dinners of watermelon, feta cheese and jam with bread on the roof. We kept a clay water cooler called a *hib* there to chill our drinking water, and on hot nights we slept on beds draped with mosquito nets and watched the stars. It was beautiful.

Delicious Memories

Many of my fondest memories of Iraq are of our wonderful family meals. My mother cooked with the help of the maid. They were marvelous cooks and when I think about the meals they made, I can still taste them in my mouth. Sometimes during my lunch break from school, I bought food from street vendors: in the hot months I enjoyed handmade ice cream called *dondermah* and flavored ices. In the winter

I ate boiled *foul* [fava beans] with sweet turnips and beets in a paper cone. My favorite treat was the classic pickled mango-and-tomato sandwich. The pickled mango is called *ambah* and tomato is called *tamata*. Sometimes I added shish kebab to it, and then it was called *laffa*. In the summer, the entire family would hire a horse and carriage to go to the river, where we had fishermen catch fish for us and prepare it over a wood fire for us: *mezgouf*, and was delicious.

My mother used to make *bamya* [okra], which was virtually a staple of the Iraqi diet and is prepared many different ways. The ends of the *bamya* were very gluey, and we would cut them off and let them dry in the sun. Then, with a *hawan* [mortar and pestle], we crushed them finely, then mixed them with water, making a gluey paste. We used that mixture as a thickener for mango sauce and other sauces. I also used this as glue for my kites in the summer.

I loved to watch my mother baking or cooking and sometimes we children would put a reed mat on the floor and help with her preparations. For instance, my mother gave one of the children the *hawan* when we made *medgugah*—which is the process of pounding dates and nuts into a thick paste with the *hawan*, but it is also the end product. The women in the family, my mothers and aunts, would sit and gossip while they cooked, chattering and laughing about which woman was pregnant, who was marrying whom, and which of them made the best rice. We had a big kitchen to accommodate our large family: eight children, my parents, and grandparents. Every day my mother and the maid cooked for at least for 15 people. When we had guests, it would often be 30 people.

Sometimes I accompanied my mother to the market because women didn't go shopping alone in those days—they usually took a male with them. At the market we would hire a *hemal*, or porter, to carry the food back home because we bought large quantities for our big family.

In the summer we had an abundance of produce and my father liked to pickle the various produce with spices, salt, and vinegar. We stored the pickled produce in big glazed ceramic vases for the winter. We stored feta cheese, pickled mango, pickled cucumbers, tomato paste, *tehina* [sesame paste] and jams made from apricots, prunes, peaches, lady apples, quince, and other fruits. In the morning I liked to eat *geymar*, which is heavy cream with *silan debes*, date honey. Every day my mother cooked a different dish and I learned to cook all of these dishes myself. I experiment with new ingredients while maintaining the flavors I love, and in some cases create new dishes.

Today, I cook the same way as my grandmother and my mother cooked, using the same utensils. Because we didn't use kitchen appliances, we had *hawan* in different sizes for various foods, as I do now. For instance, to make potato *kubbeh* [the classic Iraqi dumpling], one would boil the potatoes and mash them with a large *hawan*. I don't use electric appliances in my kitchen: I like the process of creating meals with my hands, the same way I make my art. I also use a *tachtah*, a chopping board with short legs on both sides so as to enable the cook to chop, place a bowl beneath the board, and then easily gather the food into the bowl. Simple technology, but it works well.

We would begin cooking on Thursday evening for Shabbat, when we had the biggest meal of the week. You could tell if you were in a Jewish neighborhood on a Friday because the whole neighborhood was full of the aroma of hot sesame oil. We would use beautiful ceramic and gold-leafed dishes on our white embroidered tablecloths, and our finest silverware. My mother would light the seven wicks of the *quarayee*, an Iraqi-style Shabbat lamp. We would pray for Shabbat to welcome it, bless the wine, and my father sang "Eshet Hail" [The Woman of Worth]. The children would enthusiastically join in, singing her praises, and enjoying the wonderful dinner.

In my home in New York, I have a *quarayee* that was brought by my family from Iraq to Israel. The *quarayee* consists of three parts: a wick-holder called a *belbolah* shaped like a Star of David, which was made of silver and holds seven wicks, a glass bowl in which to place the *belbolah*, and chains that hold the bowl and allow it to be hung from the ceiling. We would fuel our Shabbat and Hanukkah lamps with sesame oil, which was abundant in Iraq. We added equal parts of oil and water to the lamp, because the water would keep the glass from overheating, and the lamp would naturally go out when all of the oil was burned off. For the wicks, we would wrap small slivers of palm branches in cotton and place them in the wick-holders of the *belbolah*. European Jews typically light two candles for Shabbat, but we always lit the seven wicks of the *quarayee*.

In our courtyard, we built the *sukkah* [outdoor ritual structure for the holiday of Sukkot]. Weeks before the holiday, my father prepared all of the necessary materials needed to build it, and immediately after Yom Kippur ended, we began to work. He planned the *sukkah* with great care and thought before constructing it. I would lie in my bed at night, trying to anticipate its construction plan and how I would assist my father. We built it out of large, round bamboo beams. After assembling the structure, we hung strings of lights to light up the nights and covered the roof with palm branches. At the entrance, we attached three tall palm branches on either side and bent the ends towards each other, then tied them in the middle to create a beautiful organic archway for the entrance. My mother made the other three walls out of white sheets stretched around the posts.

My next job was to help decorate the inside of the *sukkah* with pomegranates, oranges, and other citrus fruits. I liked to paint the front of the structure with gold leaf pigment that my father brought from his shop. On the floor we placed a large mat made from dried reeds. We brought in wooden benches that were covered with fine cushions of red velvet and a wooden chair for Elijah the Prophet.

Once the festival started, our guests and relatives gathered around the long table inside, bringing the *sukkah* to life. My aunts, uncles, and cousins stayed with us for the entire holiday week, so we always made the *sukkah* especially large. In the evenings, we sat in it and ate dinner, prayed, and listened to many stories, sometimes until sunrise. We lit yellow beeswax candles that burned for hours. I loved to collect the soft, gentle wax and sculpt birds and pigeons with my hands.

The night of Hoshana Raba, which the Babylonian Jews call "Araba Night," was the most fun and joyous of all nights. As my father was a god-fearing man, he would talk about the living and the people who were no longer with us. During the day we children would play games, and my mother, with the help of her maid and my aunts, were busy making marvelous foods. They made *she'iriah* [noodles] cooked with rice and decorated with fried onions, almonds, and raisins, and served with lamb and vegetables. Our *sukkah* was a feast for the eyes—a piece of art. I will not forget its beauty, especially in 1950, the last year we were in Baghdad.

A Farewell

In Iraq, we had wonderful relationships with my father's Muslim friends who were partners in his shop. We were always treated with great respect by our Muslim and Christian neighbors, and no one from our family had ever been insulted or experienced anti-Jewish acts. People often ask me: "You recall Iraq with such love, so why did you leave?" My answer is simple: when we saw relatives leave—two of my uncles left for Israel before 1951—and then how tens of thousands of people were registering to go, including our friends and neighbors, we just felt we should not stay behind. It was a chain reaction in some way.

We left Iraq for Israel when I was 12. Like most Jews who left then, my parents were not allowed to sell their property and my father's business. We were only allowed to take one suitcase with us. We left Iraq, our homeland, with deep sadness. I remember the flight was crowded and we dressed in our most beautiful clothes and the women wore all of their jewelry. When we landed at Lod Airport the Israelis sprayed us with DDT out of sheer ignorance, fearing that we'd brought parasites from an Arab land they didn't know anything about. They put us on flat-bed trucks and brought us directly to the transition camp. It was winter. It was raining. We were given two tents, one for the men, one for the women. The bathroom was far away. Harsh winds blew the tents away, and it was very hard work to keep them secured and maintained. The winter was very cold, living in tents with no heat, and we had no running water. We missed our beautiful house in Baghdad, but we did not sit and cry. We were disappointed, but we focused and worked hard on building our new lives in our new country from scratch. We were in the *ma'abara* [transition camp] for almost a year. We were the lucky ones. I had relatives who stayed there for six or eight years.

Israel had so little housing at that time, and what it did have was given to the Ashkenazim. The government built "development towns" for the *Mizrachi* [eastern] immigrants in the Negev and the suburbs of Tel Aviv. The country was also being built in great part by way of *kibbutzim* [communes] and *moshavim* [cooperatives], but the Iraqi Jews were city people, not farmers, for the most part, and did not share the Ashkenazi ideology of settling the land by working the land. We were discriminated against by those who called us *schwartze* [black, in German]. Everything was a shock for us because we had grown up being told that Israel was the Garden of Eden. Still today, I feel that the real "land of milk and honey" was Iraq.

The Iraqi Jews created their own community in Israel because they had an instinct to stick together. Schunat Hatikva was filled with Iraqi bakers, restaurants, spice markets, fruit and vegetable markets, goldsmiths, carpenters, shoemakers, *kubbeh* makers, street food vendors, musicians, café and tea houses, and all of my father's friends and many acquaintances from Baghdad. Doctors and lawyers from Iraq mixed more with the Westerners in the wealthier parts of Israel.

My father could not practice his profession in Israel because he didn't have the network of suppliers and customers, nor the money to buy a shop and the necessary materials. So he performed manual labor on the roads. My older brother, Heskel, earned more than my father by painting lamp posts in the street. I took care of my little brothers and sisters, attended school, and worked painting houses, planting lawns, and gardening in the new houses of the wealthy in north Tel Aviv.

We became dedicated to our new country, which we loved. My family bought a little house in Jaffa where our neighbors were Muslims and Christians. We felt comfortable in those surroundings, free to be ourselves and not feel the burden of having to hide our roots. We could finally listen freely to Arabic music: when we listened to it in other parts of Israel we were told we couldn't listen in public because Arab countries were Israel's enemies, so until then we had listened in secret in our own homes. Overall, our Arabic culture was looked down upon. Eventually we went to listen to Iraqi music played by the Iraqi immigrant musicians Salah and Daoud el-Kuwaity.

I eventually moved to New York, where I feel freer to explore my art. The irony is that my art is far more appreciated in the West than it is in Israel, and my collectors are mostly Americans even though my art is infused with images of the Middle East. Part of the reason for that is that Israel has only a few museums and also that the Israeli mindset still pushes the Iraqi Jewish experience to the fringes of its consciousness. I describe my art as what I call "Arabesque lyrical abstraction sculptures." My sculptures are made up of strips and chunks of wood which I juxtapose with one another, and then cast the sculptures in bronze.

In 1975, I made a breakthrough in my work. I was making a *sukkah* for myself inside my loft because it reminded me of constructing the *sukkah* with my father in our courtyard. I decorated it with palm braches and hanging pomegranates. In Iraq, we often painted the *sukkah* with watercolors or gold leaf, so I experimented with that too. And I began to get inspired by the pomegranate. One day I was relaxing in the *sukkah*, and I looked at the pomegranate, and the pomegranate looked back at me, and we started a dialogue. I felt that the pomegranate wanted to be integrated into a sculpture I was working on, so I got up and took a pomegranate from my kitchen and added it to the sculpture. I fell in love with the sensuous shape of the fruit: round and full. Soon, there were pomegranates in nearly everything I made!

Like the pomegranate, symbols of the Middle East are in all my art. The shapes, colors, and forms are inspired by the Middle Eastern landscape and my memories of Iraq. The pomegranate is sweet and its color is a beautiful, deep red. It is an ancient and universal symbol of beauty, love and marriage, fertility, prosperity, hope, life and rebirth. Its seeds, rich and abundant, promise a generous future. It is one of the seven fruits named in the Bible, and the Bible mentions it frequently for various symbolic purposes. We eat pomegranates on Rosh Hashana, drink sweetened pomegranate juice upon breaking the fast on Yom Kippur, and hang them whole from the *sukkah*. I surround myself with pomegranates: they are in my kitchen, my studio, in every room of my home. Some are fresh, some dried, some cast in plaster, bronze, aluminum, silver or gold, and they are central in almost all my artwork today. I named both the galleries I opened in New York City and Israel "Pomegranate Gallery."

In 2001, I created the Oded Halahmy Foundation for the Arts to promote the work of Iraqi writers and artists. I want Westerners to be aware that we have a beautiful culture with wonderful art, poetry, music, and food. Iraqi poets, writers, and musicians—Jewish and non-Jewish—have come to my studio to read and perform.

I am also involved in a project to preserve and restore the Jewish holy sites in Iraq, which the Iraqi government would like to open for Jewish tourism in the future—a heritage tour of sorts. On my visit to Iraq in April, 2004, to document the holy sites, I started photographing the landscape the minute I landed, and my camera was shooting nonstop, even through the window of my car. Although Baghdad is not as clean as it used to be because of the war, it still felt like the Garden of Eden to me. I visited the museums, my father's old goldsmithing market, the el-Shorjah market where I used to shop with my mother, and my old neighborhood. However, I didn't go back to my childhood home because it wouldn't have been safe. I got to taste once more the wonderful *mazgouf* and some of my other favorite foods. My dream to visit Iraq was realized, but it was sad to witness the destruction of the country I love so dearly.

In 2003, I donated one of the *hanukiot* [candelabra for Hanukah] I created to the American Jewish military personnel stationed in Saddam Hussein's former palace. It arrived just days after the army had captured Saddam, and was displayed in the former dictator's throne room. It is called *Hanukiah with Pomegranates (Royal Palace)*, and has candleholders in the shape of pomegranates. Cast in aluminum, it is a symbol of peace and hope for the all Iraqi people.[9]

Oded Halahmy is writing an Iraqi cookbook focused on cooking with pomegranates, one about his hanukiot, and one about Iraqi date palm trees and the seedlings that were brought to Israel by new immigrants and were the basis of several of Israel's flourishing date palm orchards. He is making a film about Iraqi maqam *musicians in Israel. He also established a nonprofit foundation to collect funds in the United States for the Babylonian Jewry Heritage Center in Or Yehuda, Israel. His sculptures are in the Guggenheim Museum in New York, the Hirshhorn Museum in Washington, DC, the Israel Museum in Jerusalem, and many other public and private collections.*

* * *

Alfred and his wife Hanina were born in Baghdad and left as children, Hanina at age 7 and Alfred at 16. They married in the United States. Both enjoyed privileged childhoods in Iraq, Lebanon, Egypt, and England before emigrating to the U.S. Hanina is the daughter of Khedouri Zilkha, the banking magnate whose K.A. Zilkha Maison de Banque, commonly known as Bank Zilkha. (Hanina is the sister of Ezra Zilkha, whose account appears on page 25.) The Shasha family ran a thriving business importing cotton piece goods from Manchester, England, to Iraq. In their joint account, the couple describes life in Baghdad under the British mandate—a sweet time of prosperity and relative freedom for Jews across the region, and a city that felt more like a village.

HANINA: I was born in 1919. I left Iraq when I was seven but somehow I have many recollections. Perhaps my earliest memory is from age two: I had three boils on my face similar to those that every Iraqi child got at some point from an insect that fed off of date trees.[10] If the boils had not been well taken care of, I would have been disfigured. But my grandmother advised my mother to bring a goat to the house and every morning they would put me under the goat, squeeze its udders, and squirt the goat milk on my face. I cried because it was uncomfortable and I hated the taste of the milk. For a very long time after that I couldn't stand the smell of goat milk. The remedy helped, but the boil still left a small, round scar. You can identify many Iraqis by the fact that they have the same kind of scar.

Our beautiful house on the Tigris had a pretty garden with blue and white flowers which smelled wonderful. It made me happy to be in that garden. Gardens were highly prized because they provided fruits and vegetables and shade from the hot sun. Of course there was no air conditioning—people sought shade or the breeze from the river– but there was also no central heating. We burned charcoal at night during the winter. In the summer months, we placed mattresses on the flat roofs and slept under the sky. How many times I tried to count the stars! In our home we had a stork's nest which was considered good luck. We had many servants and our lives were easy and carefree. The home was the center of activity in all respects. Here the mother and father resided with their brood of seven, eight, or ten. They ate together, studied, played, laughed, cried, and received friends and members of the extended family. Matchmakers would bring the groom and his family to the would-be bride's home to see her and see where she came from.

ALFRED: I was born in 1920. The Iraq I knew was a blessed country with ample space. Bedouin lived in the outlying areas around the cities and when one of them decided to migrate to the city he did not have to buy a plot of land on which to build a house. He would simply help himself to a suitable site and build his mud house on it. No one challenged him.

I came from a family of eight children. Because families were large we tended to play with our brothers and sisters and cousins. Sometimes we played with neighbors too, Muslims and Christians. My mother was a housewife who devoted her time, energies, and attention to her husband and children. We had a cook and servants so we were pampered. Cooking in our home was done by a male cook, a Jewish Kurd from the north. My mother was always scolding him for his cooking but his one saving feature was that he was a great storyteller. He told stories about dragons and created suspense before he sent us to bed, and we would beg him to continue his story the following night.

We had two homes: one in the city and one on the riverbank of the Tigris. Our city house was big and solid and had marble columns on the inside with sandstone floors. In later years, it was turned into a schoolhouse because of its sheer size. But the one I remember best is the one on the riverbank, in Kerradah, because we spent so much of the year there. We had trees there that bore dates, figs, apples, and other fruit.

Because it was cooler near the river and the summers were so long and hot, we spent nearly eight months out of the year at our summer house. In order to get to school from that house, we rode a motorboat which would stop in front of the house and pick us up. There were no regular stops: you just hailed a motor boat and the driver would pull up and stop beside your house. This was great fun. The boats had wide, comfortable cushions and we used to snuggle up on them and put our hands in the cool water. When we were at our other house, we walked to school. Baghdad was not a big city and you could do a great deal by simply walking.

HANINA: People had many superstitions in Iraq. We kept a jug of water handy in the house should an owl fly by: when we spotted one, we would pour out the water to dispel a possible curse. When a family member left the house on a journey, the family spilled a bucket of water on the road behind his carriage or car so that he'd have a safe journey.

We also had many wonderful common expressions taken from Arabic. We said *bel eefi* when we wished someone good health. *Ya Allah elake* meant "with God's help" and *Allah karim* meant "God willing." *Befrahek* and *be frahahek* were the feminine and masculine forms of "to the celebration of your wedding!"

ALFRED: Families gathered around their dining room tables at dinner and sometimes at lunch. Those were happy times and the adults did most of the talking. I remember my mother telling us children at times, "Listen to what your father is saying..." Little did I realize then that she had "wound him up" the night before to repeat what she told him—essentially demands for maintaining discipline in the household. She was the power behind the throne!

There were picnics on Saturdays for the immediate family and friends, either in a garden on the outskirts of the city or at a sandbar in the middle of the river when the sandbars emerged in summertime. The boatsmen would catch fish and make *mazgouf* by simmering it on wood and covering it with tomatoes. It was an adventure for children. On Saturday evenings some families would hire a carriage and go for a ride down one of the main streets. It was not uncommon for a man's credit rating at the marketplace—always based on reputation—to plummet the day after people would see him riding on the carriage because they would think he was wasting money on frills.

The only leisure clubs were the Jewish clubs and they were quite nice. They had gardens and good food and very often Jews would invite their Muslim friends in government or business to these clubs. There was amity between the Sunnis, who ran the government, and the Jews. We played lots of sports. There was soccer and swimming, and made-up games. In the summer we played by the river and swam in it. We would swim or take a boat to the sandbars, stake a claim to part of it, erect a tent with the prongs of a palm tree, plant a few cucumber and tomato seeds in the soil, and in a few weeks the vegetables would sprout up. We were free as could be. This was our summer camp.

HANINA: Dress was no simple matter. As an outer shawl, affluent women wore a garment called an *ezagh* which was woven from a silver thread dipped in gold, in various designs. The weaver, who used a wooden loom, was a skilled man who commanded a high price for each. When the material became old or the woman tired of the design, she had the material melted down to a ball of silver. From this, the weaver would make yarn again, dip it in gold, weave it into cloth, and make a new garment.

ALFRED: Almost all Jewish families were religiously observant. Homes were kosher. The meat was bought from a community slaughterhouse under the supervision of rabbis. We ate lots of stews with either lamb or chicken or beef, though sheep were more abundant than cows and chickens. Animals were slaughtered by a *shohet* [slaughterer] in one's own house for the family's own consumption or for donating to the poor. Sometimes someone's hand would be soaked in the blood of the lamb and stamped on the wall of the house to ward off the evil eye. For us, food was ample: meat, vegetables, rice, fruits and milk, and cow and goat milk. Rice, imported from Iran, was the staple.

During the high holy days, families visited each other in their homes wearing their best clothes, and the hostess offered her best sweets, coffee, and cigarettes, all with great fanfare. Businesses were closed for a half-day on Friday, and Saturday was a full day off because so much of the commerce in the city was owned or managed by Jews. Friday night, *erev shabbat*, was a special occasion, and women cooked all day long to prepare for the Sabbath meal. We lit the candles, made *Kiddush* and *Ha'motzi* [prayers] and no one touched electricity for 24 hours. On Saturday mornings many men and boys went to synagogue and fathers would entice their sons to go by promising to take them to a coffee shop afterwards where they would drink super-sweet tea and have a roll.

HANINA: We were never allowed to go into the street alone, and we always had a guard taking us to and from school, usually a man, and in our case a man named Abbas whom I adored. Our parents felt we should be protected because we were Jewish and also because there was always a threat of harassment of females. Abbas came in the mornings, put me on one of his shoulders and my sister on the other and took us to school. He had a daughter named Circus, and every day he measured me and teased that Circus was still taller than me. I thought it was funny so on the days he forgot to measure me I called him to come back to measure me, hoping each time that I had grown taller than Circus.

ALFRED: The Jewish community had its own schools. Some of these schools were run by Alliance Israelite Universelle, which was on the French educational system, and some were on the English system. For grade school, I went to a Jewish community school named Ta'awan where the second language was English. For middle school I went to an English-oriented school, Shammash. I had teachers from Salonica, Greece, and France who had all been trained by Alliance and they were very competent. The idea of using a French or British system was to prepare students to go to universities in Europe, because in those days the best universities were European or American. These schools made invaluable contributions to the community in that they opened the community to the West. Their value cannot be exaggerated. Donors gave large sums to build these schools and families paid only a small tuition. The schools were also financed by a tax collected by the community on the slaughter of kosher meat. Government-run schools were open to everyone and many Jews attended those as well.[11]

HANINA: The biggest celebration of all was a wedding. When there was an important wedding, the people who were not invited were able to come but they had to view the event from the balcony of the synagogue while the guests and the ceremony took place downstairs. These uninvited guests—wedding crashers—were mostly women who wanted to be able to gossip about the wedding. They were required to wear a veil so nobody knew who they were, and they were allowed to be there because it was the custom never to refuse a stranger in one's home.

ALFRED: At that time, many beggars would come along to watch the wedding as well and the father of the groom or the groom himself would give money to them—usually Indian rupees, which had good value.

Births were celebrated too, and people preferred to have boys, so when a boy was born, very often there was a big party. At these parties, there were belly dancers and music, and men would drink and smoke and reward the belly dancers by sticking bills in their bosoms.

HANINA: My father, Khedouri, was a very well respected man. On several occasions, he met King Faisal who received my father beautifully. But my father was compelled to leave Iraq in 1927 after receiving a letter demanding a ransom. He paid the money but just the same he but decided to leave because he thought they might kill him eventually. Practically overnight he decided that he should go to Lebanon because he had contact with businessmen there. My mother was pregnant at the time with Selim and was so upset that she went into labor and had the baby a little earlier than expected. My mother and the seven children, including myself, left Iraq a few weeks after my father's departure. We took two cars: my mother in one and the cook in the other. My mother breastfed Selim while in the car which was bumping around quite a bit as the roads through the desert weren't paved. So when we arrived in Damascus the baby was very sick and throwing up.

On the way to Damascus we saw the Roman ruins of Palmyra and I remember how beautiful and colorful everything looked with grand columns against the sunset. My father met us in Damascus and we stayed there until the baby felt better and then continued onto Beirut. As we neared Beirut, my mother was filled with delight because she had never seen mountains before. My mother was a very cheerful person and she was so happy that day. She said she was going to love being in Lebanon because it was so beautiful. We were atop a large hill and looked all the way down into the valley, and the houses looked like dots so my mother mistook them for cemeteries and said, "Even the cemeteries are gorgeous in this country!" When we arrived in Beirut, my father had a beautiful, big apartment waiting for us, so we got settled very quickly.

ALFRED: My father, Yamain, passed away in 1936. Since I was close to him, his sadness towards the end of his life inevitably was transmitted to me and from the happy and outgoing boy that I had been I was transformed into a very serious and introverted one. He died while being treated by doctors in France, and my brother Maurice, who at 21 was the oldest male in the family, was forced to return to Iraq from America where he had been studying, to care for us all. My mother became completely lost and could not cope. In the same year Maurice thought it best for me to go England to study, and that is what I did.

My father lived and died before any problems of anti-Semitism affected him or his business. There was not perfect harmony between Jews and Arabs under the Ottoman Empire and the British occupation. Relative harmony is more accurate. I remember my father had a lot of admiration for the Ottoman Empire's *wali* in Baghdad because he thought he was fair and treated everyone equally well. There was some anti-Semitism but it was usually smoothed over by knowing people in the right places, as the Jews often did. In fact, life in Baghdad during my childhood was very tranquil. It was really quite similar to living in New York today: Jews were prominent in business and professions, including engineering, medicine, law, et cetera. Even plumbing and carpentry were dominated by Jews. Jews felt quite free to move about and had business relationships with Muslims and Christians but socialized mainly among themselves. Generally speaking, the Jewish community had equal legal protection.

But relationships between Muslims and Jews often involved negotiation and compromise. Once, my father built a house for my newly married sister behind our house on the river. He bought the land from a Muslim neighbor, but another Muslim neighbor was jealous. This man thought, "Why should my neighbor get all this money from this Jew when the Jew could have bought my house instead?" And how did he register his protest? As we were building, he came along looking very angry and wanted to see my father. He announced to my father, "You're encroaching on my land!"

My father said to him, "Tell me, my friend, where the boundary should be." The man moved the boundary back by about a meter. My father turned to the builder and said to him, "So that's where the boundary should be." After all, what could be the value of the strip of land my father gave up? Nothing, in the scheme of things. Then my father turned to the man and said, "Tell me. You have two grown sons. What are they doing?" He said, "Odd jobs. Not much." My father said, "Why don't they come and work in building this house?" So the man said, "Sure. I would love that." The man went home and was able to tell his wife that he made the Jew retreat and change the border and that he got two jobs for their boys out of the deal. And on our end, my sister still got her new house built.

The Arabs are very emotional people. I contrast them with the Hindus. You'd see two Hindus arguing in the street for hours but they never came to blows. But the Arabs came to blows almost before they began arguing. The Jews learned either to negotiate with the Arabs, or to turn the other cheek.

HANINA: In Lebanon, four of my siblings and I were sent to boarding school. I was only eight when I went for the first time. I was too young and it made me unhappy. The school was Lycée Français. That is where I learned French and until today I think in French and count in French. I was a good student, so once when the teacher asked, "How can I reward you? You are such a good student." I said, "Teach me English."

When I was 17, I was sent to Switzerland to another school. I missed my family constantly. Then the family moved to Egypt because my brother Selim had asthma and the weather in Lebanon was bad for him. So my father opened a bank in Cairo and Alexandria and relocated the family. I loved Cairo and began to study Islamic art with a lady named Mrs. Devonshire who took me around to all the mosques chronologically from the oldest one to the newest one. That sparked my love of art. In 1941, we came to America.

ALFRED: My livelihood was a direct outgrowth of the business that my father established with his brother Joseph in Manchester a century ago. Together, they traded cotton piece goods from Manchester, which was the main source, to Iraq.

Before the business began, Joseph traveled with Hanina's father Khedouri to Istanbul. They traveled on horseback in 1905 to get exposure to the West. Joseph was stationed in Manchester and my father in Baghdad. They shipped the goods to Basra and from there, river boats took the shipments up into Baghdad. From there they were distributed throughout Iraq and Iran, where we had agents—our relatives—in Kermanshah, Hamadan, and Tehran, who received them. It was easier to get goods into Baghdad than into most places in Iran because Iran is mountainous. The business was highly successful and eventually expanded beyond textiles to anything customers asked for. Father also began exporting some goods from Iraq as well.

By the time my father died, the business had contracted because of the Depression and because Japan had become a considerably cheaper producer of cotton piece goods. My brother Maurice turned the business around by focusing on exporting wool for carpets, though World War II hampered that business. In 1946, I opened the Shasha Trading Company in New York: Baghdad supplied the wool and it was sold to customers, carpet mills, in the U.S. and, with my brothers stationed in various cities around the world, we imported wool from other countries to the U.S.

Alfred and Hanina met in 1941 in New York. They have three children.

* * *

Sami Michael was born in 1926 in Baghdad and was active in the Communist Party in Iraq. During the government crackdown on Communists, he escaped to Iran to avoid an arrest warrant against him in 1948 and immigrated to Israel shortly after. He became one of Israel's most respected novelists. In his account, he describes the basis for his affiliation with the party and that of large numbers of Jews—and how they were brushed aside in Israel by an Ashkenazi-dominated Communist Party and ultimately disillusioned by the Israeli party's more radical ideology. These experiences, together with his happy childhood memories of Iraq and relationships with Muslims and Christians, form the backbone of many of his novels.

I was born Salah Mujalid. In Iraq, a person's last name was selected either according to the place where he came from or the family profession. Our family profession was making accounting notebooks, so we were called Mujalid, like Bookbinder. When I arrived in Israel, the pronunciation of Mujalid became Muglid, which sounds like *mugla* in Hebrew, pus, so I adopted the name I had used in Iran when I bought a counterfeit ID—Sami Michael.

I was born into a middle-class family. My father was a distributor of textiles. My grandparents lived in the old alleys of Baghdad, which didn't even have names. I grew up in a big house with my *hamula*: the extended family including my immediate family, grandparents, and aunts and uncles—close to 50 people in all and a total of

10 immediate families. There were three things in addition to kinship which held us together: my charismatic grandfather, our beautiful house, and the source of our livelihood, which was a workshop in the house for producing notebooks. Although there were plenty of quarrels and outbursts, members of the *hamula* would be there to support one another and collectively they provided material and emotional support. Everyone came together for holidays which were the pinnacle of my childhood happiness.

There was a funny tradition in Iraq of moving from house to house once a year. I don't know why people did it. It was a very ancient custom. Every year after Sukkot, there was a giant reshuffling—people exchanged apartments and houses and every extended family would rent a new, large house. In my family, this went on until I was seven or eight when my mother decided, "enough"—she needed a house of her own.

So we left the *hamula* and moved to our own home in Betaween, then a new neighborhood, which was mixed at first—Jews, Muslims, and Christians—with modern villas and houses. The streets were straight, with electricity and asphalt. And then a huge gap was created between me and the rest of the family as a result of our new residence because in Betaween all the kids, my new friends, came from families much richer than mine. We had moved from an environment where poor and middle-class families lived together in a densely populated ghetto to a neighborhood where most of the residents enjoyed economic prosperity and valued education. So it was like moving from one homeland to another, from one country to another.

I attended Al-Wataniya, Shem-Tov, and Shammash schools, all run by the Jewish community. So in fact I had two groups of friends: friends from the new neighborhood who were my classmates, and friends from the old environment in which I grew up who were very simple folk. The friends from the old environment never held a newspaper, never read. I describe this reality in *Victoria*[12] which is about life in the Jewish ghetto of Baghdad, and in *Handful of Fog*.[13] In the second reality, Betaween, everyone wore suits, went to school—girls included—and read newspapers. In the house to our right was a Christian family. The father of the family was an officer in the British army and an adviser to the Iraqi army, and the mother was from Lebanon. They spoke English in the house. On our left was a Muslim family. All of the children who lived on the street played together. We had very close relations with non-Jews.

Muslims joined us in every celebration until the tensions between the Jews and Muslims were created because of two things: the bloody conflict between the Jewish *yishuv*[14] and the Palestinians on the one hand, and the intensifying Nazi propaganda and the rise of Nazi Germany on the other. Eventually Betaween became an exclusively Jewish neighborhood as the Christians and Muslims slowly left when housing prices rose.

Betaween was a neighborhood of parks: huge gardens like you see in London, straight streets, highly developed. It was planned in a British design. There were three large parks in the neighborhood and the neighborhood abutted the Tigris River, where there were modern cafes—not for backgammon and men-only talk, but with lemonade and soda, where we played dominoes or billiards and where women could also come. The clothing was different and new, not the traditional attire: men wore suits and girls wore dresses without the *abaya*.

In *Storm among the Palms*,[15] I drew extensively from my own life in this period in order to describe the life of the adventurous Jewish boy Nuri in Baghdad's streets: becoming part of street fights and pranks, standing up to bullies, and grappling with first love.

The Tigris River was a central part of my life. I have wonderful memories from the river. At the age of 10 I took a swimming course with a teacher named Sasson. He used to take 40 or 50 kids with him at once to teach them how to swim. We began with floats and the final exam was to swim across the Tigris and to return. We did this every day of the week during the summers until we grew up and swam by ourselves. We also used to rent boats and go on hikes. We swam or took a boat to the sandbar in the river, made bonfires and grilled fish.

Later on, when I joined the Communist Party, we took advantage of the river as a safe haven, giving lectures on boats as we floated along on the current.

People played musical instruments and some drank arak. I used to go alone along the river's promenade, on foot or by bicycle, and learned to ride a horse there. The river was part of my daily life. When I was older I sat in cafes next to the river, read books, and wrote. We prepared our homework in cafes from the age of 14 onwards because the houses were filled with children and noise—and my house was quite noisy, with five boys and three girls in all. It was an amazing sight to see the cafes in the middle-class areas filled with students doing homework. The sound of rustling paper, the quiet hum of people reading and memorizing. As I grew older, my activities in the Communist Party began to eat up much of my time, and in addition I didn't like to do homework, so I used to join one of the groups of good students and I would prepare for an exam by listening to them.

Ever since those days on and around the Tigris, water has been a central part of my existence. I worked for 25 years as a hydrologist in Israel's Hydrological Service, part of the Ministry of Agriculture. I measured water—floods, springs, wells. Today I live in Haifa with a sweeping view of the bay. I love water. I love touching water, I love looking at water. Water is good for my soul.

Evolution of an Iraqi Communist

My opinion is that most of the Israelis who write about Jewish life in Iraq have actually tried to reconstruct the reality there, which has been done according to the needs of Zionist education. Israelis have been brainwashed regarding the past in Iraq and the integration here in Israel to believe that the Zionist narrative is the main narrative. People have been led to believe that the Jewish community in Iraq was largely Zionist and readily picked themselves up and made aliyah. But the entire Zionist story is a myth that has no basis in reality, according to the reality I saw and experienced. The Iraqi Jews were like American Jewry of today, that is, we cared about the well-being of the Jews in Palestine but at the same time we enjoyed the lifestyle of the land in which we were born and had no intention of moving.

The shaping of our philosophy and national identity began in the 1920s with the Balfour Declaration. At that point, the leadership of the Jewish community discussed among themselves which orientation the community should have: an Iraqi identity or Zionist identity. Whether to educate the children as Iraqi patriots and to integrate into Iraqi society or to sit on their suitcases and to adopt the Zionist approach. Apparently before there was even any readiness to lean towards the Zionist orientation, emissaries from Eretz Yisrael arrived in Iraq. As a result, Iraqi Jews sent donations to Israel and purchased land in Kfar Yehezkel in the Jordan Valley and in the Lower Galilee near Kfar Tavor, which the Laura Kadourie School helped finance. Somehow the decision was made, and Zionist clubs and societies sprouted up, although the leadership's eventual decision was to become part of the Iraqi community, not the Zionist one.

At that time, the Jews were well integrated into Iraqi society. In addition to their domination in commerce, the first prose literature was written by Jews like Anwar Shaul and Shalom Darwish and Jewish poets wrote in Arabic. There was no newspaper editorial staff in Iraq without Jews on it. The integration was so complete that Jews even began engaging in local political activity. That was a unique case in the Middle East, though it existed to a more limited extent in Egypt. In Iraq the Jews were involved in politics even before the trend towards Communism in the 1940s. They rallied at demonstrations and speeches, and felt like Iraqi patriots.

The British gave the Jews the opportunity to enter any university in England. In school, we were oriented towards Europe, not Israel. We studied math and science in English. At Shammash we had teachers from England and India. Many of them didn't even know Arabic, only English. I was familiar with world literature in English, not translated into Arabic and certainly not in Hebrew.

I became involved in the Communist movement because it was the single attractive alternative to the political reality in Iraq at the time for me. My graduation from high school coincided with the increase in Nazi propaganda in Iraq. I remember the Farhoud clearly. I was 14 and had taken 2 of my brothers and a sister to visit my grandfather and grandmother in the old part of Baghdad. At the end of the day we took the bus back home and then I saw the masses outside, as if prepared for something. I believe ours was the last bus that passed that mob safely before it began to riot. The bus after us was stopped and Jews were taken out and slaughtered.

The areas that really suffered in the pogrom were the poor areas. The army protected the middle class and the rich, and we were protected in Betaween. After it was over, we realized that the Iraqi army had saved us from further slaughter. The British army, on the contrary, sat outside the city and waited for all the rage to be taken out against the Jews before it entered the city and took control. When we woke up on the morning of June 3, the entire street was filled with Iraqi soldiers. Out of pain, anger, and embarrassment, some of the poor people emigrated[16] immediately after to Palestine. There were only a few hundred, not more, that immigrated in '42, '43.

So the anti-Jewish riots came as a shock—hit me hard in the face. And then World War II broke out and on the way to school we saw graffiti that Hitler was destroying the "germs." I knew that they meant me, a Jew, and my generation that was coming of age then and had previously felt so secure and happy. The world around us was crumbling. The Germans were marching from victory to victory and their intention was to conquer the entire Middle East. We began worrying about the Jews in Palestine.[17] So to think in those days about Zionism as a solution sounded not only impossible but also stupid. Furthermore, the British army wasn't gearing up to protect Iraq against the Germans but instead dug into hiding, seeking protection against a German invasion in Palestine. Yet many Jews did join the Zionist movement in Iraq starting in the early '40s.

At this stage of the war we discovered that the one and only power that managed to stop the German advance into their territory was Moscow. How did it happen that the most un-Western, seemingly weak country managed to do that? We wondered. So suddenly we admired the Russians. We didn't understand what Communism was because in Iraq we had a very weak Communist Party at the time with perhaps just a few dozen adherents and it was underground. But we had heard about it.

So my friends and I began reading all we could get our hands on about Communism. It was all in English—there was nothing in Arabic about Communism. So in addition to Balzac and Shakespeare, we started reading Marx and we began translating the books into Arabic for others to understand. Then we discovered an interesting thing: we could find no books or articles published in Iraq that spoke out against anti-Semitism—except for the Communist material. So we said to ourselves: "Here is our address." Many educated people found this was the path for them: all my friends—girls and boys, men and women.

But being a Communist was very dangerous because we became a real force—a threat to the regime—as the movement grew. The government denied us licensing as a political party in 1946. In the early and mid-'40s, the Iraqi government did not recognize Zionists and Zionism as enemies in any formal way because the Zionists did not challenge the regime—they only wanted to leave Iraq. All the heroic stories about the secrecy of the early Zionist underground were made up later on. The regime knew exactly when and where the Zionists operated and who they were. And in fact the regime was pleased about the Zionists, because one Zionist is one less Communist.

The Communists became popular: we even wielded influence within the ranks of the Iraqi army and military training academies. The Communist Party became the strongest party in Iraq, despite being underground. And the most amazing thing of all was that it was a sort of Jewish-Shiite-Kurdish coalition against the ruling Sunni minority. It was a very strong coalition, and very popular. We were considered heroes. If I said, "I am a Communist," I was immediately protected. Every door was open to me. We had press and we sold our newspaper, *Al-Usba*, almost openly, with the certainty that we would be protected, and we had a circulation of about 6,000.

Then arrests began as early as '43, '44, and continued through '49. *Al-Usba* was banned in 1946 shortly after its founding. The prisons were full of Communist women too—even Arab girls. The Jewish Communists were charged, ironically, with the crime of Zionism as well in many cases. But we continued to function. Communists were often given 10 years to execution. And the CID [Central Intelligence Department]—also called the *Muhabarat*—which were the secret police, acted mainly against the Communists, not against the Zionists. On the contrary, it regarded the Zionists as allies. Only just before the State of Israel was established were discriminatory measures imposed against Zionists.[18] With the establishment of Israel, the Iraqi government was glad to get rid of the Zionists and the Jews in general, and used that event as the pretext for ordering the arrests or executions of Jewish Communists.

Erased

Then came the historic period that was later expunged from history, as if it never existed. The prohibition of publicizing the events of the Communist Party as they occurred was the result of a tacit agreement between the Iraqi, British, and Israeli establishments for decades to come.

What happened was that the issue of the Baghdad axis came to life. Iraq was preparing to sign the Portsmouth Treaty, which set out terms of cooperation and alliance between Iraq and Britain and thus was essentially a pact against the Soviet Union and Communism. We took advantage of this to organize demonstrations against the treaty and against the government in late 1947. We organized mass protests with rabbis, Muslim sheikhs and vicars, and Christian leaders, and we held hands and talked about Jewish-Arab brotherhood. The movement became known as the *al-Wathba*, like an *intifada* [uprising].

Jews and Arabs fought together against the government and the Jewish community supported it in a big way—on the streets, with their wallets, ideologically. There were street battles with many fatalities. We beat the police and the army didn't interfere. It wasn't prepared to do so, and it turned down the command to fire on us. On the contrary, soldiers as individuals also participated with us. And we won. We won to the extent that the government in Iraq fled for several days.[19] In the final stage the party's Jewish secretary and my friend, Sasson Dallal, was hanged. It was the first case from the time of Mohammed and until today that the head of the opposition in Iraq was a Jew. Several top leaders in the party were Jews as well, and I personally helped found new cells and organized officers and members of the Shiite community.

The government didn't start harassing and persecuting the Jews until it broke the Communist Party. But at the same time, Jews and Arabs were fighting each other in Eretz Yisrael following the UN resolution for the partition of Palestine so this window in time became obscured by the conflict there. So the Iraqi authorities used the Palestine conflict to divert attention away from the unrest at home and economic difficulties, and thus attempted to erase this piece of history. The Arabs erased it because the Arab nationalist line after Israel's establishment became that all Zionists and all Jews are monsters and thieves, and that you can't make peace with them. And the Iraqi Communist Party erased this chapter to avoid admitting that Jews and Arabs could cooperate.

Israel also has tried its best to abolish this storyline from memory because it does not fit the Zionist narrative in which all the Jews sat on their suitcases and waited for the Zionist redemption. And it did not fit the reality of what was happening in Israel at the time. Few wanted to hear that Jews and Arabs have lived together in peace and harmony and, moreover, were ideologically aligned. In addition, Israel had chosen an anti-Soviet, pro-American path in diplomacy so it shunned Communism. In the same way, the most amazing chapter of the Holocaust was ignored—that the Red Army liberated the Jews from most of the concentration camps. So if such a big story can be obliterated, then of course a small story like the Iraqi Jewish Communists can be as well.

Bound for Israel

In 1948, the Iraqi regime and the British embassy, which had an enormous influence on it, had arrived at the conclusion that they could not accept Iraq into the Baghdad Alliance, which was similar to NATO, without totally breaking the Communist movement, so they began a brutal campaign against the underground. They hanged, killed, and jailed many people. They tore the party to shreds. After those who were imprisoned were released—some had been in jail more than a decade—the authorities put them on planes straight away and sent them to Israel.

That spring, an arrest warrant was issued against me. I was nearly caught in a coffee house and then I moved between my relatives' homes until my father hired a smuggler to steal me over the border to Iran that spring. He hid from the smuggler the fact that I was a Communist because that affiliation was extremely dangerous at the time and he feared the smuggler would therefore decline the offer. My father gave the man a large sum so he could hire a bodyguard and someone who knew the way. I was alone with three people guarding me and the whole escape took a week before I got to Tehran. It was a deluxe escape. Every day we stopped at a new place.

The smuggler was a "Don Juan"—in every place he had a woman with children waiting to host us. A large part of the way we traveled by car and I was dressed as a Bedouin sheikh.

In Tehran I didn't have a passport or money, and I faced the danger of getting extradited by the Persians to Iraq because of my party affiliations. Then an offer came from the Soviet embassy in Tehran to go to the Soviet Union. I accepted the embassy's proposal and traveled in the direction of the Soviet border. I arrived at Mashad, a holy city for the Shiites which the Jews were forbidden to enter. There were Marrano Jews there who had converted to Islam and who hid us in a mosque. I was at the border for four days, thinking about how if I crossed over, I wouldn't be able to come out. That didn't suit my character. I like being free. I turned around and returned to Tehran and registered with the Jewish Agency to make aliyah to Israel. Nine months later I arrived in Israel.

When I and other Communist activists arrived in Israel, we felt like heroes. I didn't go into the *ma'abarot*, because they were not yet set up. I moved to Wadi Nisnas [an Arab neighborhood in Haifa] and began working with the local Communist Party, organizing Arabs and Jews. I began working as a journalist for the Arab newspapers, *Al-Jadid* and *Al-Ittihad*, usually under the name Samir Marid. I used to give speeches about Communist ideology to residents in the transit camps and I was attacked by Mapai and Herut bullies[20] wielding metal rods and axes. I was spit on and cursed. Many other Iraqi Communists in Israel experienced the same aggression against them. But despite everything, the Communists got 20 percent of the vote in the first elections for the Knesset in which the new Iraqi immigrants participated, thanks in great part to the transit camp population.

The Iraqi Communists in Israel were discriminated against from within the party itself, which was an Ashkenazi party and racist. The strongest racism against Sephardim and Mizrachim was from within the Communist Party and among the *haredim* [ultra-orthodox]. So despite all the votes it received from the Mizrachim, its leadership didn't see fit to promote a single one of them and take him to the Knesset.

The Jewish Communist in Iraq was a Communist because he was a Jew, because the ideology was one of equality irrespective of religion, and thus affiliation was in the interest of the Jews. Meanwhile, the party in Israel emphasized equality only for the Arabs. Eventually it evolved from an Ashkenazi party of mostly Russian and eastern European immigrants to an Arab party, so the Iraqi Jews were ignored again. On a personal level, I didn't experience the phenomenon of the exclusion by Arabs from the party. In fact, at *Al-Ittihad*, the Arabs promoted me. The first thing Arab Israelis did when they got their newspapers was to open them to read what I wrote.

Yet over time I began to feel that something stank in Communism: it started to adopt a bit of an anti-Semitic policy. At the newspaper, I also used to translate from English into Arabic and I read between the lines in the articles and sensed a tone of anti-Jewishness. I thought to myself, "I came to Communism in order to protect Jews, to fight anti-Semitic propaganda." Something that later made me especially angry was an article that appeared in the *New Times*, the mouthpiece of international Communism, which said that the pioneer of liberation in the third world was the army—armies that generate revolutions, military coups. This scared me. An army? The armies I knew were the ones of the Third World that abused their power. I understood that the Soviet Union started to implement a policy of empire and not a policy of spreading Communism according to the ideas of Karl Marx. And I was disillusioned by Stalin, especially his fabrication of espionage charges against physicians, mostly Jewish, in what was known as the "Doctor's Plot." So I said, "goodbye," and left the party in 1955.

New Country, Same Cause

In Iraq we didn't know about the terms Ashkenazim, Sephardim, and Mizrachim. Those concepts didn't exist: we thought Jews were Jews all over the world. When people spoke about the east we didn't think they meant the Middle East. We thought in the terms of the Cold War. To us, the east was Russia, Poland, Hungary, et cetera. Yet I arrived in Israel and saw two peoples: people that identify with the Ashkenazim and the other people like me, who look as if they came from the desert.

When I got off the plane from Tehran in Israel, an official speaking English asked me, "From where did this plane come?" I told him, "From Iran." He asked me, "Are you Iranian?" I told him, "No, I'm not Iranian, I'm Iraqi." He said, "Ah, you're Sephardi." I said, "No, I didn't come from Spain. I'm telling you, I'm an Iraqi who came through Iran." He said, "So you are *Mizrachi*." I told him, "No, I'm not from Poland or Hungary. I'm telling you, I'm Iraqi." I wasn't being argumentative. I simply didn't understand his categories. Later I understood that in Israel, Mizrachi means from an Arab country.

These new differentiations started to become clear to me as a journalist and an ordinary person. I spoke only English in the beginning. I didn't know Hebrew, and all my friends were Ashkenazim. I also married an Ashkenazi. But the Ashkenazim didn't guard their tongues in my presence and referred to Iraqis as Arabs. When I moved to Wadi Nisnas, the Arabs started treating me like an Arab and spoke of the Jews as of non-Arabs. So I was in this bizarre in-between place. I came to the conclusion that I was living in a racist country where people considered Arabs inferior. It wasn't simply a nationalist-based hatred. It was deeper than that—a condescending distaste perhaps. All my youth and adulthood was spent in a war against racism. Now I found myself in a state of racists. That is still my feeling today, despite my great love for Israel.

Once I began to relate to Israeli literature and to read in Hebrew, I found that Zionism's fortress was Hebrew literature. More than politics, more than the army.

So after nearly two decades in Israel I decided to write about racism in Israel, and that became my 1974 book, my first novel, *Equal and More Equal*,[21] about life in the *ma'abara*. It had taken me 15 years to completely transition from Arabic to Hebrew, and I had to work very hard to convey the flavor of Iraqi culture and Iraqi people in a language that was not Arabic and without alienating my readers. I also describe life in the transit camp in *Tin Shacks and Dreams*,[22] as well, a youth book.

Equal and More Equal divided the reading public in Israel into two camps because it dealt with sensitive issues about Israeli society that were previously cloaked in silence. Half of the country hated me for it and the other half said "bravo." The book entered the literary establishment like a bomb, outraging much of it and causing a great storm. I was almost lynched as a Jew-hater, an anti-Semite, the whole gamut. But luckily all the Ashkenazim who were familiar with the societal problems I described defended me. They said, "He's right." And all of a sudden I became a hero to the Sephardim. I didn't mean to be, and I don't hate Ashkenazim. Many of those who read it and hated what I had to say wanted to turn me into an Ashkenazi-hater. Students don't read it at school—it would be like teaching Torah in a Gaza mosque. For the same reason, I believe, there has never been much interest in translating it to English, because in the U.S. and overseas in general they prefer the idealist Zionist picture that depicts Jews in Israel as brothers and heroes.

Then came *Refuge*,[23] about Iraqi-born Marduch—a Communist who survived 13 years in an Iraqi prison—and his Ashkenazi wife Shula, who have a retarded son, Ido. Shula wants more kids, but Marduch is afraid of having another Ido. Shula's mother pushes her, saying, "Tell your husband he's making a mistake. He's from back there in Iraq, and when it comes to complicated matters like this, he obviously doesn't know the first thing."[24] Marduch also embodies the Iraqi Jewish Communist I've described here: the Zionist by default who goes on to fight for Israel, which gave him refuge. After he was released from prison, he was sent to Israel against his will. Then, when the Communist Party demands that Shula provide refuge for an Arab comrade, she is torn between loyalty to the party and to the state.

In these early years of my writing, this establishment hostility was two-dimensioned: I was identified as an Ashkenazi-hater and as a Communist, because people had no understanding of the basis for Iraqi Jews becoming Communists. That was despite the fact that the Communists attacked me all the time. So many doors were closed to me, but I was lucky that literature teachers began to teach my books and I eventually moved from the periphery to the center of the Israeli literature scene. To me, that is a sign that the themes and ideas I express have become part of the Israeli consciousness and that I have succeeded in conveying the reality in Iraq for the Israeli reader, which I've done in order to show that the Jewish Iraqi past is part of the ordinary Israeli, and part of Israeli culture. I've tried to introduce the reader to an otherwise unfamiliar world.

I continue to write about these themes, in new ways, and all my novels explore the complicated, interlocking relationships between Arab and Jew. *A Trumpet in the*

Wadi,[25] which takes place before the first Lebanon War, is about two Israeli Arab sisters whose lives change when a young Russian Jewish immigrant and trumpet player moves into their home. In *Water Kissing Water*[26] I write about Yosef, a new immigrant from Iraq who came to Israel during the mass aliyah in 1950. Much of this story is drawn from my own experiences as an immigrant and an Israeli: Yosef works in the Water Authority as I did and makes his first steps in literary writing in Hebrew.

But I still find myself pushing the envelope and colliding with Israel's limitations—in some cases with bizarre outcomes. After the first Gulf War, the Iraqi people were in great distress because of the sanctions against Iraq. There were food shortages, lack of basic medicines and other needs, and poverty. So several friends and I—Israelis of Iraqi origin—decided to establish a movement to identify with the Iraqi people, in order to at least recognize their plight and create a mechanism through which we could sell them food and supplies. I personally hoped to carry out a humane act: because they were lacking many medicines and suffering from many diseases, I and a group of some other well-known Israelis decided to organize a group of doctors from Israel that would volunteer to work in Iraq. But the Registry of Non-Profits didn't give us a license because, we were told, there was suspicion that we could be Saddam Hussein's spies. We laughed—and cried. The turn of events was all over the media, but the story ended with that.

Sami Michael has authored 12 books, mostly novels, many of which have been translated in several languages. Victoria *has been translated into Arabic. Many Israelis consider the publishing of* Equal and More Equal *as marking the beginning of contemporary ethnic literature in Israel, according to Nancy Berg, an American academic who has written about Michael's literature.*[27] *He translated the Egyptian author Najib Mahfouz's famous trilogy to Hebrew, and has won numerous prizes, including the Israel Prize for Literature and the President's Prize. He is president of Israel's Association for Civil Rights.*

Notes

1. The word *maqam* has two different uses in the Arab world. In Arab countries other than Iraq, the word means "scale." Its equivalent word into Iraq is *nagham* that is used in other Arab countries as a synonym for *maqam*. *Nagham* and *maqam* in this usage simply mean a particular set of pitch levels employed. The word *maqam* in Iraq has a second meaning as well: it denotes a group of existing songs that are collectively called *Al-Maqamat al-Iraqiyya*, the Iraqi Maqams. Kojaman, p. 11.
2. Shiekh Ahmad Al-Jaber Al-Sabah served at Kuwait's emir from 1921 to 1950.
3. According to Shlomo el-Kevity, this article is "Thirty Years after His Death in Tel Aviv, Saleh's Family Releases New CD in Israel," by Ahmed al-Sarrat, *Al Qabas*, March 11, 2006.

4. Salima Murad later married a Muslim singer named Nadem al Razali and converted to Islam.
5. The currency used in Iraq until the dinar was established as the national currency at Iraq's independence in 1932.
6. Considered the most important prayer in Judaism, *Shema Yisrael* is the centerpiece of all morning and evening prayers and echoes Judaism's monotheistic message.
7. The others were Zionist activists Shalom Saleh Shalom, Yosef Basri, and Shafiq Adas.
8. Literally, "Gate of Immigration," a large, temporary transit camp for immigrants in Haifa. From there, immigrants were assigned to other transit camps.
9. The *hanukiah* is now in the collection of the American Embassy in Baghdad.
10. This boil was called an *ukht*, also nicknamed the Rose of Baghdad, and virtually all Iraqi children were marked with one. It was a lesion caused by a parasite carried by the sand flies and mosquitoes that thrived in areas where date palms grow. It appeared on exposed areas of the body where flying insects could access, took a long time to heal, and left behind a scar in addition to immunity to the parasite. Hillel, p. 252.
11. Alliance opened its doors on December 10, 1864, in Baghdad, then closed for several years as a result of opposition by the religious hierarchy who saw their *istadhs* (yeshivas) emptying out. It reopened in 1872 thanks largely to Chief Rabbi Abdallah Somekh who pushed aside the protests of his fellow rabbis and even went so far as to send his own son there. Decades later, Sir Elie Kadoorie of Hong Kong and Shanghai donated funds for the establishment of a girls' Alliance, opened in 1893, which he named for his wife Laura. It was the first girls' school in Iraq. Later, Alliance schools were established in Basra, Mosul, Hilla, Amara, Kirkuk, and Khanaqin. Rejwan, pp. 181, 185–190.
12. Am Oved Publishers, 1993. *Victoria* is the only one of Michael's books that has been translated into Arabic. It was published by Arab Publishing House in Cairo in 1995.
13. *Hofen Shel Arafel (Handful of Fog)*, Am Oved Publishers, 1979.
14. The "yishuv" is the term used by the Zionist movement to describe the Jewish settlers in pre–state Israel.
15. *Sufa ben ha-D'kalim (Storm among the Palms)*, Am Oved Publishers, 1975.
16. He used the passive form of "immigrated" in Hebrew—as if they were brought.
17. The Allied victory in El Alamein, Egypt, prevented the German incursion into the Middle East.
18. Following the UN approval for the partition of Palestine in November, 1947, the Iraqi government took a number of discriminatory measures against the Jews, including forbidding the issuance of passports to Jews and prohibiting the acceptance of Jews to universities. After Israel's declaration of independence in May, 1948, a host of other discriminatory measures were put into place. The measures were enforced with greater and lesser severity over the following decades. Rejwan, pp. 234–239.
19. Even as the terms of the treaty were being negotiated, mass demonstrations were taking place in the streets of Baghdad against it by both nationalists and leftists. The protests became so serious—several demonstrators were killed by police—that the government was forced to resign for a short period. Jewish participation angered the pro-British establishment, thereby strengthening the anti-Jewish stance. Rejwan, pp. 236–237.

20. Mapai was the social democratic party that dominated Israeli politics until Menachem Begin's election as prime minister in 1977; Herut was a rightist party.
21. *Shavim V'Shavim Yoter (Equal and More Equal)*, Bustan Publishers, 1974.
22. *Pahmonim V'Halomot (Tin Shacks and Dreams)*, Am Oved Publishers, 1979.
23. The Jewish Publication Society, 1988. The Hebrew edition, *Hasut*, was originally published by Am Oved Publishers in 1977.
24. English edition, pp. 6–7.
25. English edition by Simon & Schuster, 2003.
26. *Maim Noshkim L'Maim (Water Kissing Water)*, Am Oved Publishers, 2001.
27. Berg. p. 1.z

SECTION TWO

An Audacious Plan

Introduction

When a 2,500-year-old community that has played a central role in the life of a country disappears, one must ask why. For the Jews of Iraq, a community firmly integrated into Iraqi society by the 1930s, the prospect of leaving behind their way of life in a culture they knew in order to begin a new life in the hardscrabble land of the Bible went from unthinkable to inevitable in 10 tumultuous years.

While persecution was increasingly pervasive throughout the 1940s, two events in particular—the Farhoud in 1941 and the hanging of Shafiq Adas in 1948—compelled many Jews to begin to consider a life in the new State of Israel. Israeli emissaries and local Zionist activists were active in encouraging the groundswell of interest among Jews to leave, but the Iraqi government was opposed to all Zionist activity within its borders. Therefore, all such activity was done in secret. In the following pages, we'll hear from Shlomo Sehayek and from Mordechai Ben Porat, two of the first half-dozen members of the Zionist underground, the "Young Halutz."[1] The movement formed in 1942 in response to the pogrom and growing anti-Semitism, and promoted and coordinated immigration to Eretz Yisrael. But the movement's views about the need to organize and leave for Eretz Yisrael did not sit well with all Iraqi Jews. So the 1940s was a decade fraught with debate within the community about which homeland to choose: Iraq or Israel.

Throughout the decade, a network of smugglers, both Jews and Muslims, facilitated the escape of thousands of Jews over the borders, mostly to Iran, but also via Jordan and Syria. Ultimately, the Iraqi government's anger at these smugglers, the work of the Young Halutz, and that of secret Mossad emissaries like Shlomo Hillel from Palestine and Ben Porat resulted in the passage, on March 1, 1950, of a bill that allowed Jews to renounce their citizenship and emigrate. Law No. 12, as it was, resulted in the mass exodus of Jews from Iraq in the early 1950s. Of the approximately 137,000 Jews who resided in Iraq in the early 1940s, 124,000 had left by 1952, most on some 950 flights destined for Israel in what became known as Operation Ezra and Nehemiah.[2]

Ongoing clandestine communication between the Mossad in Tel Aviv and its emissaries was critical to the operation throughout this decade and played a major role in the orchestration of the mass emigration. We hear from Ilana Marucs, code-named "Chris," an Egyptian Jew who as a young woman served as a stewardess on hundreds of those airlifts and who meanwhile ferried key documents between the Mossad in Israel and its emissaries in Iraq. The messages conveyed by Marcus and others—including a team of wireless operators like Yitzhak Saieg*—relayed information about political and security issues in Iraq, Jewish fugitives headed toward Eretz Yisrael, and a myriad of operational instructions.

As a woman, Marcus wasn't an anomaly in the Zionist network: one of the earliest female activists, for instance, Raya Azar,* was an instructor who hid weapons and Hebrew books and materials on Eretz Yisrael in a secret space beneath her living room floor. But the movement was so controversial even within families that she and her siblings and mother hid her involvement, and that of a sister and brother, as well as their knowledge of the hidden cache, from her father. When the crackdown on the movement forced hundreds of activists to flee in 1949, Azar escaped Iraq as a teenager through Basra to Iran, and then to Israel, with only the clothes on her back.

The Farhoud and the story of the mass exodus of Iraq's Jews and their immigration to Palestine, later Israel, occurred during the same decade as the flight of Arabs from Palestine during and after 1948. The difference between the reception Jews received in Israel compared with that of Palestinian refugees in Arab lands goes to the heart of a conflict that seems never to end. It was a decade that continues to resonate.

*Her interview is not included in the collection.

* * *

For five years starting in 1946, Shlomo Hillel was the undercover Mossad³ emissary who is credited with orchestrating the mass exodus of Iraqi Jews to Israel. Iraqi Jewish emigration to Palestine began in small numbers in the 1930s and 1940s but accelerated quickly upon Hillel's arrival. Born in Baghdad in 1923, Hillel moved to Palestine as an 11-year-old and, after witnessing the arrival of illegal refugee boats from Europe during World War II, became inspired to help Jewish immigrants from Iraq. In his account, he recalls using a half-dozen aliases and identities to achieve his first major success in airlifting Iraqi Jews to Palestine, known as Operation Michaelberg. Soon after, he opened up a route via Iran that enabled thousands of Jews to leave Iraq. His efforts culminated in the massive airlift now known as Ezra and Nehemiah.

I was the youngest of 11 children. I don't remember the neighborhood in which I was born, but when I was two years old, we moved to Bab-el-Agha, which was on the main road in Baghdad, El Rashid Street. At the time, there was only one road going through it. It was a mostly Jewish quarter.

By the time I was born, my brothers had already started to go abroad—to India and other places in the Far East, but mostly to Bombay, where they had a commercial relationship with my father in Baghdad. Eventually some of them went to Manchester, England, and one went to Japan. The business was importing clothes and tea to Baghdad. We had a very big piece of the market on tea in particular, which we brought from Sri Lanka [then Ceylon]. There was quite a big Hillel family in India involved in the business and other businesses and I had many other relatives there too.

When I was young, my parents used to visit my brothers in Bombay every other year so I went to Bombay about four times with them while the other children stayed behind. I got to go because I was the youngest. To go from Baghdad to India at the time was a major ordeal because one had to go by train to Basra, which took about 24 hours, and then take a ship to Bombay, which took 8 days.

Until Iraq got its independence in 1932, Zionist activity was semilegal. At least it was not illegal. With the Hebrew teachers who came from Palestine to teach in the Jewish schools in Iraq came the Zionist ideology and Achi-Ever began as a movement of high school students who decided they wanted to learn Hebrew seriously and prepare for aliyah. They received Hebrew newspapers from Palestine and studied intensely, meeting a few times a week to speak only in Hebrew. I used to follow my brother Eliyahu to these meetings when I was small, and he was an inspiration to me as one of the group's founders.

But the tide turned in 1932 as Faisal's health was declining and his son Ghazi, a hot-headed Arab nationalist, garnered greater influence and the Nazi influence began to grow. Ghazi sent home the teachers from Palestine and he forbade modern Hebrew instruction in the schools. That's when Eliyahu decided to leave for Palestine. He was the first sibling to come to Palestine. All my sisters were still in Iraq but all my brothers, with the exception of Eliyahu and myself, were abroad, either in India, England, or Japan. And then, in 1933, hundreds of Assyrian Christians were massacred in Iraq. I remember the victory parade of the Iraqi army through the main road of Baghdad. My father said, "If this is what they do to Christians, what's going to happen to us?"

That year, I went with my parents to Palestine because my sister was sick and we brought her to Jerusalem to be treated. Two of my brothers then came to Palestine to work as British government employees. After we arrived, I insisted on staying as it was clear to all of us that we would have to move there permanently because Iraq was beginning to change dramatically.

I was 11 years old on that visit, and I could already speak some Hebrew because I had spent so much time hanging around with Eliyahu at his Achi-Ever meetings. Eventually my father agreed to leave me with my two brothers in Tel Aviv. But my brothers were working and out enjoying themselves and they used to come home late at night, so after returning from school, I used to spend the rest of the day alone. I went to the Herzliya Gymnasium in Tel Aviv, which was the most prestigious school in Palestine in those days. In 1935, most of the rest of my family joined us, and my married sisters followed afterwards with their families.

Witnessing the arrival of the illegal immigrant ships carrying Jews from Europe to Palestine was a major turning point in my young life. The *Tiger Hill* arrived to the shores of Tel Aviv on September 1, 1939, at the outbreak of World War II. Two years later, the Farhoud took place and it was clear that we needed to find a solution for the Iraqi Jews.

With the arrival of the British army in Iraq in 1941 came Jewish Palestinian soldiers in combat and auxiliary forces in which they helped to build airports, roads, and other infrastructure. Due to the Farhoud and the general anti-Semitism, some of the Jews of Iraq wanted to leave but were not allowed passports, and they saw an opportunity to be smuggled to Palestine with the help of these Jewish British soldiers. And that's what began to happen: Iraqi Jews, disguised as British soldiers, went in the backs of army trucks. These were mainly daring youngsters and a few hundred of them managed to flee this way. If they came with the British army, they went through the British colony Trans-Jordan, which was renamed Jordan upon its independence in 1946. Others went with truck drivers or vacationers going through Syria to Lebanon: first from Baghdad to Damascus, where local Jews fed and housed them for a few days before they continued on to Beirut, and from Beirut, they paid for rides with drivers transporting goods to and from Palestine.

By that time, I was one of the founding members of a kibbutz which was later renamed Ma'agan Michael. The founding members were graduates of Herzliya Gymnasium and the Reali School in Haifa. We received two groups of European youngsters who came before and during the war, mainly without their families, part of the Youth Aliyah.[4] In one of the groups was my future wife, Tmima. She had come on the *Patria*.[5]

In 1945, our kibbutz, at that time called Kvutzat Ha'tzofim Alef [First Scout Movement], was located in Pardes Hannah. We were ordered by the Haganah to move from there to Rehovot, where the Haganah wanted us to build a secret underground factory for the manufacturing of bullets. I was responsible for overseeing the factory's construction and operation of the factory. At that point, it had become clear that there was a strong possibility that a Jewish state would be created. Until then the Jews had been involved in small skirmishes with local Palestinian Arabs in which villages were attacked and a few people were killed here and there. But if a Jewish state were to be proclaimed, we knew we would be attacked by the armies of the neighboring Arab countries—organized armies with tanks, airplanes, huge weapons arsenals. Real armies from Egypt, Jordan, and Syria. So we realized that the Haganah wasn't enough—we needed a real Israeli army. And one of the things that was badly needed was bullets for the locally manufactured Sten submachine gun used by the Haganah in those days.

Still, preparing for such a war was the second-most important thing on our minds. Our main focus was dealing with illegal immigration: getting more Jews to come to Palestine from Europe after the Holocaust and preventing their interception by the British. So although I was involved in the factory, my bigger desire was to be involved in helping illegal immigration. I asked my superiors in the Haganah if I could get involved somehow. They agreed, and that's how I first began working for the Mossad L'Aliyah Bet.

Initially I thought I'd be sent to Paris or Rome to help the European Jews. After World War II ended, the British withdrew from Iraq and as the possibility of the creation of Israel became more and more real, life became worse for the Iraqi Jews. One day, my friends from the Haganah came to me and said, "Iraq is the place. The underground activity there has just gotten much more difficult. You'll fit in well there. You were born in Iraq, you have an Iraqi face, you can speak Arabic—not very well, but well enough for everyday life." So in 1946 I was sent to Baghdad. At first, my mission was to organize the underground Zionist movement and to teach the activists Hebrew. Gradually, I took on the illegal immigration issue. That first stint in Iraq lasted one year. It was a very difficult year because the ease of transporting Jews with British military convoys to Palestine had ended with the departure of the British from Iraq in 1945 when World War II ended. So our only option at that point was to find Iraqi truck drivers willing to smuggle out small groups of three or four youngsters through the desert. At that time, Iraq used to import and export goods to and from Europe through Haifa's port. Iraq's major export other than oil was dates, so trucks went to Haifa carrying dates and brought back other goods to Baghdad.

I moved around Iraq under various aliases and identities, including "Shammai" within the Mossad and in my correspondences via wireless with my bosses in Tel Aviv, or "Amu Yusuf" for my interactions with the local Zionist activists. We experienced a number of successes that year. We also experienced a number of tragedies in which people were killed along their escape routes, including the time we brought 40 youngsters to the desert to be picked up by truck and two of them were killed during a sandstorm; the rest were returned to Baghdad, battered by the horrifying experience. I returned to Palestine in 1947 exhausted.

The Michaelberg Mission

I began to feel that this system of helping people escape individually or in small groups was challenging and inadequate if our goal was to enable the escape of thousands. Yet at that time we had no other ways or means. I felt frustrated because I thought we were not doing enough to smuggle Jews out when they were clearly facing danger and hardship. It was evident that priority was given to Holocaust survivors, which was understandable, but I thought we should do more for Iraq as well.

Then the American pilots appeared—pilots who had served in World War II and were bored after its end and eager for some new action and money. Some of them were taking advantage of all the postwar corruption and began flying planes with smuggled gold, hashish—whatever—from place to place. Someone in the United States had told two of them: "Look, in Palestine there are some crazy people who are willing to pay a lot of money to smuggle Jews to Palestine." The pilots, who were not Jewish, agreed, saying, "As long as they pay well, we're in." Their names were Leo Wessenberg and his copilot, whom I just knew as Mike—hence the plan that transpired became known as "Operation Michaelberg."

At the time I was raising hell about the need to get the Jews out of Iraq: I was complaining and cursing and shouting at my bosses from the Mossad, kicking up a big fuss at every opportunity. To shut me up they let me go ahead and become the first to experiment with an airlift rescue operation. And that's how I was given the opportunity to organize the first illegal airlift from Iraq.

It would have been much easier to bring European Jews by plane, or Jews from practically anywhere, other than Iraq. The Iraqi government had revoked all Jewish passports and prevented Jews from leaving the country, let alone go to Palestine, whereas European countries were more than willing to let the Jews leave. For the European Jews, the only challenge—albeit a serious one—was bypassing the British to enter Palestine. So Iraqi Jews were constrained on both ends: leaving Iraq and entering Palestine. In addition, by that year, the neighboring countries of Syria, Jordan, and Lebanon had become terribly hostile to Jews, so escaping through those countries had become difficult and dangerous.

But then, suddenly, I was faced with figuring out how I was going to make this work—even the pilots couldn't envision it. There were no seats; it was a cargo plane. Our main idea simply was to take 50 passengers back with us without the authorities finding out—ideally, arranging a passenger pickup in the middle of the barren desert outside Baghdad. The arrangement was made so quickly that I didn't even have the time to think it through. I literally left the kibbutz in the morning for a meeting with my bosses in Tel Aviv, and they asked me to leave immediately for Iraq.

The three of us—the pilot, the copilot, and myself—took off the same day for Baghdad. As we neared the Baghdad airport, I gazed down on the vast desert to try to identify a good spot from which to pick up the passengers and take off. I realized there was no way for me to determine such a thing from the air. I suddenly panicked, feeling that I was in way above my head—that this whole secret airlift thing was a whacky idea. We were only supposed to take a day or two to organize the operation once we were in Baghdad. I started to think, "How are we going to do this? To find the precise place in this vast desert? And to bring people to the middle of the desert after midnight?" I started to be scared, but it was already too late to be scared.

What was certain about our plan was this: we had to arrive very early in the morning in Palestine—early enough that the British would still be sleeping, but that there be enough light for the pilots to see our makeshift landing strip because we could not land publicly in the airport. We were to land in Yavniel, a village near Tiberias, beside the Kinneret. Taking into account a three- or four-hour flight, we would therefore have to leave Iraq after midnight.

Funnily enough, it was my experience flying—by then a grand total of three times, to Baghdad and back on my first mission, and now back to Baghdad—that enabled me to come up with a solution. Until then, my friends and I in the Haganah spoke only in terms of ships when we spoke about illegal immigration. Most of them had never flown in their lives. Even before I left on my third trip, they considered me some kind of expert on air travel, which I thought was hilarious. But the truth is my little experience was what made the Michaelberg operation work.

I had learned that after the passengers and pilots boarded the plane, the plane taxied to the end of the runway where it paused for five minutes or so in order to rev up its propellers and prepare to take off. In Baghdad, as most everywhere else, the end of the runway was about a mile away from the airport building—in the middle of nowhere. There was a fence around the edge of the runway, but there were no buildings, no police, no one around. So it occurred to me that if I could get my 50 youngsters through the fence and waiting at the end of the runway, we could use those minutes at our disposal to bring them to the plane. Yet I had been ordered by my superior in Tel Aviv, Moshe Carmil, to pick up passengers from the desert, and this is what the pilots originally had in mind too. So when I told the pilots that I wanted to run the operation out of Baghdad's international airport, and explained my idea, they thought I was out of my mind. Eventually I convinced them. After agreeing, they teased me, saying, "You have flown three times in your life, so now you are an expert?"

We had the plan set. The night before we left, Wessenberg, Mike, and I went to a cabaret club and Wessenberg asked for his payment. I was shocked. Our people in Tel Aviv had told me that the pilots would be paid upon delivery of the passengers the sum of 5,000 British sterling in gold coins, worth $20,000 in those days, and the payment had already been arranged. I explained this to Wessenberg. But now he refused to fly unless they were paid ahead of time. "No money, no flight!" Wessenberg said to me. I assured them that they would be paid in full upon safe arrival in Yavniel, but when they refused again, I told them I could get half of the amount in Iraqi dinars and I would write my own personal check for the other half and that if the Mossad didn't pay them within two weeks they could cash my check. Because I had rummaged through their belongings earlier, I knew that Wessenberg had an account in Chemical Bank in New York. So I bluffed. I told him that I had an account in the Chemical Bank of New York but that I didn't have a checkbook with me. He was thrilled to hear the coincidence that we both had accounts in the same bank, and he said, "No problem. I have an account there too! I'll give you one of my checks and you just write your account number on it." The deal was sealed: I wrote out a check with a made-up account number to the tune of $10,000.

The operation went ahead. We had arrived in Baghdad on a Wednesday afternoon, and by Friday night, I had my 50 passengers waiting at the end of the runway. I organized a few people who selected the passengers and took them from the main road alongside the fence and through the part of the fence that we had broken through, and positioned them next to the runway. I shuffled them onto the plane and no one saw us, as far as I could tell. We took off and arrived in Yavniel at dawn with ease. No British troops and no commotion. When the plane came to a standstill, several Mossadniks came over and handed the pilots a satchel filled with the proper sum of gold coins. I demanded my check back, and the pilots apologized for the spat over their payment. They revved up their engines and took off.

We had succeeded—we had a system in place. The next flight was handled without me. I sent a telegram to our local underground people in Iraq about how to manage the next flight and they replicated precisely what we did the first time. The next flight actually went from Yavniel to Italy where it was supposed to pick up 50 refugees from Europe to bring them to Palestine. The challenge wasn't as great because we didn't care so much about secrecy in Italy since we knew they wanted to be rid of Jews anyway. The next day the *Corriera della Sera*, the most important paper in Italy at the time, published a story about a "bizarre occurrence" the night before in which a plane landed near Rome, took off with 50 Jews and headed for Palestine. The story seemed so bizarre that no one really believed it!

We were only able to complete one more Michaelberg flight from Baghdad. In September, 1947, the commander of the Haganah stopped us because it was clear at that point that there was going to be a State of Israel and that we would be going to war. So the Haganah decided that it was much more important for the time being to use the Michaelberg system to bring heavy ammunition into the country, not passengers. The story in the Italian newspaper also had made them nervous that others might catch on to our secret flights and their plan of smuggling arms this way would be destroyed before it began.

Shortly before the UN resolution on the partition of Palestine,[6] some of our people in Iraq took a truck convoy through the desert carrying about 77 passengers— the biggest single escape until then. I was in Lebanon at the time working on other tasks for the Mossad. There, on November 30, I witnessed the angry reaction in the streets to the partition. Before that, with the success of the last big convoy and of Michaelberg, we started to believe that we probably had the system down pat—a combination of airlifts and desert convoys that would enable us to increase the flow of Jews from Iraq. But the UN resolution made it impossible to cross the desert via Jordan or Syria anymore, even by air. The last time we were able to get a convoy through that way was in February, 1948.

The Haganah began smuggling arms from Czechoslovakia, Italy, from all over. They continued using the same system we developed, wherever they landed: sneaking the arms onto the plane while the plane was at the end of the runway. Still, in early 1948, we did manage to smuggle small numbers of people via plane. The flights took off from Baghdad for Cairo and stopped over in Lod Airport [now Ben Gurion Airport] en route, where our passengers entered Palestine on forged passports. This way, we smuggled one or two couples at a time: I used to wait for them at Lod and sneak them into Tel Aviv, which was very complicated because of British checkpoints along the way. But when the airport fell into the hands of the Arabs in April, 1948, that was the absolute end of that system. With the War of Independence, there was no longer any way to bring people out of Iraq.

The Priest and Persia

After the war broke out, we began to receive telegrams from our emissaries in Baghdad through our secret wireless system. The telegrams said, "The situation is horrible. Jews are being arrested and harassed. Please come and help us." Carmil told me, "You have to go back to Baghdad."

I was reluctant at first, I have to say, because I didn't think I could succeed there given the situation. But I recall thinking, "Let us not put ourselves in the position later in which we will have to answer when people say that we never responded to their calls for help when they were in the midst of such dire circumstances." We had the conscience of Holocaust on our minds and the fact that the Jews in Europe felt that we did not do enough to rescue them. So we felt that even though there would be so little we could do, we should at least give the Iraqi Jews the feeling that we were trying to come to their aid. It was really almost a symbolic gesture. In general, to be honest, along the way I never contemplated the big picture. I just kept working bit by bit and hoping something would come up that would enable us to help some of the Jews to escape.

It was June, 1948, and this time, I could not take a plane directly to Baghdad because we were at war. So by the end of the first truce, in the end of June, I was told to go to Paris and from there I would be able to take a plane to Baghdad. I was given a forged passport to take to Baghdad. But when I got to Paris, our people stationed there determined the passport wasn't good enough.

At that time, the Mossad L'Aliyah Bet was working morning, noon, and night orchestrating the smuggling of young immigrants from Europe and arms to the newly born State of Israel, and no one in the Paris office had time to deal with me. I thought I'd be stopping off in Paris en route to Baghdad just for a few days, but it ended up being about a month until I could get a satisfactory passport. So, to make myself useful I began going to the office to help them answer the telephones and do whatever they needed done. In the process, I learned something important. In Europe, we were moving thousands of people from Italy to France in order to get them on a ship to Israel. And the next day we moved hundreds of people from Switzerland to Norway, where they boarded a ship. Step by step like that.

So I came up with the idea that if we couldn't get Iraqi Jews westbound directly to Israel then we could smuggle them out in a different direction. I was primarily concerned at that point with smuggling out our local activists who were sought after by the police. I thought, "How about moving them through Turkey or Iran, for safety, and then we could even try to send them out, ideally to Israel?"

I told my superiors about my idea. At that time, few people in Israel even knew that Iran was not an Arab country. For us, all the Middle East countries were the same—we figured all Muslims were Arabs, with the same culture and the same hatred for Jews and Israel, and most Israelis did not know the history of the centuries-long animosity between Iraq and Iran. So they laughed me off, but said, "Do what you want. You will get your new passport and your ticket, and off to Baghdad!" No one took me seriously except for the priest, Abbe Alexander Glasberg.

Glasberg had been born to a Jewish family in Russia and converted to Catholicism. I had first met him in Palestine when I came back from Syria and Lebanon in December, 1947. He was very much respected by our people in Israel because he rescued many Jewish boys during the Holocaust by hiding them in monasteries. The Germans wanted to arrest him, but instead they arrested his brother and killed him in a case of mistaken identity.

After the war, Glasberg continued to help French Jews immigrate illegally to Palestine. One of the amazing things that he did was when the ship the Exodus was intercepted by the British who then sent it back to where it had come from, Marseilles, he organized mass demonstrations in France to protest the return of the ship. And the French, being the anti-Semites they were, didn't want the Jews either, and said, "We are not going to oblige the British."

The British would not take the ship back to Palestine. So the protest caused the British to find another port to which to send the ship, and they took it to Hamburg, Germany. That created an uproar. Everyone—Jews and non-Jews alike—cried, "How could the British take Jews who were rescued from the Holocaust back to Germany?" This incident, in my mind, is one of the factors that compelled the UN to vote for the partition of Palestine. It really caused people to say, "It is impossible to have a situation in which the British are bringing Jews back to the place where they were slaughtered. There must be a place for the Jews to find refuge." So Glasberg was seen by Israel as a real hero for helping precipitate the UN resolution. Because of what he did, Glasberg was invited to Palestine to meet with officials from the Mossad L'Aliyah Bet.

When I met him that first time, a few months earlier, I began to speak to him in English. He said, "I don't speak English. Let's speak French." My French at that time was fairly weak. So I said, "I can't speak French." So he said, "Ok, so let's speak Yiddish." I said, "I don't speak Yiddish." So he said to me, "How on earth is it that a Jewish boy in Palestine does not speak Yiddish?" So after a pause I almost asked, "How is it that a Catholic priest can speak Yiddish?" I didn't know at that point that he was a convert. But I didn't ask him, out of respect and timidity.

While I was in Paris, one day out of the blue he entered our office. He asked me, "What are you doing here?" He took me to lunch. He managed to squeeze out of me the whole story about what I was doing and where I was supposed to go and I even told him about my idea to smuggle some Jews to Iran. He said, "Look, you said you don't speak Yiddish, but you have a *Yiddishe kop*.[7] This is an excellent idea and I'm going to help you." At this point we were speaking in French to each other—I had bad French, but we managed. "How?" I asked. He said, "There is a group of Assyrian Christians who live on the border between Iran and Iraq. They have been persecuted, sometimes by Iraq, sometimes by Iran. I am in constant touch with them and try to help them all the time. I send them money, et cetera. And because their monasteries are located on the border they have been able to help some of their own people escape from Iraq into Iran. So I will bring you to them and they will help you." Then he called my superiors in Paris to tell him, "I've heard Shammai's idea and it's an excellent one. I want to go with him to Iran and help him." Since Glasberg was so respected by all of us, no one dared to tell him, "It's rubbish." They said, "All right. Go for a week. Let's see what happens."

And so it was decided that I would go to Iran and a week after that, he would come with his secretary—he never went anywhere without her. She was half-Jewish. It was somewhat surreal, the whole thing: a once-Jewish Catholic priest and his half-Jewish secretary go to Iran to meet with an undercover Mossadnik with a French alias—with my new French passport, I became Maurice Perez—to get Assyrian Christians living in mountaintop monasteries to help Iraqi Jews escape to Israel.

Once in Tehran, we drove together to the border of Iraq and Iran to the monastery. But ultimately, the idea didn't work out. The Assyrians were so miserable themselves that they couldn't possibly help anyone else. They were worse off than the Jews: poor and persecuted. In the end, I gave them a truck which we intended to use ourselves, but I saw they were in desperate need of a vehicle in their remote location.

Yet I learned from that experience that it was possible to smuggle people over the border to Iran because the border was long and porous. And in the meantime, I had made connections with Jews in Tehran who could be helpful in my effort. One of them was a Jew from Palestine who spoke Hebrew. We made a connection with the police in Tehran and got their consent that if we got Jews out of Iraq and into Iran they would not be sent back to Iraq. Instead the refugees would pay a fine to the Iranian authorities. In short, a major bribe. The police also agreed to let the Jews leave Iran for another country if we arranged visas for them. This was very important achievement. So now the question was: how could I get visas? And that was Glasberg's second contribution.

Glasberg said, "Don't worry. My best friend is now the minister of interior in France. How many visas do you want?" I just threw a figure out. I said, "250." And he said, "All right, give me the names." I didn't know what to say—I had no names because I didn't even know who the people would be. He said, "Without the names, I can't get you the visas." So I sat down and in one night, out of thin air I made up the names of 250 people—entire families with fathers, mothers, daughters, and sons. Later, I would have to match real families with their aliases. The list was flown to Paris. A few days later, I got a telephone call from the French consulate in Tehran. An officer there told me, "Monsieur Perez, we have here waiting for you a long list of visas we have issued for you. Please come and collect them."

We had to take photos of the people for their laissez-passer and in some cases to disguise them—a girl to look like a boy and so on. But because the Iranian police were getting their money they didn't care to check the validity of the people appearing in the photos. They looked the other way and let us operate. Now, the key challenge was getting the people out of Iraq to Tehran, and I was having difficulty staying in touch with my people in Iraq. We had the wireless connection from Iraq to Israel at that point. But in Iran I had nothing. To be in touch with my people in Iraq, I had to go to the post office to send an open telegram to Paris to relay things to them in all kinds of convoluted, mysterious language and hope that they would understand. I sent messages like, "Have Baghdad send me three parcels," or "We're ready for 10 laborers," that is, Jews. In many cases, they didn't understand exactly what my messages meant so they sent them to Israel and our people in Tel Aviv couldn't figure them out so they sent them to Baghdad, and they didn't get it either. No one understood what's going on. For several weeks I couldn't get anyone to understand what I wanted.

In the meantime, I found a group of eight or nine Communist Jews who escaped from Iraq on their own because they were being persecuted as Communists and as Jews. They were hiding out in Tehran but they were afraid to go out on the street and take the chance they'd be seen by the police because the Iranian police really hated the Communists. I got in touch with them and asked them, "If you're Communists, why don't you go to Moscow?" They said, "Are you nuts? We would be killed in Moscow." I went on, "So why don't you go back to Baghdad?" "In Baghdad they will hang us," they said. I asked, "Why don't you go to Israel?" "Will they take us?" They asked. I said, "Yes." And they became the first group of Jews that used our visas to leave Iran for Israel. I convinced them to be ready to go to the police, as I had arranged for all the incoming refugees, and say that they had run away from Iraq and were willing to pay the fine so as not be sent back to Iraq. The thought of going to the police scared them at first, but I convinced them. I sent them to Paris, and from Paris they were sent to Marseilles. From Marseilles, they waited in a refugee camp called the Grand Arenass for a ship to take them to Israel. They served as my test case in getting Jews out of Tehran: once I had completed their escape successfully, the system was in place for everyone else.

Eventually, our people in Iraq understood the meaning of my messages and began sending people to me in Iran. First it was 2 people, then 10, and then 15, and so on. Suddenly I had so many people I didn't know what to do with them all because they had to wait in Tehran for a period of time while I arranged their visas and flights. At first I put them up in a hotel. But soon there were too many of them to do that. That's when I set up a camp in an old Jewish cemetery. The conditions were poor and the Tehran cold was a shock to the Iraqi Jews, but we transferred huge numbers of people through there: in less than a year and a half, about 12,000 to 13,000 Jews from Iraq stayed there en route to Israel.

To fly them out of Iran, we came up with an arrangement with Trans-Ocean, an American charter company through which the Mossad was already bringing people in from Bombay. Our main contact there was Ronnie Barnett, a British Jew who had volunteered to work in the cause of illegal immigration and was serving as a liaison between Trans-Ocean and the Mossad as an employee of Trans-Ocean. We used Iranian Airways as our local carrier, which meant that Trans-Ocean paid the airline—Mossad money, in short—to fly the Jews from Tehran to Israel. Our Mossad code for the arrangement was the "Big Deal," and many Iranian Jews, a good number of whom were extremely poor, took the opportunity to leave for Israel as well.[8]

Shlomo Hillel a.k.a Richard Armstrong

I left Tehran at the end of 1949 and came back to Israel where I continued to work on the "illegal aliyah"[9] from afar. I believe that it was the opening of this smuggling route that eventually brought the Iraqi government to the conclusion that it must let the Jews go legally. About 2,000 Jews per month were attempting to escape from Iraq via Iran, and Iraqi police arrested and sent many of them to prison. But the Jews kept coming, undaunted: they were running for their lives. The phenomenon was both an embarrassment to the Iraqi government and a major expense and trouble. It was overwhelming the government and the international community was taking notice: the *New York Times* had sent reporters to the border between Iraq and Iran to write about what was going on. At that time, Iraq elected a new prime minister, Tawfiq el-Suweidi, the man who had been in charge of the Iraqi delegation to the UN in 1949. And in 1949, Israel raised hell against the Iraqis in the UN. It worked. When Israel's delegates began speaking about the persecution against Jews in Iraq, with the Holocaust still fresh in people's minds, there was a small international outcry.

El-Suweidi's next-door neighbor and very good friend happened to be a Jew named Yehezkel Shemtob, a second cousin of mine. Shemtob had recently been elected head of the Jewish community to replace Hahkam Khedouri, who was forced to resign when the community protested that he hadn't done enough to protect those Jews who were arrested and persecuted.[10] Shemtob was a good man and a good Jew, I would say, but he knew nothing about our activity, nothing whatsoever.

El-Suweidi called Shemtob and said, "My friend, what should I do? If I close my eyes the numbers will only rise—from 2,000 this month to 3,000 next month. But if we continue to arrest them, the outcry at the UN will grow louder." Shemtob said to him, "Probably the whole story is about hot-headed youngsters who have finished school and now your government is not letting them get public sector jobs and they are unemployed. Let them go. There can't be more than five or six thousand of them. Why do you want to keep them here against their will? You get rid of them and we'll be rid of them too." And Shemtob really believed this. He didn't have a clue about the groundswell of interest in leaving.

And so the Iraqi government brought a resolution to pass in March, 1950, allowing Jews to renounce their citizenship and leave Iraq legally and permanently.

The minister of interior, Saleh Jaber, who presented the resolution to the parliament, said openly that it was a necessity because recently people had been running away from Iraq, breaking laws, and the phenomenon was damaging the security of Iraq. The resolution didn't state where the Jews would be going to, though it was tacitly understood that their destination was Israel.

So it came as a huge surprise to the Iraqi government and to Shemtob—and to us, frankly—when, over the period of several months, nearly the entire community registered to leave: about 104,000 people. I went to Carmil in Tel Aviv and told him I was prepared to go back to Baghdad to help organize a mass exodus. As the numbers grew rapidly, we began working on a way to airlift everyone out—and swiftly, before the Iraqi government could have a change of heart.

But the overwhelming response also caught Israel by surprise. A few days before I was to leave for Baghdad, I was invited to the office of Levi Eshkol, the treasurer of the Jewish Agency.[11] Eshkol was very concerned about the plans to bring all these Jews. He asked me for an estimation of the number of Iraqi Jews who would take advantage of the resolution and come to Israel. "About 70,000," I told him. At the time, the registration had only begun and I thought I was exaggerating, but I wanted to err on the side of caution. He replied, "We'd be delighted to have them all, but not yet. How are we going to handle all these immigrants? We don't have a place for them. We can't do it. We can barely support the people we already have here. We don't have housing or employment. They'll have to live in the street. If you bring them, it must be clear to them what kind of conditions await them. I don't want them protesting outside my window—if they do, I'll send them to protest at your kibbutz, Ma'agan Michael!"

I left the meeting fuming and went straight to Carmil, who tried to explain to me Eshkol's position and reminded me that Eshkol was still grappling with the absorption of European Jews. But then Carmil took me to Ben Gurion himself. [David Ben Gurion, Israel's first prime minister]. I told Ben Gurion, "I have to resign because I can't go and risk my life just to tell people they can't come to Israel." And Ben Gurion said, "Eshkol is right. We have no houses, no work, no food. We are going to have a problem. But you go and bring them as fast as you can because who knows when the Iraqis [the government] are going to change their minds."

Together with Ronnie Barnett, I left days later for Iraq, this time as "Richard Armstrong" from the Near East Air Transport Company, another American charter company. The only counterfeit part of the operation was my alias—the company really did exist, and Ronnie was employed as a senior manager after moving over from Trans-Ocean. The idea was to obtain the local franchise for transporting the Jews out of Iraq, which meant convincing the Iraqi authorities to give our company the concession, because we wanted to be in full control of the whole operation—numbers, departures, timetable, et cetera.

The owner of Near East was an American named James Wooten, a non-Jew who as the head of Alaskan Airlines had overseen the transport of Jews from Yemen to Israel a year earlier. Following that event, Wooten established Near East Air Overseas, in hidden partnership with El Al, and we hoped the slight change of its name in Iraq to Near East Air Transport would sufficiently obscure the connection.

While working for Trans-Ocean, Ronnie had taken people to Mecca on pilgrimage, and in that capacity had met the director of the travel agency Iraq Tours, Abdul Rahman Raouf. They had hit it off together, so Ronnie contacted him and arranged to meet him in Rome. I came along—it was my debut as Richard Armstrong. We told him that he could make a lot of money bringing Jews out of Iraq if he could secure the bid with the Iraqi government. He said, "I have something to tell you. The prime minister, Tawfiq el-Suweidi, is on the board of my company." So we realized that we could turn this into a business opportunity for Suweidi, which would smooth the plan at the top levels of government.

We went back to Baghdad and Raouf arranged for us to meet el-Suweidi. Ronnie and I met el-Suweidi in his home, and I was sickened with worry the whole time, realizing that what I was doing was the height of chutzpah—visiting the prime minister under an assumed identity. He began to explain to us how the illegal immigration was terrible for Iraq because the Jews were likely smuggling property out and not settling their debts or paying off their taxes. I pretended to be sympathetic to this nonsense, and then we got to business: Raouf said he believed no less than 60,000 would leave, and we discussed how much we'd charge per ticket—12 dinars [about $48]. We gave el-Suweidi the pitch about the strength of our fleet and the company's experience, but we all refrained from discussing the biggest seller to him personally—the projected revenues to Iraq Tours—but that was understood.

In the middle of the conversation, he and his aides decided to invite Shemtob to join us. I hid my panic. Shemtob, my mother's cousin, hadn't seen me since I was a young boy, but I worried he'd recognize me, which would blow the whole operation to pieces and I'd end up in jail. Shemtob came in moments later and sat down. I expected him to look at me and say, "Excuse me, aren't you Selim, Aharon and Hanini's boy?" Thankfully he didn't recognize me, or if he did he acted as if he didn't.

Eventually we closed the deal: Ronnie, Raouf, and I proposed to take the flights to Cyprus—we didn't raise the option of direct flights to Israel—and Shemtob committed to ensuring the Jewish community would collect the fares, absorbing the costs of anyone who couldn't afford to pay, and transferring the funds to Iraq Tours.

The deal sealed, the Meir Tweig synagogue transformed into a government center for renouncement of citizenship, and the Mesouda Shemtob synagogue became a departure station from which the denationalized Jews left for the airport. At first, we flew the planes to Cyprus, landed for a short time, and took off from there to Israel. But then, in 1951, the flights were able to go directly to Lod because there was a tremendous backlog of Jews waiting to go. The Iraqis were happy to expedite the process. The *New York Times* wrote at the time that it was the biggest air migration in history, though it doesn't hold that title anymore—the Soviet Jews arriving in Israel in the 1980s and 1990s trumped our numbers.

At first we didn't have a name for this massive immigration. Every newspaper in Israel chose a different name. Even the name "Ali Baba" appeared in one of the newspapers. Moshe Sharret, then our foreign minister, suggested "Operation Babylon," which I took later for the title of my foreign language translations of my book about the operation. One day the newspaper *Ma'ariv* used the name "Ezra and Nehemiah" and it stuck. Ezra and Nehemiah are the names of two chapters in the Bible that tell the story of the Jews who were exiled to Babylon and returned to rebuild the Second Temple in Jerusalem, and Ezra and Nehemiah were the main leaders of that return.

That was the end of my activity in Iraq. I returned to my kibbutz and married Tmima. A year after passing its resolution the Iraqi government shut the floodgates, in March 1951. Earlier, it had declared that anyone who registered to leave and renounce their nationality would have their money and property confiscated, though formally freezed. It was a nasty, nasty trick. So most of the 104,000 Iraqi Jews who arrived in Israel with Operation Ezra and Nehemiah arrived virtually penniless unless they had been able to transfer funds via relatives already in Israel years earlier.

Later, when I became a member of the Israeli parliament, visiting the transition camps was initially my main activity. In the 1950s, about 100,000 Mizrachi Jews, many of them Iraqi, were living in the *ma'abarot* and the majority were jobless. When the Iraqis in the camps heard about the much-improved conditions of those who remained in Iraq—indeed, that their former community was prospering—they complained about their own situation. Some of them criticized us for having brought them here and for not doing enough to improve their lot. Those complaints gradually quieted as stories of the worsening lot of the Jews in Iraq reached Israel, and simultaneously economic conditions in Israel improved.

Shlomo Hillel successfully advocated for improved conditions and employment opportunities in the transit camps and among Iraqi immigrants overall. He became an elected member of the Knesset in 1953 and in 1959 he joined the Foreign Service and helped establish ties between Israel and Africa. He served as a minister in the governments of Golda Meir and Yitzhak Rabin and held a leading diplomatic post at the UN. In 1984, he was elected Speaker of the Knesset. Hillel's full account of his years as a secret Israeli emissary appears in his autobiography, Operation Babylon: The Story of the Rescue of the Jews of Iraq *(1987). Hillel spent most of his life in Jerusalem and now lives with his wife Tmima in Ra'anana, where their son resides. Their daughter, Hagar, died in 2005.*

* * *

Ilana Marcus was born and grew up in Egypt. After making aliyah in 1947, she was recruited by the Mossad L'Aliyah Bet to become the stewardess on the flights for the airlift operation of Ezra and Nehemiah. Code-named "Chris," she also served as a courier for the Mossad between Iraq and Israel—the secret part of her job—carrying thousands of letters and documents between Mossad emissaries in Iraq and headquarters in Tel Aviv that enabled the coordination of the exodus. In her account, she describes conditions on the approximately 200 airlifts on which she was the sole air hostess—personally caring for many of the Jews who were part of the year-long airlift of some 950 flights.[12]

The departure process for the refugees began at the Mesouda Shemtob Synagogue, which became transformed into an exit camp—a way station from which all denationalized Jews were given the necessary travel documents and taken to the airport. Posted outside the synagogue walls were lists of flight schedules and names of the travelers booked on each plane. Kiosks for food and drinks nearby were teeming with activity. Inside, people prepared to leave while relatives came to bid them farewell.

Each traveler was allowed to take 50 dinars [one dinar was equal to about four dollars at that time], a wedding ring, a watch, and a bracelet, though some tried to smuggle gold and jewelry in the one suitcase each that they were allotted. Suitcases were often slashed by the customs agents, and any outlawed valuables were sent back to the synagogue to be retrieved by family or friends. When the inspections became increasingly vigilant, the Mossad paid off police officers and customs officials to turn a blind eye to the contents of the suitcases, often to the tune of as much as 500 dinars per month. After crossing the customs checkpoint, the emigrants waited, often for hours, outside in the hot sun until they were allowed to board the plane. Eventually, a tent was erected for them.[13]

I was born in 1924 in Alexandria but grew up in Cairo. When I was about 23 years old, I made aliyah alone. I wanted to work on a kibbutz. My family thought I was completely crazy—leaving my nice life to go work in the fields. In 1950, I took a boat to Israel and arrived in Haifa. I stayed there for two days because there was cholera at the time in Egypt and everyone coming from Egypt was quarantined. Then I was sent to Bror Chail near Ashkelon to help develop the tiny outpost into a kibbutz. I remember that first winter there so well because it was the only year we had significant snow in the Negev in all the 65 years I've lived in Israel. The winter was very difficult. Right away I realized my family was right—I was crazy—because the conditions in the Negev were harsh. It was a very hard life.

Bror Chail consisted of two caravans and two tents. We were 5 girls and 12 boys, and we were surrounded by Bedouin. And we were right next to the border with Egypt—so close that we could hear the Egyptians talking. It was impossible to work in the fields because it was so cold and there was no food, little water, nothing. It was so harsh that I said to myself, "I can't continue." After a short time there, I was sent to Kibbutz Nir Am [also near Ashkelon] to work in the kitchen. One morning in Nir Am I woke up and began to read in the tent. My bed was just a piece of wood and a mattress and that day the rainwater came up above the bed. Walking through the kibbutz, the mud came up to my knees. The toilet was far away from our tents. We ate salty smoked fish every day which the Askenazim liked but I couldn't stand. So I decided, "Enough is enough."

I knew some people at the port in Tel Aviv so I went there and asked them if they had a job for me. They sent me back to the kibbutz and said they'd think about it. A week later, someone called me and said he had a special job for me but he wasn't sure I would accept it. I told him, "Anything, anything. I'll take anything—I can't stand the kibbutz anymore!" One day I was called for an interview in Tel Aviv, and only learned when I got there that it was with the Mossad L'Aliyah Bet. I was asked very strange things, like whether I knew who Baron de Montesquieu[14] was and whether I knew that he went to Persia. "Yes, I learned that in school," I answered. I went back to the kibbutz and asked my friends, "Why are they asking me about Persia and France? I think they want to send me to Persia."

It turned out it wasn't Persia, it was Iraq, and they were trying to test my knowledge of the Middle East and of French. So they said they were going to send me to Iraq but didn't say what for, and told me I had only two weeks to prepare. It wasn't very hard to leave Israel, to tell you the truth. It was really difficult there and the pay that I was getting from the Mossad was marvelous. I didn't know what to do with all that money.

They got me a French passport, but they made the most horrible mistake with it. I went to Tehran first and from there to Baghdad because I had never flown before and the leg to Tehran was kind of a test run. So I needed visas for Iraq and Iran. They gave me the passport after I boarded the plane to Tehran, and when I looked inside I noticed they had given me a visa for France instead of Iran. I said, "What is this? Are they out of their minds?" Making matters worse, I was all alone on the plane—just me and the two pilots—and I was so terrified I couldn't speak because it was the first time I had flown. It was pure luck that the officials in Tehran didn't even open the passport when I arrived. If they had, I surely would have been arrested. I told the Israeli emissary there: "Do me a favor. If you want to send me to Iraq without my being caught on the first day—and killed—exchange the passport." So they flew me back to Israel to get a new passport and then flew me through Nicosia, in Cyprus, to Iraq. In Tehran I was given a gun which I knew how to use because I had been in the Haganah while in Israel.

I remember vividly my first flight into Baghdad. From the air, Iraq looked very flat. There were a lot of palm trees along the rivers. The Tigris is something out of this world—stunning and gorgeous. As the plane descended, the pilots searched for the famous Hanging Gardens of Babylon.[15]

I was given a uniform that had belonged to some other stewardess. Whoever she was much taller than I. And it was the first time I saw pleats in the back. All my life I wore pleats in the front. So I put the skirt on backwards. Then somebody said to me, "Hey, what happened to you? Are you drunk?" And then I realized and turned it around. But I wore that silly uniform on all the flights back and forth from Iraq.

I was on one of the first aliyah flights out of Iraq, on May 19, 1950. Initially during this period I was living in Nicosia because the flights had to go through Nicosia before going to Israel and it was safer for us to live there than in Baghdad. Near East Transport took the passengers to Nicosia and El Al took them from there to Israel. Nicosia was lovely. Then, Cyprus was run by the Greeks and we stayed at a beautiful hotel called Lidra Palace. We swam in the pool during the days and danced in the evenings. An Iraqi policeman accompanied all the flights out of Iraq to ensure we didn't go directly to Israel, though eventually we were allowed to go directly to Israel.

At that point I was told I'd have to move to Baghdad. Living in Baghdad was difficult because no one understood who I was, what I was, or what I was doing in Iraq, yet I couldn't explain it to them because I had to keep my identity secret. There were sometimes three flights a day so I couldn't be on every flight. Eventually, the Mossad hired two more air hosts, a Greek girl and a French boy, but in the beginning it was only me. I was also a courier. I took papers back and forth between Israel and Iraq: intelligence information gathered by the Israelis working in Iraq, documents that needed to go the other direction, passenger lists, and even letters between the emissaries and their families or girlfriends. I used to take love letters back and forth for Mordechai Ben Porat and his girlfriend at the time, Rivka, who later became his wife!

My biggest problem was that I had so many papers that I didn't know where to put them all. When I got to the hotel in Baghdad, which is where I lived for many months, I fretted about where to put the letters because I knew that my suitcases were being opened and inspected by the Iraqi police many times. I don't think they were specifically looking for reasons to arrest me but it was just that I was a foreigner and they searched many of the foreigners' belongings.

One day I looked at the window drapes in my hotel room and got an idea: I opened the hem at the bottom, put the letters inside and sewed it back up. I kept the letters there until I was able to deliver them to their destinations. The work I was doing was very dangerous but I was young and daring, I suppose, and never really even thought about being caught. I was confident in myself so I was never scared. Actually, I ended up really enjoying myself in Iraq. I used to go dancing with the crew at the American club and I lived the life of a foreigner on vacation.

My code name in the Mossad was Chris, but my public identity was a French woman named Lilian Milian. I was indeed named Lilian in Egypt before I came to Israel, although I was usually called Ilana. When I asked my parents about the meaning of my name they told me, "a tree." Because I'm so short, I said, "Really, you are making fun of me. You couldn't come up with anything else?" They joked, "There are small trees!" Milian was the last name of my neighbor in Egypt, who was French. I thought it sounded nice with Lilian. The pilots knew that I was Jewish and working for the Mossad, though I continued to be Lilian Milian even on the plane.

While I was living in Baghdad, I didn't associate with the Jewish community. People were supposed to think I was a Christian, and a few Christian friends took me to church with them on Sundays and I hated to go. I made up all sorts of reasons not to go, like, "I forget where it is"—even if I'd been there before. Or, "It's such a small place. I don't like it."

In Iraq I became friendly with some of the American diplomats and only when I was with them did I really feel secure. During that period, there were numerous Americans in Iraq, many of them working in oil export. I would usually tell them that I was taking Jews to Israel, because the airlift was not a secret, but I kept my work as a courier for the Mossad secret, of course. One time, I was walking in the street with a lot papers that I was planning to take to Israel when I saw two American pilots driving in a car. They asked me, "Lilian, where are you going? Are you going to the airport?" I said, "Yes." And they said, "Come with us." They put me in their jeep and we arrived directly to the plane because they were in a diplomat car so they didn't have to go through any security checks and questioning as I usually did when I boarded the flights to Israel. They didn't ask me what I was doing and I didn't tell them anything, and that was marvelous. I never knew whether they suspected I was doing more than being an air hostess.

Ironically, the only place I was afraid to arrive was Israel. That's because I had to maintain my fake French identity when I landed at the airport so that it wouldn't get out—through passengers, for instance—and somehow get back to the Iraqis that I was really Ilana, an Israeli from the kibbutz! But it was such a small country that Israelis I knew used to recognize me at the airport all the time and nearly blow my cover. One time when I landed, one of the boys I worked with on the kibbutz was stationed as a guard at the airfield and saw me. He said, "This one is French? No way! She was with me in the kibbutz. She worked in the kitchen." Somehow I managed to slip by him without a problem. I always said to the pilots and the others I was working with, "I prefer to arrive in Baghdad, Tehran, anywhere, but not Tel Aviv."

Women never walked alone in Baghdad, but I was a foreigner so all the unwritten rules didn't apply to me, and I walked by myself a lot, though not past 10 o'clock in the evening. Those things you can do in Nicosia, but not in Baghdad. That is why I liked Nicosia so much. Iraq was a poor country. It was not very clean. The children came up to foreigners in the street and asked for *baksheesh* (charity). They were nearly naked and what they were wearing was just terrible. There was a great deal of poverty. I frequently walked alongside the Tigris on the wealthy side, which was beautiful, but a few times I crossed over its bridges and walked into the neighborhoods on the other side. There, I saw the mud houses of the poor people, almost all Muslims. The children, especially, were so miserable. I came from Egypt where there is a lot of poverty, but not like in Baghdad at that time. It was much worse. The irony of course is that Iraq was a rich country with all its oil.

I took about three flights per week to Israel. There were only 50 seats, but about 100 or 120 people were stuffed onto each flight. People sat in the aisles, on laps, anywhere they could. We used the same plane for all those flights. The experience was very difficult for all the passengers. Everyone came on with suitcases and women sometimes wore three dresses, one on top of the other, because they were only allowed to take out of Iraq what they were wearing and what they could carry in one suitcase. I remember seeing a Kurdish woman from Mosul wearing seven dresses. It's cooler in Mosul, in the north of Iraq, but in Baghdad she was very hot with all those dresses. And it was especially hot on the plane because there was hardly any air conditioning: we'd have it for half an hour, then it would stop, and then it would come back on weakly. So everyone was thirsty, but I never had enough water for them. There was no food on the plane because the flight was only four hours long.

I was the only person in a position of authority in the passenger area other than the Iraqi policeman. Basically, my job was to assist people in any way I could—getting them comfortable, fetching them water, and calming their nerves, as almost no one had flown before. When passengers boarded the plane, the toilet was always clean, but after one hour it became a mess. Many vomited from air sickness, but we didn't have enough sick bags. On the first few flights I was air sick all the time and was so ashamed of myself because I was supposed to be taking care of the passengers, who were also sick—more sick, even. I never took care of the pilots. In fact, they feared my touch because of all the sickness that I came in contact with when helping the passengers.

There was one death on these flights and one birth. I recall that a young boy came onto the plane looking very pale and sick and a doctor cared for him on the plane, but he died before we got to Nicosia. After arriving in Nicosia, I wrote a report about the death and then went straight to the bar and drank a cognac.

The birth was also of a boy. The laboring woman's mother-in-law helped deliver the baby and I assisted. I remember that when the baby was born I thought it was a girl and the women made fun of me because it was a boy but they just hadn't let me get in close enough to see. So they joked, "Ilana, we didn't know that you don't know a girl from a boy. At your age, it's really ridiculous!" Years later, in 1994, when Mordechai Ben Porat made a big party and reunion for the flight crew, I saw this boy who was, of course, then a grown man. He told me that for years his family has called him "the boy who was born on the plane."

Once, one of the pilots said to me, "Come here, Ilana. Stay with us. Let them be alone. They can fend for themselves." So I went to the cockpit, and he continued, "You don't have to take care of them so much. They are walking baggage." This infuriated me. I argued, "But they are very thirsty. I have to bring some more water on these flights. It is impossible to leave them like that. I have to go back." Later, I told the Mossad folks what he had said and this pilot got the sack. He never knew why, and, thank God, I never saw him again.

Those flights were of course a very emotional moment for all the passengers, but, I have to say, not a really happy moment for them except for those who were really Zionist and were delighted to be coming to Eretz Yisrael. Most were weighed down with worries about being destitute—about how they'd earn a living in a place they'd never been and where they don't speak the language. They worried about whether they'd have a house and where the children would be educated. They didn't know what to expect and in many cases they didn't really know why they were going except that it was what everyone was doing. But the worries were silent usually. I just became so familiar with the looks on their faces that even if they didn't say anything I knew what was going through their minds.

My last day in Iraq was the day I was almost caught by the Iraqi police. It happened after they caught Mordechai [Ben Porat, in his fourth and final arrest before escaping], and I was supposed to bring mail and documents to him. But that day I decided to get a pedicure at the hotel. The woman who did my pedicure cut my foot badly by accident and I couldn't walk. I telephoned the house I usually delivered the papers to in order to explain to them that I couldn't come because I was hurt. I heard a strange voice on the other end of the line. A man asked me in Arabic where I was, what I was doing, and why I wasn't coming. I usually spoke on the phone in English or French when I was at the hotel and never Arabic, so I just put the phone down and knew something was wrong. Two hours later, a Mossad agent came to the hotel to tell me that Mordechai had been arrested and I shouldn't go to the meeting place and instead must leave the country immediately.[16] I said, "You are a little late, you know. I realized two hours ago that something was amiss." I left most of my things behind, including a beautiful Persian carpet I will never forget. I took all the remaining papers to the hotel bathroom and burned them and prayed that no one would smell the stench and catch me.

I left the hotel for the airport at night with the French air steward and some others in our group. We left at night. Usually the planes took off during the day but we had to escape quickly so we left immediately, and passengers were told to get ready to go. We didn't give any signals to the passengers that something was amiss—that practically the whole Israeli operation was escaping on their plane—and they didn't notice anything.

After completing her work in Iraq, Ilana Marucs briefly lived in Tel Aviv where she worked for the Mossad typing correspondences between Egypt and Israel. Her family left Egypt in 1956 and joined her in Israel. She moved to Kibbutz Sdot Yam, and then back to Tel Aviv where she married and worked in a bank. She lives in Ramat Aviv with her husband, Alfred Marcus. She says that when she "gets depressed" because of her old age, the passage of time, and considering her life's accomplishments, she thinks back to her days in Baghdad and says to herself: "Ilana, really, you're not so bad."

* * *

Shlomo Sehayek was born in 1920 in Baghdad and was one of the early leaders of the Young Halutz. He describes here how in the early 1940s, his home became the base for undercover Israeli emissaries who came as representatives of the Mossad L'Aliyah Bet to cultivate the Young Halutz and coordinate the smuggling of Iraqi Jews to Palestine. As one of the emissaries' local point persons, Shlomo carried out missions for the cause as did his brother Shaul, also an activist. Also in their home, emissaries began to operate the first wireless machine used to communicate with Mossad headquarters in Tel Aviv for the purpose of coordinating activities and exchanging information.

My name before I made aliyah was Salman, a translation of the name King Solomon. In my early childhood I was educated by my father to dream of making aliyah. My father said that making aliyah was the greatest and most important mitzvah of the faith and he tirelessly repeated the phrase, "Next Year in Jerusalem."

I attended the Shammash School, where we were taught both Torah and modern Hebrew. Our Hebrew teacher was a man from Eretz Yisrael, Avraham Rosen. With his help, several pupils aged 12 and 13—among them my brother Ovadia, who was 5 years older than me—established a Hebrew library that ordered books and textbooks from Israel, and a biweekly newspaper called *Itonenu* (Our Newspaper). Ovadia and his friends called the group Achi-Ever and a growing number of students joined it, all intent on making aliyah. When the educated Arabs in Iraq started to understand that Zionism was a nationalist movement which intended to put down roots in Palestine, they started persecuting the Jews. In 1936, the Iraqi authorities banned the teaching of modern Hebrew and expelled Avraham Rosen and the rest of the Jewish teachers who came from England and Eretz Yisrael.

I graduated from high school in 1938 and started working for a Jewish bank, Edward Aboudi and Co. Limited, one of several Jewish-owned banks. In banking, like in trade, partnerships existed between Jews and Muslims because the Muslims wanted smart and experienced Jewish merchants to manage their businesses, and the Jews wanted the Muslims for protection from official or social discrimination. Both sides had an economic interest in maintaining strong, cooperative relations.

My brother Ovadia finished school in 1932 and father allowed him to make aliyah. That year, Jews could still get passports for Palestine, and he traveled there as a tourist with our cousin Sasson. They were the same age and both were members of Ahi-ever. My grandfather, father's father, was already in Jerusalem and he took them both under his patronage. Ovadia joined the *Noar Haoved* [Israel's youth labor movement] and a group at the *moshava* [rural community] of Migdal which founded Kibbutz Genossar, where I eventually became a member.

Then in 1934 or '35, suddenly Ovadia appeared in Baghdad. He arrived in his clothes and shoes from the kibbutz and with a man named Benzion Yisraeli from Kvutzat Kinneret [a kibbutz]. Yisraeli came to Baghdad to smuggle date shoots back to Eretz Yisrael, and Ovadia was supposed to help him by contacting date merchants. However, Ovadia had an additional goal: he was given 10 aliyah licenses by the Jewish Agency to bring some of the Ahi-ever members to Eretz Yisrael. He organized a group of nine members and he set aside one certificate for himself, so that he could arrive legally in Eretz Yisrael this time. But in order to renew his passport he needed father's signature.

My father asked him what work he was doing in Eretz Yisrael. Ovadia told him, "I'm a kibbutz member." Father didn't know what a kibbutz was but he asked him how much Ovadia earned there. Ovadia answered that on the kibbutz one works without receiving a salary. My father said, "That's nonsense! How could that be, work without receiving a salary?" So Ovadia explained to him the principles of the kibbutz. "Do you observe Shabbat on the kibbutz?" he asked. Ovadia told him, "No." Father said, "So you desecrate the Shabbat?" Ovadia answered, "Yes." "Do you pray and put on *tefillin* [phylacteries] at all?" My father asked. "No," Ovadia answered. So my father told him, "You are a heretic! Do you think that I will sign for you to return to Eretz Yisrael only for you to continue abandoning religion?" Ovadia answered, "Father, if you force me to stay in Baghdad and refuse to sign, do you think I will change my habits?" Father consulted his rabbi, and returned and signed the papers for Ovadia.

To grasp the extent of the internal conflict this request created for my father, I must describe his deep devotion to his faith. Until the age of 13 or 14, he wrote prayer books by hand in Hebrew using color and ornamentation, and he later donated these books to the National & University Library of Israel in Jerusalem. He was deeply religious. During Shabbat meals father talked about the Torah portion of the week and told us about the longing for Eretz Yisrael and the yearning for aliyah. He instilled in us the desire to unite with the world's Jewish people in the Jewish homeland.

His devotion to Israel only intensified over time. When my aunt and uncle wanted to marry off one of their daughters, she did not consent because she wanted to make aliyah. What could the parents do? They looked for someone to talk to her and convince her to marry. Since my father was a respected man in the family, they came to him and asked him to convince her. But my father was loyal to his faith and principles. "No," he said. "I will not talk to her. And if she will come to ask me for advice, I'll tell her to make aliyah. So please go to someone else."

The Rise of a Movement

When we walked down the street in Baghdad in the months leading up to World War II, we could feel the hatred against the Jews was growing. Then on Shavuot of 1941 the horrible pogrom against the Jews happened in Baghdad. The Farhoud made my father think seriously about aliyah for the whole family. We were five brothers and five sisters. Ovadia was in Eretz Yisrael, so father asked him to get aliyah certificates for three of the sisters and one brother. In the beginning of 1942 the sisters and the brother made aliyah. (The two elder sisters were married overseas.) The four went to Kibbutz Genossar and then to the Meir Shfeya youth village in

Zichron Ya'akov. I stayed with my brother Shaul and our youngest brother with our parents in Baghdad.

After the Farhoud, the Jews slowly trickled back to life again. But the Jewish youths didn't accept the new reality, and a number of young Jews between the ages of 16 and 19 united and said, "Enough. We will not allow another slaughter of Jews. We need to get organized to learn how to use weapons and to protect ourselves and our families if, God forbid, another pogrom breaks out." In order to recruit more youths, they wrote flyers inviting others to join their group, which they signed *Shabab al Ilqaad* (Young Halutz) and handed them out secretly among the Jews. One of these flyers somehow reached the "institutes"[17] in Eretz Yisrael.

The institutes' leadership declared, "If there is such enthusiastic youth in Iraq we must help them, and in order to help we must be there. We must send emissaries who will teach them how to use weapons for self-defense, teach them Hebrew and find ways to smuggle youths to Eretz Yisrael."[18] At this point, each Jewish passport issued in Iraq had a stamp indicating that it was valid for all countries "except Palestine." The only way to get a passport without this restriction was to bribe the clerks. So young Jews fled to Eretz Yisrael through the desert by bribing professional Arab smugglers, and emissaries began to arrive from Eretz Yisrael to Baghdad to help coordinate more of these escapes.

The British had reoccupied Iraq after the Farhoud so Baghdad began to fill up with soldiers: British, Indian, Australian, et cetera—each army with its individual uniform. One day, a guy I knew from school from the Itach family came to my workplace and told me that there is a soldier from Eretz Yisrael at the Rashid Hotel who wants to see me because he has a letter for me from my brother Ovadia. I went to the hotel and met the soldier, who introduced himself as Shaul. He handed me the letter from Ovadia but I couldn't read it because I had forgotten the Hebrew I had learned in school. He asked me, "Are you Salman?" I said, "Yes." "Sit down please," he said. "Tell me about the pogrom, about what happened." In my broken Hebrew I tried to tell him the story of the pogrom. He asked me to come back with my brother Shaul to see him again.

I brought the letter home to Shaul, who read the letter, as his Hebrew was then better than mine, and together we went back to the hotel. The man welcomed us nicely, and Shaul spoke to him in Hebrew. We learned that the man's full name was Shaul Meirov and he was from Kvutzat Kinneret. The following day Itach came to me again and said, "Shaul the soldier sent me to you because my family and I are making aliyah, so he asked to know whether you were ready to meet two people who have come here illegally from Eretz Yisrael, and then to bring them to a young man called Salim Halifa." I discovered later that Halifa was the head of the Young Halutz. I said I was ready. He gave me a password, "Gabriel," which the two men would use when they came to me.

Several weeks later I walked into my office and two soldiers were waiting for me. A throng of people were gathered around them out of curiosity. I immediately realized who they were and started speaking to them in English. Then I got closer and one of them opened a button on his shirt and I saw that under the uniform he was wearing a suit and tie. I didn't wait for them to say "Gabriel"—I said it first and they said "yes" quietly. Meanwhile, I had to shake off all the people around us, so I said, "You should be ashamed of yourselves. I want to make a deal and it's not nice that you are sticking your noses in it. Go look for your own deals." Smuggling money was so commonplace and accepted in those days that they immediately understood, and left. I led the two men into one of the rooms in the office. We began to talk. One of them, Ezra Khedouri, had been born in Iraq and made aliyah at the age of nine and had become a member of Kibbutz Maoz Haim. The other, Shmaryahu Gutman, was from Kibbutz Na'an. They had arrived with an Egged convoy as drivers because the British army was using Egged buses to transport soldiers throughout the Middle East.[19] They said they must reach the place where the buses were parked so that the drivers' manager could see them with me and understand that they had reached their destination. They said they hadn't showered in a week.

I took both of them to our house, and after they washed and ate I introduced them to my parents as friends of Ovadia. After dark I took them with my brother Shaul to the place where the Young Halutz members met. The head of the group, Salim Halifa, sat with them alone and after an hour he came to us and said that he didn't have room for them to spend the night. He asked us to take them to our home and that a decision on what to do with them on a more permanent basis would be made the following day. The next day it became clear that Halifa and his friends weren't able to have them stay in their homes. So Shmaryahu and Ezra said to Shaul and me, "We understand that we can't expect Salim to take us in, but now we have two choices: to return to Eretz Yisrael or stay with you at your home. But you should understand: we are walking explosives. If we get caught our fate will be very serious—we could even be executed by the Iraqi or the British government. We came here to organize groups of youths for three goals: to buy weapons and train Jewish men to use the weapons for self-defense, to teach Hebrew, and to smuggle young Jews to Eretz Yisrael in any possible way." Shaul and I both agreed that we must let them stay at our home, but we couldn't do so without father's consent.

The men asked to meet father together with us. They explained to father their purpose in coming to Iraq and warned him about the danger of their staying at our place, both for them and for us. Shaul and I waited for our "idol," our father, to speak—the man who had preached to us throughout the years about the longing for Eretz Yisrael and his belief that, as he used to say, "Israel is bought through suffering."[20] It was a real test for him.

And then he spoke: "My sons, for Eretz Yisrael, 'til the gallows. My house is your house. Do what you want, on condition that you don't desecrate the Shabbat in my home." They thanked him but then said, "The house you live in doesn't suit our needs. We need a huge house in order to host the many activities we will hold. We need a house we can escape from if there is a need in a time of danger, one which has room for *sliks* [secret hiding places for weapons] to be built, and which has windows overlooking the street so we can be on the lookout. And such a house needs to be closed off such that what goes on inside can't be seen from the outside." Father agreed to move. And so we found a huge house in the Abu al Sa'ad neighborhood that answered all these requirements and we moved into it with Shmaryahu and Ezra.

The house we rented was adjacent to the Alliance girls' school and close to the Beit Zilkha yeshiva and synagogue. The house was huge—it was the size of a palace. In the basement we could carry out weapons-training activities, and the walls were one-meter thick so the activities would not be heard from outside. We also managed to get false identity cards for Shmaryahu and Ezra that belonged to two deceased people, for a bribe of 20 dinars each. Ezra received a card of a man named Naji and Shmaryahu received a card that belonged to someone named Khedouri, and we began to refer to them by their assumed names.

Soon after, the emissaries told us that they needed to bring a wireless operator in order to maintain daily communications with Eretz Yisrael. One day I came home from work for lunch and found a blond girl with blue eyes and fair skin in the house. We had been expecting her: her name was Malka Rofeh. She arrived from Eretz Yisrael dressed as a British soldier with a British convoy. Only one person on the convoy knew her real identity. Because she was a young woman with cropped hair she looked like a 15-year-old boy. She told us later that the British soldiers saw her and went mad, saying, "What, they're bringing kids to Iraq to serve in the army?" In order to bring her through the streets to our home, we asked a woman named Tikva Shochet to help us. She had been organizing women's groups for Hebrew study. She agreed to the task and brought another woman with her: Simha, who later married Ezra, the emissary. The two women went to the other side of the Tigris to pick up Malka from the British camp. They dressed her in traditional Arab clothes—a veil to hide the face with holes only for her eyes, and a black *abaya*. They told her: "You can't move around without this. Get used to it. There is no other way." And that's how they brought her back to our place.

Malka began the communication with Eretz Yisrael on the wireless machine. Initially there were problems: she could hear them but they couldn't hear her. It was a primitive machine. Shmaryahu returned with one of the convoys to Eretz Yisrael, where they explained to him how to search the innards of the machine and operate it. He returned to Baghdad and did as they said. One day at the designated transmission time Malka tried and got a signal—they could hear each other. What joy! We were dancing. *Ya allah*. Every day at a certain time Malka pulled out the wireless machine from its hiding place in the house and brought it up to an attic room where she would work, receiving instructions, passing on instructions, and passing back information to Eretz Yisrael.

Soon after, another emissary arrived, Enzo Sereni. He was officially the representative of Solel Boneh[21] with the British army so he lived freely in a Baghdad hotel. One day Sereni appeared at my office and introduced himself. I was expecting him and led him to Shmaryahu and Ezra. Together, the three of them formed the core of the Israeli leadership.

That was about the time that my brother Shaul got an opportunity to go to Eretz Yisrael, and he took it: in May, 1942, he disguised himself as a Polish soldier in a convoy transporting a Polish army unit from Iraq, and entered Palestine illegally. A few days later, we received a telegram from Ovadia. "Shaul's surgery was successful." We understood that Shaul had arrived safely. Before Shaul left, however, he had arranged for a meeting between the emissaries and six members of Achi-Ever. This group formed the core of the Young Halutz. These people agreed with enthusiasm to cooperate secretly—and thus the underground movement was born at our house. The group and I were sworn in by the emissaries as Haganah members and we became the first group trained in the use of weapons (by Ezra), as well as face-to-face combat with knives and sticks. Then a group was formed to look for ways to acquire guns and weapons, called *Shura* [rank and file]. The activities of the Shura and the Young Halutz expanded to multiple cells of 10 to 15 people each.

The Underground at Work

We tried various routes by which to smuggle youngsters to Eretz Yisrael. But we didn't always have success. Early on, we organized a group of five youths, and the plan was to use a Jewish driver we knew who was familiar with the transit routes from Iraq to Trans-Jordan to Eretz Yisrael who would take them across the border in a rented car. I knew a Jew who owned a private car who was ready to rent it out for a week in return for a large sum. Our driver, Naji al Aswad—al Aswad meaning "the black," because he was very dark-skinned—took the youths and went. Several hours later we learned that they had been caught by the police and arrested. Naji was released on bail but the five youngsters were required to provide guarantors in order to be released until their trial on charges of trying to flee Iraq illegally.

One of the boys was the son of a rabbi named Hacham Yosef. This rabbi came to our house—having learned that we were responsible for his son's escape—and threatened that if we didn't secure his son's release he would disclose to the police our underground activities. My father, who knew the rabbi well, told him: "Rabbi, are you ignoring the saying, 'The land of Israel is reached only by suffering?' Isn't this the situation now? You are suffering for your son. You mustn't threaten us. But you can be sure that your son will be bailed out." Eventually, the youths were given fines.

The police in the meantime had tracked down the owner of the car and wanted to charge him with attempted smuggling. He denied any connection with the case and led the police to me. One day a policeman appeared in my office and ordered me to follow him to be investigated. The investigating officer tried to accuse me of conspiring to smuggle the five youths to Palestine. I told him, "Sir, I don't know what you are talking about. I was just mediating for two dinars between the evil driver and the car owner." The police had to verify my story with Naji, but they found out that he had fled Iraq together with the man who was the guarantor for his release. Thus they had no way to cross-check my story, and the case was closed.

Every few days, the movement coordinated the escape of individual Jews to Eretz Yisrael, either by taxi or by foot through the desert to Jordan. In addition, many Polish Jews—about 4,500—who came with the Anders' Polish army through Europe to Iran and Iraq defected and were smuggled to Eretz Yisrael through our underground network. The Jews in the Polish army were hated deeply and bullied by the other soldiers, so the moment they arrived in Baghdad they looked for ways to reach the local Jews in the Jewish neighborhoods. They made contact with Jews they found in synagogues. The local Jews took them in, put them up for a few nights, and connected them with underground members who hid them until it was possible to smuggle them out.[22]

Meanwhile, the British convoys continued to arrive from Palestine to the center of Baghdad in Egged vehicles, and when the vehicles parked on the city's main streets, local Jews gleefully gathered around them, thrilled to see Hebrew letters—the holy language—for the first time out in the open, and began kissing the words as if they were Torah scrolls. The Iraqi authorities were not pleased with these occurrences and demanded that the British park these vehicles outside the city beyond the Tigris, several kilometers away.

In 1942, Moshe Dayan[23] came to Baghdad from Palestine, disguised as an Egged driver with one of the British convoys. He told Sereni that he had brought three suitcases, two filled with weapons and the other filled with Hebrew textbooks. Sereni took Dayan to our house for a meeting with the emissaries and activists, including myself. It was a Saturday. Dayan was tall, wore an Egged uniform, and had a black eye patch. He explained to me how to get to where he was going to be parked that evening so that I could fetch the three suitcases. He instructed me to bring along two Jewish Polish soldiers who had defected. Sereni interjected, "Salman needs to find a taxi owned by a Jew to carry out the operation." I said, "Have you gone mad? A Jewish taxi owner is unheard of—it is an Arab-only occupation." I also pointed out that because it was Shabbat it would be difficult to find a Jew to drive. Eventually we agreed that a Jewish-owned vehicle must be found, at any cost.

There were a few Jews who had private cars, like the son of the owner of the Zilkha bank, Abdullah, whom we knew. He had visited Israel and had a positive affinity to the Zionist movement. After a search a colleague and I found him and told him about our mission. He was enthusiastic and said, "No problem. I'm ready." At the agreed-upon time we picked up the two Jewish Polish soldiers and crossed the bridge over the Tigris to the camp where Dayan was waiting for us. Beside the camp there was a grove of trees and Dayan appeared from between the trees at the expected spot. We slowed down and let the two men off and they went to Dayan, who later took them back with him to Palestine. Dayan threw the suitcases into the car. Though I didn't know their names at the time, the Poles were Adam Gillon and David Azrieli, who later became the owner of the Azrieli Center in Tel Aviv. (Some 58 years later, when I went to see David Azrieli in his office with my brother Shaul, I recognized him immediately and we had an emotional meeting.)[24]

When we started driving back from the camp with the suitcases, we—the driver, Edward Shochat, and I—were stopped at a roadblock manned by two policemen, one British and one Iraqi. Before us was a long line of cars waiting for inspection. We were scared to death. When it was our turn to be inspected, the driver was requested to present his driver's license, and by some miracle we were allowed through. At the house the emissaries were anxiously waiting for us, and we quickly unloaded the suitcases and hid the weapons in the secret hiding places.

From then on, our weapons cache continued to grow steadily. Weapons were stored in caches in various Jewish homes which were well hidden and only one or two members of the families knew where they were.[25]

We had other close calls. One day Enzo Sereni came to the house and told us: "One of the Jewish soldiers in the British army brought two batteries from Israel, one of which is filled with grenades and the other with safety caches. One of us must cross the bridge over the river, meet the soldier and pick up the two 'batteries.'"

It was decided to assign the mission to my cousin Shaul Shemesh, but he was warned not to cross the bridge on foot but rather to hire a carriage. It was dangerous to walk on foot over the bridge because policemen stood guard there looking for goods stolen from the army and for other smuggled goods. My cousin arrived at the designated location, met the Jewish soldier and received the two batteries from him. However, he decided to save money and walked on foot instead of hiring a carriage. He was stopped on the bridge by two policemen who asked him to explain where he got the batteries. Instead of giving them bank notes as the acceptable bribe, he started to joke around with them, and only when he understood that he was in serious danger did he try offering a bribe. The policemen refused and took him to the police station. They recorded the event in the police log and told him that he would stand trial for smuggling, but that he could be released until the following day after paying bail.

The emissaries and I waited impatiently for Shaul Shemesh to arrive with the batteries. A policeman came to our house to discuss the situation with my family, and when Shmaryahu and Ezra saw him coming they climbed to the roof and fled. Father said he was willing to sign for the bail and went with the policeman to the station. He signed, but the batteries remained at the police station. We knew that if we didn't get the batteries back fast we would be in terrible danger.

I had ties to Arab merchants who had commercial ties to the bank where I worked. One of them, a grain merchant named Abed al Razeq Mullah Hajo, lived across the river, close to the same police station. I telephoned him early in the morning and told him about my cousin Shaul who foolishly had bought batteries stolen

from the British army and was caught by the station policemen. When I identified the police station, Hajo told me, "Salman, relax, I am a good friend of the station commander and I will immediately see to fixing the matter. But it will cost money." An hour later he called me and said, "Salman, the affair is settled. It will cost you six dinars. But your cousin must return to the station. The policemen will welcome him, give him the batteries, and even escort him to the carriage and make sure he passes the bridge safely. He mustn't forget to buy the policemen tea." And thus Shaul Shemesh got the batteries and brought them home. The Arab merchant told me that the officer tore out the station log in which the event was reported. But the affair wasn't cheap for us: six dinars nearly amounted to a typical government officer's monthly salary.

The underground activity did not escape the eyes of the British and, together with the Iraqi police, they tried to find intelligence on us. For this purpose the British found an Iraqi Jew in Eretz Yisrael who was prepared to cooperate with the regime. He was sent to Baghdad and he tried to follow the underground activity in a crafty manner. He spread the word that he had returned to Baghdad to find a bride. But meanwhile, in Baghdad we received notice from Tel Aviv through the wireless about the arrival of the "snitching traitor" and were told to keep alert. We spread the word about the snitch arriving in Baghdad pretending to look for a bride, and after a short while almost all the Jews knew the story. The man understood that his cover had been blown and left Iraq.

There were other betrayals. When defection from the Anders army increased, the Poles decided together with the British to follow the Jewish underground members who were assisting in smuggling Iraqi Jews with groups of Jewish soldiers in the British army. So they planted a Jewish spy named Landes—whom Shmaryahu had once smuggled out of Iraq to Eretz Yisrael—among the Polish soldiers in Baghdad. He was ordered to follow the deserters and to learn which Jewish homes the deserters stayed in until they were smuggled out. In this way he made aliyah to study the entire procedure. He was then returned by the British to Baghdad so that he could show the Iraqi policemen and the Polish army the homes where Polish Jews were hosted.

We received word of this scheme from Tel Aviv and were ordered via the wireless to immediately "search for the leavened bread." We notified the families who hosted the Poles and ordered them to hide all traces of Hebrew textbooks and anything else that would expose them. The Iraqi police searched the homes Landes pointed out, but found nothing indicating the Polish soldiers had stayed at those homes. Meanwhile, Shmaryahu, who knew Landes well from the days he had smuggled him to Eretz Yisrael, began walking on the main street where the Polish soldiers gathered and one day he identified Landes among them. Shmaryahu was disguised as a peddler selling gum and cigarettes and offered his goods to the Polish troops. When he got close to Landes, who was standing among them, he said, "Landes! We know about your betrayal." Shmaryahu immediately disappeared, and Landes understood the hint: he knew he had been exposed and he ceased his spying activities.

One by one, the emissaries and those in the original underground group left for Eretz Yisrael, to be replaced by new local activists in Baghdad. One of the biggest challenges, however, was orchestrating the return of Malka Rofeh. She couldn't leave in the same way she came in because we feared it would be discovered that she was a woman, which could lead to the unraveling of our network. Therefore, we considered the possibility of preparing a long crate with holes on the top and sides and sending her inside of it as freight with the Jewish unit, together with other crates and materials. Such a crate was even prepared and the operation was almost launched despite the danger to her.

However, a better option arose at the last minute. A young Jew named Alber who had excellent relations with the Iraqi clerks who issued passports bribed the clerks to issue passports without the limitation of entrance to Palestine. During those days we managed to obtain a number of immigration certificates for girls from the Palestine government, as we knew women could not be smuggled the way boys were. One of the girls for whom we got a certificate changed her mind and decided not make aliyah. So we tried to get a passport in this girl's name and to glue Malka's picture on it. We asked Alber to do this. He agreed, but several days later he returned and said that he was willing to do this if we would include him on Malka's passport as her husband and get an aliyah certificate for him too. We agreed and the passport was issued with pictures of Malka and Alber. The British embassy stamped the passport with an authorization to travel to Palestine. So we started running around looking for a way for them to travel. We were able to get them two seats on a flight leaving the very next day, to the tune of 1,000 dinars, a huge sum in those days. That evening, we interrupted Alber while he was sitting with friends in a café and told him that he must come with us to where Malka was staying and to be ready to leave for Eretz Yisrael the following day. He resisted a little, saying he wanted to notify his family, but we insisted that he not discuss his departure with anyone. Alber had not yet met Malka in person at this point. Alber came to meet Malka at our house, and we promised him we'd notify his family after he left. And off they went.

I felt satisfied that we managed to establish the underground framework, made a number of great accomplishments, and trained many successors. I was eager to go to Eretz Yisrael myself, finally, and I made aliyah in December, 1943. I dressed in a British army uniform and stood with a unit of Jews serving in the British army, and together with other Iraqi Jews disguised as British soldiers I was smuggled out by the head of the unit in a British convoy returning to Eretz Yisrael.

Shlomo Sehayek was a member of Kibbutz Genossar until 1950. He lives in Tiberias with his wife, Rivka, and they have four children. Shlomo's brother Shaul lives in Ramat Aviv and has authored several books about Iraqi Jewry and the underground movement.

* * *

Born Murad Murad in Baghdad in 1923, Mordechai Ben Porat became a Zionist activist in Baghdad. In 1945, he escaped to Palestine by car and foot through Jordan and Lebanon with five other men. In 1949, at age 26, he was sent back to Iraq as an undercover emissary for the Mossad L'Aliyah Bet in order to assist Jews escaping to Iran, and ultimately helped organize Operation Ezra and Nehemiah. When his identity was exposed in 1951, he was forced to flee, this time for good. In his account, he describes his secret work in Baghdad in those tense years.

My parents were Regina and Nessim Yehezkel Murad. I was the eldest of 11 children. I was named Murad after an uncle who was drafted into the Ottoman army and disappeared during World War I. My father later changed our family name to Kazzaz when we began to attend school, as we attended a Muslim school and Murad was an obviously Jewish name. Kazzaz, which means "silk trader," was my grandfather's profession. Later, in Israel, I changed my name again.

We lived initially in Taht-el-Takia, Baghdad's Jewish quarter, and in 1934 or 1935 we moved to El-Adhamiya, a township north of Baghdad and east of the Tigris, near the Shiite holy city of El-Kathemia. The neighborhood was considered a resort area and many Jews purchased land there and built homes on the riverbank, but it was otherwise a Muslim area. When we moved there, my father convinced 10 other families to buy homes there as well, and a Jewish street was created and a temporary synagogue erected.

We were mostly cut off from the center of the Jewish community and our Muslim neighbors became our friends. Generally, we had very good relations with them. It was because of one Muslim neighbor, in fact, that we survived the Farhoud. On the eve of the Farhoud, our neighbor, Colonel Taher Mohamed Aref, came to our house to warn us about what was to happen the next day. We barely knew him and our families normally kept a distance from one another. My father took him seriously and began barricading the house and preparing for the worst.

On June 1, we began to be attacked on all sides by Arabs, including different neighbors from across the street whom we had considered friendly to us. We heard the shouts of *Allahhou Akbar!* (God is great!), *Idbah Al Yahud!* (Murder the Jews!), and *Mal el Yahud—Halal!* (Sanction to rob the Jews!). We had no weapons to defend ourselves and were utterly helpless. We put furniture up against the doors and windows to prevent the rioters from breaking in. Then, Colonel Aref's wife came rushing out of her house with a grenade and a pistol and shouted at the rioters, "If you don't leave I will explode this grenade right here!" Her husband was apparently not home and she had either been instructed by him to defend us or decided on her own to help. They dispersed, and that was that—she saved our lives. We had not known her before that incident—never had any connection with her. And then Jewish families from our neighborhood began flowing into our house to be sheltered from the riots. All in all, more than 100 people took refuge at our house, and we fed them and they slept there for two days until the riots subsided.

One of the guests was my cousin, Sasson Naim, and my mother traveled to Taht-el-Takia by bus to inform his family that he was safe, because we had no telephone service in those days. When she got off the bus, she faced a mob: she was covered with an *abaya*, but when the rioters spoke to her they discovered she was not a Muslim. She was attacked and fainted. Luckily, a soldier extracted her from the mob and brought her to our relatives' home nearby.

After the Farhoud, in 1942, I joined a growing underground movement, the Young Halutz. I was one of its first members.[26] Because of the Farhoud, my mother decided in 1943 that it was time to leave Iraq for Palestine. My father, however, wanted to go to India. She said, "No. Palestine. I am not interested in acquiring wealth. I want only security for my children." So that year she traveled to Palestine alone to try to figure out whether to move the family there and if so to establish some kind of footing. She was pregnant and hired a Jewish driver to take her across Iraq, through Trans-Jordan and into Palestine. She was an amazing woman—totally independent. She stayed with relatives in Jerusalem. During her stay she was able to get an immigration certificate from the Jewish Agency. At that time, the British were allowing the agency to give out a small number every year—the quota was extremely small. She returned to Baghdad with one aliyah certificate.

She tried without success to acquire passports for the whole family, so the Halutz put pictures and names of my whole family into her passport, so it was as if the certificate was valid for the whole family. Then one day in 1944, the family went to Lake Habaniya, which was about a half hour north of Baghdad and where the British were stationed, and they bought tickets on a sea-airplane that took off from the lake and landed in the Dead Sea. Two of my brothers flew to Palestine two days later and I stayed in Baghdad with my grandmother to continue my underground activities. The family settled in Tel Aviv.

I came to Palestine in 1945. The trip was long and dangerous. My family was very worried because they knew I had left Baghdad but then didn't hear from me until I showed up in Tel Aviv a month later. On my final night in Baghdad, I went with my fellow travelers, a group of six other men, to a club to hear the famous singer Salima Pasha Murad. Shimshon Levy, one of our group and a bit of a daredevil, requested that she sing her song, "Tomorrow is Our Journey." She understood the significance and sang to us with special feeling but without giving away our plans.

The next day, with the help of a Muslim smuggler, we traveled from Baghdad to Anah, in the north of Iraq, where we stayed with local Jews for five days, and across Syria, where we were hosted by Jews in Aleppo—and where we stayed in the attic of the glorious Yoav Ben Zrouya Synagogue in the Jewish quarter—and then into Lebanon. In Beirut, local Jews took us to the synagogue in the Jewish quarter of Wadi Abu Jamil, where 70 Jews, most of them Lebanese, were waiting to go to Palestine. We took the entire group. We were young and strong, so we escorted them across the border to Palestine by foot. There were many women and children in the group. For food, we took only hard bread with us and dipped it into the water from the Hatzbani River to make it more edible. We walked day and night for 48 hours with only a flashlight to guide our way in the darkness. For much of the way, I carried a small five- or six-year-old child, and we didn't even stop to let the kids urinate, so at times I felt a warm trickle down my back!

We crossed the border into Eretz Yisrael on September 8. A man from a special Palmach unit called Shahar brought us to Kfar Giladi [a kibbutz in the Upper Galilee, overlooking Mt. Hermon and the Hula Valley]. The unit was responsible for receiving refugees and bringing them to settlements in Palestine. It was midnight, and we crossed an apple orchard. It smelled so sweet. We hadn't eaten anything substantial since we had left Beirut. We just picked the apples off the trees—it was like a dream. At the kibbutz, we were given hot and cold drinks and sandwiches with marmalade. An hour later the Shahar men took us to another kibbutz because they feared the British army would come looking for refugees on the kibbutz. Around the time we arrived—a week previous or a week after, I can't recall—the British located a group of new refugees at a kibbutz, and there was a clash of fire between the army and our people.

At midnight, we were taken to yet another kibbutz and then to Rosh Pina, and by then it was morning, and we were taken to Kibbutz Yagur, and from there to Haifa. In Haifa, everyone in the group was asked where he or she wanted to go. All I knew was that my family was in Tel Aviv, though I didn't know where in Tel Aviv. We were given money, and when I made it to the bus station in Tel Aviv, I began roaming around, searching for the faces of my siblings and parents. Suddenly, I saw my sister Bertha! It was a small country in those days, so that kind of luck was strange but not totally out of the ordinary. She took me to their house. I greeted my parents and siblings with joy, and then learned that one of my brothers and a sister were living in Kfar Giladi, where I had just been! So I made my way back up there to find and greet them.

The year 1949 was a terrible one in Iraq: in September, about 450 Jews were in prison, of them some 40 women, and more continued to be arrested throughout the summer and fall. Most were underground movement members or Communists. Many had been sentenced for up to 10 years, some with hard labor. A group of female prisoners went on a hunger strike to protest the terrible prison conditions, and prison authorities force-fed them. In late November, the chairman of the Jewish community, Sasson Khedouri, tendered his resignation in the face of mounting protest by many Jews of his inability to protect the community. The news of the persecution of the Jews of Iraq reached many countries, which began supporting some kind of solution.

It was a moment of serious crisis for the Halutz, and in fact the reason so many members had been arrested was because some of the new young recruits who had been tortured in 1949 had cracked under the pressure and revealed many of the names of activists and secrets of the movement. Many people within the movement called them "informers." We arranged for their escape to Israel so they wouldn't continue to create problems. In addition, many key figures in the underground were arrested, including Aziz Kashi, a member of the editorial staff of the movement's newspaper who knew the location of the arms caches and the printed material which included hundreds of pamphlets and some 3,000 books; and Yitzhak Shamash, a Shura commander. After many confessed under torture, and long lists of movement members were attained by the government, there was a mass exodus of movement activists from Iraq, mostly over the border to Iran.

Nineteen hard months of suffering by the Jews under military courts were brought to an end in December, 1949, when the cabinet of Prime Minister Nuri el-Said resigned and a new cabinet announced the end of 10 months of martial law.[27]

Back to Babylon

In Palestine, I worked for the Haganah, which, by 1948, had become Tzahal [Israeli Defense Forces] and I was a company commander. In late 1949 I was approached by the Mossad L'Aliyah Bet to become its undercover aliyah emissary in Iraq, and in that capacity I was supposed to intensify awareness within the Jewish community of the dangers they were facing and promote the idea that emigration to Israel was their only solution.

I had only about three or four hours to read the material I had been given about my assignment. I said goodbye to Rivka—my girlfriend, who became my wife—and I left. My code name with the Mossad was Dror, which means "free" or "liberty." I moved around Baghdad with the identity card of a Baghdadi Jew, Nissim Mandelawy, whose family had taken me in. Nissim left his house and moved in with relatives so there wouldn't be two people by the same name in his house. When I traveled outside of Baghdad, south to Basra or north, by air or car to Mosul and Kirkuk, I was a Muslim merchant named Ibrahim Salman. I also used the names Habib and Zaki, depending on what I was doing and who I was communicating with. The Iraqis later discovered with surprise after I left that Nissim was Habib, Zaki, and Ibrahim—they had been on the hunt for all of them separately.

I was only responsible for the underground's aliyah branch, not the Shura or education branches. However, I gave lectures all the time at the Shura, and I was responsible for communicating with Israel through the wireless with the help of the wireless operators.

When I arrived in Iraq, about 20 or 30 Jews were escaping over the border to Iran per month with the help of smugglers. My first objective was to map out improved escape routes—most Jews were going through Basra, but also via Amara and Khanakin—and many were being nabbed at the borders and imprisoned. I also set out to develop a wider network of smugglers, including police and military men, usually through bribery. A few thousand Jews were escaping with our help but there were many others who located smugglers independently and escaped on their own. Many of them had nasty experiences because they didn't know how to deal with smugglers—often they were robbed, abandoned or arrested. But those who were smuggled out with our operatives also ran up against problems, including a terrible incident before I arrived in Iraq, in October, 1949, that still haunts me today, in which several Jewish boys disappeared without a trace in northern Iraq. We began to feel that a better solution was necessary.

Apparently, so did the governor of Basra, who was furious about the escapes and voiced his frustration to the government in Baghdad. He suggested that the government would be better off if it let the Jews leave legally. All in all, more than 15,000 Jews fled Iraq for Persia over the border over a decade between the early 1940s and early 1950s.

In the meantime, I developed relationships with Jews who were close to key government officials. Thus I had access to all the important information immediately and I would wire it to Israel. For instance, if a decision was made in the cabinet on cracking down on smuggling Jews across the border, or how to deal with the Jewish emigration, the next day I had the minutes of the meeting in hand. In particular, I started to work with the head of the community, Yehezkel Shemtob, who had taken Rabbi Khedouri's place in 1949. We had a very good relationship, and he had a close relationship with the new prime minister, Tawfiq el-Suweidi. Shemtob communicated messages to el-Suweidi when I asked him to, primarily requests to release prisoners and to grant permission for Jews to emigrate legally. In return, Shemtob asked us to use our influences to bolster el-Suweidi's government, and through *Kol Yisrael* [Voice of Israel Radio, whose Arabic station could be heard in Iraq] we accused el-Suweidi's political opponents of corruption and bribery.

I believe that passage of the Citizenship Revocation Bill was a direct result of the corruption and chaos that we had helped create at the borders, which was a disturbance and an embarrassment to the government, as was the humiliation that the Jews were escaping to Iran, Iraq's archenemy. But the real embarrassment came only later, when the government began to witness the large numbers of Jews registering to leave. El-Suweidi believed that no more than 12- to 14,000 Jews would leave Iraq. I figured it would be more like 40,000. But nobody anticipated that within two months of the announcement of the new law, 63,000 Jews would register to leave, and the numbers kept climbing, ultimately to 110,000. Israel kept sending us cables saying, "Please find a way to slow down the pace [of emigration]. We don't have accommodation for such numbers." Israel had only a few hundred tents from the British army in India. If the Iraqi government could have predicted what really happened, it probably would never have passed the law because the vast number of emigrants was a sign that something indeed was terribly wrong in how the government had been treating the Jewish community.

The task of figuring out the logistics of transporting the emigrants to Israel was daunting and complex. We discussed various travel options—by sea out of Basra via the Suez Canal, by ground transport via Syria, via Jordan, or via Saudi Arabia. I tried to secure an arrangement with a British airline company named Fowler, owned by Major T.A. Cayton, which I felt was a good plan, especially since it was supported by the British government. But in the meantime, Shlomo Hillel had arranged an agreement with an American company. My superiors in Israel preferred this plan, and this was what we ended up doing, though Cayton was furious when his deal was cancelled and there was a great amount of friction over this conflict within our ranks. But this was only one of the many conflicts that I had to negotiate during my time in Iraq given all the actors involved: the Halutz movement, myself and the other Israeli emissaries, our bosses in Israel, the local Jewish community leadership, and others.

The American deal undermined my relationship with Shemtob, with whom I had been working on the British deal (though Shemtob ultimately helped broker the American deal). In addition, Shemtob wanted to manage the emigration himself, something that he and I could not agree on. He was unaware of the wireless connection between Iraq and Israel and of the financial arrangements we had made for the emigration. We also disagreed on how the queue for immigration be managed: we requested that the first emigrants be families of prisoners as well as members of the underground who knew Hebrew and who we thought would be useful in Israel because they could assist subsequent immigrants in the absorption process. He had other ideas.

With our disagreements piling up, we erupted into an argument one day. He lost his temper and said to me, "Stop this emigration!" He said, "Six million Jews have gone. Let another hundred thousand go!" I was astonished. I said, "If that's what you think, you ought to resign!" He snatched his *sidara* [hat] from his head and threw it on the floor.

When Jewish community leaders also began to object to Shemtob's handling of the emigration, Interior Minister Salah Jaber responded by assembling a Jewish communal committee comprised of its existing leadership which would control the emigration. He was made a member in spite of my efforts to ensure that he be kept off the committee and of objections by community leaders. We worked very closely with the committee, which included Sasson Abed, chairman of the council, Moshe Shochet (who was deputy director general of the railways in Iraq and thus had many important connections in the government), Abraham Alkabir (who was general manager of the Treasury in Iraq), David Sala, and Sasson Nawi.

When the first emigrants were airlifted out of Iraq on May 19, 1950, and arrived in Israel the Israeli and international radio and newspapers pounced on the story. The numbers of emigrants were staggering, and the fact that their departure was all done by airlift was unprecedented. The Mossad spent more than a half-million dinars [about two million dollars in 1950s currency] bringing the Jews of Iraq to Israel.

The sheer logistics of the citizenship revocation, ticketing and travel arrangements throughout those years was tremendous. Prime Minister Nuri el-Said worried about the initial slow progression of the flights and, wishing to hurry up the exit of all Jews who had registered to leave, tried to find alternative exit routes. He traveled to Jordan to convince the Jordanians to allow the Iraqi Jews passage to Israel via Jordan, but the Jordanians objected. The Jordanians declared the idea "inhuman" but they were really worried that the Palestinians would decry the move as enabling Jews to occupy Palestinian land and possibly cause chaos in Jordan, which had many Palestinian refugees.

The Demise of the Underground Network

I remained in Iraq for another year, until June, 1951, to continue to coordinate the aliyah. I also worked to release many of the underground movement members who were imprisoned, which required a good deal of bribery. In the process, I was arrested four times. The first time was as I was dealing with a group of smugglers who were underground activists. I discovered only afterwards that the house they operated from was known to the police, and the police surrounded the house while I was inside. They arrested us and put us in prison for one week.

Soon after that, I sent a cable to Israel that I was ready to finish my mission because I had been in Iraq for more than one year. They wanted me to stay longer. I said, "I want to get married." So they managed to get Rivka a passport and they sent her to Iran so I could meet her and we could get married, and then I would go back to Iraq. I tried to cross at Basra with four other people, but the police surrounded us and arrested us. When they asked what I was doing, I told them, "I finished secondary school, graduated, and I have no work. You don't give us work in this country. I want to cross the border to find work in Iran." I was brought to the police station in Basra and fined, and I was let go after 12 days. I never got to Rivka and she returned to Israel.

The third time I was arrested was after having a traffic accident when my car collided with a bicycle rider while on my way to deliver documents to "Chris," Ilana Marcus, our stewardess and courier. After the accident, a mob gathered around. They didn't know whether or not I was a Jew, but one of them was very nasty—he cursed me and I cursed him back. We took the injured man into the car and went to the police station whose manager, it so happened, we had been bribing to get prisoners released, though I didn't know the man personally. We took the man to the hospital and I arranged for one of our people, Yosef Basri, to get him four days of treatment. The matter went to court and I was subpoenaed. I entered the room where a judge was sitting with a captain standing beside him. I realized that the captain was the same man who had cursed me in the street. It turned out he was a very high-ranking army officer. The judge sentenced me to two weeks in prison. In prison, I recognized many members of the underground, though they didn't know my role—they just knew that I was an activist.

The final arrest happened in May, 1951, when I was caught in a store with "Ismail Salhoon," code name for the Israeli Yehuda (Yudka) Tajer—the man who had been sent to replace me. It was my error. Yudka, unlike me, had been properly trained for intelligence work and was better suited than I for the job. I had relinquished my responsibilities and was excited to go home. But on that day, I was overly confident in myself. If I had to be in a highly visible public place, usually I went alone and disguised. But this time I pushed too far. Two Israelis shopping in broad daylight was very dangerous.

Yudka couldn't find what he wanted so we started to leave but by the exit a Palestinian Muslim recognized him from Acre [in Israel]. The man immediately informed a CID [Central Intelligence Department, equivalent to the FBI] officer nearby. In a matter of seconds, three CID officers came after us and arrested us 15 meters outside the store. They stopped a taxi and ordered us to enter it. I knew one of the officers because we had been in elementary school together. In fact, he used to copy off of me during examinations and the teacher always managed to blame me. So I *really* didn't like him! In the taxi I was in the back with two officers on either side of me and Yudka was up front with the man I knew and the driver. In my back pocket, I had a newspaper article attacking the interior minister for holding underground activists as prisoners. We had previously tried to bribe him with 5,000 dinars to release them. He said he would only accept the money and help us if the newspapers attacked him for keeping them so it wouldn't look like he had taken a bribe, so we instigated this article. I was handcuffed in the back, but I was able to reach into my back pocket and slip the article out and bury it deep into the cushions in the seat. Later I discovered that Yudka had a small notebook on him with names and telephone numbers of activists which the police later discovered during his interrogation.

At the police station, Yudka and I were separated, and I was asked, "Who is the man with you?" I said, "I don't know him." I identified myself as Nissim Moshe Mandelawy. Yudka identified himself as Ismayil Salhun from Persia, and he showed them his Iranian passport. But when they started to speak to him in Farsi, he couldn't answer. The police went searching for evidence of our real identities in the Masouda Shemtob synagogue and homes.

They took me to another station, El-Sarai in the center of Baghdad, and then to the Dora station. There, they tied me up, interrogated me, beat me with chains and cursed me because I wasn't forthcoming with information. In beating me, they broke my eardrum and I couldn't hear in one ear for about three months. I was there for three nights and four days. They took me to a judge who cross-examined me and Yudka. When asked how I knew "Ismail," I said that we had met at the orchestra and then he asked me to come shopping with him. Yudka then gave his testimony in English which they had to translate into Arabic. It turned out they didn't know how to translate it, so they asked me to. But I was very careful not to change his words too much because I was afraid that it was a trick.

I was bailed out with the help of Yousef Fattal, a Jewish lawyer, and his Muslim partner. However, I had to return to prison for two weeks for the traffic accident—or rather, that episode was an excuse for imprisoning me longer.

For decades after Ezra and Nehemiah, the Zionist movement in Iraq lived under a cloud of suspicion about its role in five bombings in Baghdad, most of them at Jewish shops and sites that took place in 1950 and 1951. The Iraqi police falsely accused the movement of throwing these bombs, an absurd claim supported by other Arab governments and many Iraqi Jews and Israelis who were opposed to our work. It is something I consider nearly a blood libel. It was a ridiculous claim particularly because there was no need to encourage more Jews to leave Iraq by bombing Jewish sites, as so many Jews were leaving without any added manipulation.

After the third attack, a grenade thrown at the Masouda Shemtob synagogue, I immediately went to the site in order to track down evidence and I talked to one of the men who had been critically injured, a Jew, who had been inside the synagogue when the attack occurred and told me he saw who threw the bomb: an Iraqi policeman, a Muslim dressed in khaki, while standing on the balcony of a building facing the synagogue. I also confirmed that all the Muslim peddlers on the street disappeared to safety minutes before the attack. Two young Jewish boys died in the attack. I took five of our activists to the hospital and we gave blood to the injured Jew, Moshe Baghnou from Irbil, and the other injured people. We asked the police to come immediately to get testimony from this man. But Baghnou was badly injured and died at 8:00 the next morning, a half hour before the investigating officer showed up. The government didn't take the investigation seriously, nor the investigation of any of the other bombings—though it felt free to lay the blame on Zionist activists.

The men who paid the price for these falsities were Yousef Basri and Shalom Saleh Shalom, whom the government accused of throwing some of the bombs.

In prison, I had overheard conversations and understood from my interrogations that several movement members were in danger and therefore, I determined, must leave Iraq immediately. I realized that my days in Iraq were numbered too, as I overheard that the police were looking for "Habib" and "Zaki." The bomb attack of a government-owned bank and the store of Stanley Shashou, a Jew, occurred around this time and the police were looking for the perpetrators. They believed that Yousef Khabbaza was involved, and went to search his house, but Yousef Basri, a lawyer and one of our activists, was hiding there in a cupboard, and they took him instead. Basri, who had been in elementary school with me, had previously left Iraq for Israel through Iran. But in Iran our people sent him back to Baghdad to operate as a spy, and he had done a very good job.

Shalom Saleh Shalom, a shoemaker, was responsible for preparing arms caches in the Shura, and he knew the location of all the hidden caches. Shortly after my release from prison, I told him, "Shalom, tomorrow morning you have to leave." He told me, "All right. I'll go but I have to go get my trousers tailored." And while he was waiting for his trousers the police caught him and arrested him. Both Basri and Shalom were tortured terribly, and the police forced Shalom to sign a statement identifying three of the bomb throwers, which he did under duress. During his trial, Shalom retracted his statement to the police for this reason. In catching Shalom, the police were able to uncover many of the arms caches, lists of movement members, and other secret material. The movement was unraveling, and fast: activists were fleeing and hiding and often being caught in the process, then arrested and tortured. Shalom and Basri were hanged on January 21, 1952, six months after I left Iraq. Yudka Tajer was imprisoned in Iraq for nine years. He came to Israel after his release.

Several years later, a left-wing Israeli reporter living in the U.S. published in the *Spanish Federation Journal* in Jerusalem that Israeli emissaries had carried out the bombings. I sued him, and he apologized in court, admitting that he had no evidence to back up that claim. But until today there are many Jews who believe that Jews carried out the attacks, and the Palestinians use the incident to argue that Israel used cruel techniques for pushing the Jews to leave Arab countries.

As I readied for my escape, I hid out with Naim Mandelawy, my "brother," on his roof for about five days. He would bring me newspapers where I read that the police were looking for "Zaki" and "Habib." My people came with Ronnie Barnett at night to give me a map showing me my escape route to the airport. I was taken there at midnight. It was June 14, 1951. At the airport, I had to sneak under the fence and walk more than one kilometer to the plane—one of those taking the emigrants to Israel. The plane approached me and stopped to let down a rope for me and I climbed aboard. The passengers didn't know who I was. I just kept to myself during the flight. When the plane landed in Israel, I had no passport, no documentation of who I was.

Years later, in 1993, we threw a party for the pilots of Ezra and Nehemiah, Shlomo Hillel, and others who played key roles in the rescue of Iraqi Jews. Arthur Lipa, one of the pilots, stood up and told the story of me climbing onto his plane that night. He said, "We stopped the plane as we saw someone come towards us, and he was very dirty—covered with mud. We took him in but we didn't know who he was."

In Israel, Or Yehuda became the site of four large transit camps containing 12,000 Iraqi Jews. In 1955, when I was elected head of the Or Yehuda Council, they were still living in tents and wooden huts. That was not an easy job: life was very difficult here. I lived with my wife and family in Holon, and when it rained and was cold, I used to come home and say to Rivka, "I feel awful that we are here lying in a warm, comfortable bed with a ceiling over our heads and people are freezing and wet in tents and huts." Getting the immigrants out of the *ma'abarot* was a difficult process that took up to eight years for many families. In 1958 we started building apartment houses and homes in Or Yehuda. They were small and very basic, but they were homes. I was mayor for 14 years, until 1969, while overseeing this major transition. Now this city has 34,000 people. During the last four years as mayor I was also a member of Knesset, which was a great help to the city because I was able to get a good amount of national funding for Or Yehuda in those years.

I became interested in documenting the history of the Iraqi Jewish community in the early 1970s. Hebrew University called to notify me of large quantities of documentation and information it had acquired on Mizrachi Jews. I went there and was brought down to the cellar, where I saw boxes upon boxes of material. I asked, "Why is all of this sitting in a cellar? Take it upstairs and sort through it and make sense of it all." There was material there on all the various groups of Mizrachi Jews—Yemenites, Syrians, Iraqis, et cetera—all jumbled together. Until then, they hadn't thought to sift through the material and divide it into the various countries of origin. That experience made me think seriously about creating a museum documenting the community's history and educating Israelis about the story of the Zionist underground, and soon after that incident, in 1973, several colleagues and I decided to realize the idea. Over the following 15 years, we gathered items, pictures, memoirs, documents, and testimonies. The Babylonian Jewry Heritage Center, containing the only museum in Israel that explores a particular Diaspora, was finally opened in 1988, in Or Yehuda.

Most recently, Ben Porat has spearheaded an effort to identify the Jewish graves in Baghdad, about 35 percent of which have names and another 10–20 percent are marked with numbers. The remaining graves are unidentifiable, in large part because of the destruction and transfer of the cemetery during the regime of President Abdul Karim Qassem in 1961. Ben Porat continues to gather books and documents including property registrations, marriage certificates, death certificates, and other items belonging to the community.

Ben Porat's full story about his years as a Mossad operative appears in his book, To Baghdad and Back: The Miraculous 2,000 Year Homecoming of the Iraqi Jews *(1998). Since the opening of the Babylonian Jewry Heritage Center, nearly a half-million guests have visited its exhibits and archives, and the museum continues to collect artifacts and record historical information about the Jews of Iraq, particularly the Zionist underground and the work of Israeli operatives in orchestrating the mass aliyah. Ben Porat serves as its chairman. He was a member of Knesset from 1965 through 1983 (with a short break in the middle). He served as a minister in the governments of Menachem Begin and Yitzhak Shamir with the portfolio of managing the needs of Jews from poor countries. He founded the World Organization of Jews from Arab Countries (WOJAC) to raise awareness of the history and suffering of Jews from Arab countries. One of WOJAC's other objectives has been to contrast Israel's absorption of Jews from Arab lands with the treatment of Palestinian refugees by Arab countries that have allowed the Palestinians to persist in squalid conditions in refugee camps for generations. In 2001,*

Ben Porat received the Israel Prize in 2001 for his work in the Haganah, in organizing Operation Ezra and Nehemiah, and for contributing to Zionist education. He was awarded the Ben Gurion Prize and the Begin Prize, also for these successes. Rivka died in 1995 and in 1999 he married Nechama. He has three daughters.

Notes

1. In this context, *Halutz*, which also means "pioneer," translates as "rescue" or "savior." The Young Halutz was part of the Haganah, the Jewish paramilitary organization during the British mandate of Palestine, which was succeeded by the Israeli Defense Forces at the creation of the State of Israel.
2. Figures from the Babylonian Jewry Heritage Center.
3. Mossad here refers to the Mossad L'Aliyah Bet, which was responsible for illegal immigration to Palestine and purchasing of arms. This is a different organization than (and the predecessor of) the Mossad of today, Israel's intelligence agency responsible for intelligence collection, counterterrorism, and undercover operations. The Mossad and Mossad L'Aliyah Bet are used interchangeably in this collection.
4. Youth Aliyah was initially established to bring and absorb Jewish youth from Germany, though it later helped Jewish youngsters from elsewhere. Sachar, 189.
5. In 1940, the British navy intercepted an illegal immigrant ship to prevent its passengers from reaching Palestine and transferred some of them to another ship, the French ocean liner the *Patria*, which the British chartered in order to exile the refugees to Mauritius, an island in the Indian Ocean and a British colony. While the *Patria* was at anchor off Haifa, the Haganah (the Jewish underground organization for the protection of the Jews in Palestine) smuggled a mine on board the *Patria* with the intention of creating minor damage and enabling the rescue of its passengers to the shores of Palestine. But the explosion was unexpectedly large and inadvertently sank the ship, killing more than 250 people on board. The Haganah drew the surviving 1,900 Patria passengers to shore and they were ultimately granted permission to stay in Palestine. From Gilbert, *Israel: A History*, pp. 105–107.
6. The UN voted for partition on November 29, 1947.
7. "Jewish head" in Yiddish, meaning a clever mind.
8. From 1949 through 1951, the years in which Hillel was working in Iran to facilitate the escape of Iraqi Jews, 24,805 Iranian Jews also immigrated to Israel. Hillel, p. 197.
9. Since the creation of the State of Israel in May, 1948, there was no need to enter Israel illegally. The only illegality was to take Jews out of Arab countries, which had restrictions on emigration, as did the Soviet Union.
10. Jewish mothers protesting their sons' imprisonment organized a demonstration against Rabbi Sasson Khedouri, calling on him to act for the release of their sons. The Zionist underground worked against Khedouri as well, and eventually Khedouri resigned in the summer of 1949. From Rejwan, p. 244.
11. The Jewish Agency was responsible for immigration. Levi Eshkol later became prime minister, in 1963.
12. Figures from the Babylonian Jewry Heritage Center.
13. Ben Porat, pp. 120–122.

14. The French writer and prodemocracy advocate, famous for his 1721 satire *Persian Letters*.
15. One of the Seven Wonders of the Ancient World, the Hanging Gardens are on the east bank of the River Euphrates, about 50 km south of Baghdad.
16. This occurred on May 22, 1951, according to Ben Porat. Ben Porat himself left Iraq on June 14, 1951, after his release from prison.
17. The main Jewish bodies in Palestine were loosely referred to as the "institutes" (*mosdot*): the Histadrut, the Jewish Agency, and the Mossad L'Aliyah Bet. The Histadrut is the Israeli trade union congress. It was founded in 1920 and early on it assumed responsibility for the Haganah that involved the illegal purchase of arms from Europe and the training officers. Sachar, p. 213.
18. At a meeting of Haganah volunteers in Palestine in 1943, David Ben Gurion, Israel's future prime minister said, "The Jewish communities in the Middle East are hostages to our Arab neighbors. If there were to be any upheavals here in the country, we will be alerted, but we have no guarantee whatsoever that Iraqi Jews won't all be massacred by then. I also wonder what would happen to the Jews in Egypt and Yemen even without the present 'riots' (anti-Jewish riots in Mandatory Palestine) in the country. We are not prepared to wait until a disaster occurs." Ben Porat, p. 42.
19. Egged is the Israeli bus company, established in pre–state Israel.
20. From the Talmud, in *Brachot* 5A: Rabbi Shimon Ben Yochai said: "The Holy One, blessed be He, gave three good gifts to Israel, and all were received through suffering: The Torah, the Land of Israel, and the World to Come."
21. Solel Boneh Building and Infrastructure Ltd. is a major construction and infrastructure contractor in Israel.
22. Shlomo's brother Shaul authored a book entitled *Parasha Aluma* (2003) (*An Unknown Episode*), about the escape to Palestine of some 6,000 Jews, of them 4,500 in General Anders' Polish army. The army was formed in the Soviet Union after Germany invaded the Soviet Union on June 22, 1941, and included Poles who had escaped eastward during the war, many of them Jews. The army moved through Iran and Iraq and accompanying them were thousands of relatives of the troops and other Polish civilians, including Jewish men, women, and children. Many of them managed to flee to Palestine with the help of Iraqi and Iranian Jews in 1942–1943. The coordination of their escapes helped solidify the framework for the escape of Iraqi Jews to Palestine. From *Parasha Aluma* by Shaul Sehayek.
23. Moshe Dayan was a Haganah leader at the time. He later became the Israeli Defense Forces' Chief of Staff and held other top political positions.
24. David Azrieli recalls the events of his escape to freedom in his 2001 book *One Step Ahead* published by Yad Vashem in Jerusalem.
25. Some weapons were bought individually and many were bought by the Jews of Basra, who had excellent connections with arms traders in El-Zubair City, which was within the boundaries of Kuwait before its independence. The contact man in Basra was Barukh Daniel, a local merchant, who used to travel in disguise in order to buy weapons for the Halutz movement. He was later arrested and sentenced to 12 years in prison. Ben Porat, p. 44.
26. Ben Porat was among the first group of members to be sworn in in the ceremony Shlomo Sehayek describes in his account.

27. Martial law was declared on May 15, 1948. Nuri el-Said returned to office after a 22-month hiatus on January 6, 1949, but his government lasted less than a year, a result of his inability to solve Iraq's economic problems, make up for his government's disastrous foray into Palestine in 1948, and boost Iraq to a position of leadership in the Arab world. After a short-lived government that followed, Tawfiq el-Suweidi took over the premiership in January, 1950. Hillel, pp. 210, 224–225.

Photo 1 Jews lining up en masse at Meir Tweig Synagogue to revoke citizenship and file for emigration, 1950. Courtesy Babylonian Jewry Heritage Center.

Photo 2 King Faisal visits Meir Elias Hospital in Baghdad in the presence of the chief rabbis, Sasson Khedouri and Ezra Dangoor, 1924. Courtesy Babylonian Jewry Heritage Center.

Photo 3 Students at the Alliance School for Boys. Courtesy Babylonian Jewry Heritage Center.

Photo 4 Baghdad on the west side of the Tigris River. Courtesy Babylonian Jewry Heritage Center.

Photo 5 Typical alley in the Jewish quarter of Baghdad. Courtesy Babylonian Jewry Heritage Center.

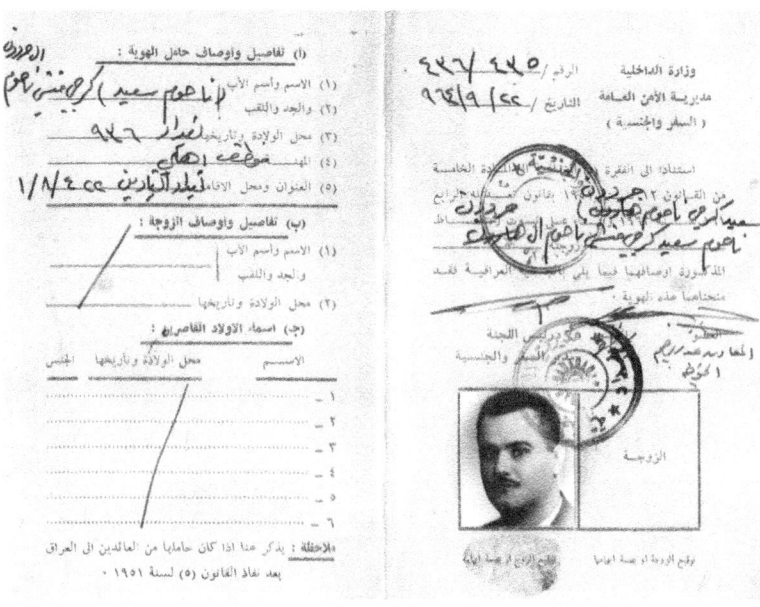

Photo 6 Typical yellow identity card Jews were required to carry starting after the Six Day War in 1967. This one belonged to Saeed Herdoon. Courtesy Saeed Herdoon.

Photo 7 Typical large extended Jewish family at the turn of the century. This photo is of the Somekh and Masri families, relatives of Linda Masri Hakim, circa 1900. Courtesy Susan Lawi.

Photo 8 Hakham Sasson Khedouri, Abdullah Obadiah (headmaster of the Frank Iny School) and Hakham Daoud Meir, Baghdad, August, 1965.

SECTION THREE

Our Country No More

Introduction

The final chapter in the history of the Jews of Iraq begins with the Ba'ath Party, which, under the leadership of General Hasan al-Bakr, seized the government in a coup in 1963 after ousting the Communist leader Abdul Kareem el-Qassem. The Ba'ath Party was overthrown 10 months later in a countercoup, but mounted a second successful coup in 1968 and ruled Iraq for the next three-and-a-half decades—until the American invasion in 2003.

By the late 1970s, President al-Bakr's health was declining and his nephew and Vice President Saddam Hussein wielded the real power until he formally became president in 1979. The Ba'ath Party was greatly influenced by the Pan-Arabism of Egypt's Gamel Abdel Nasser and used its discourse to help unify a factious Iraq divided on ethnic, religious, economic, and social fault lines. Saddam held a tight grip on Iraq largely through a corps of ruthless security forces and his own heavy hand.

After the mass exodus in the early 1950s, the Jewish community lost many of its institutions. Many Jewish social clubs and the Meir Elias hospital belonging to the Jewish community were seized by the government. Only two Jewish schools, Menachem Daniel and Frank Iny, remained in Baghdad, once home to some 60 Jewish schools. Only a handful of synagogues, where there had once been dozens, continued to function.[1]

In this section, we will hear from Jews who remained in Iraq in the two decades after the majority of their community had left. They stayed because their families, deeply entwined and flourishing in Iraq, hoped anti-Semitism would diminish. Those who stayed the longest soon found themselves in a country-wide prison.

The Jews of Iraq began to experience a new level of discrimination shortly after the Six Day War, when Israel defeated its Arab enemies (including nominal forces from Iraq) on three fronts in an overwhelming victory. The Arab defeat sent shock waves through the Arab world. Unable to win on the battlefield, Arab countries lashed out at their own Jewish populations. On March 3, 1968, the Iraqi government passed a retroactive ad hoc law, Law No. 10, which instituted a series of restrictions on Jews. Jews were ousted from their jobs, had their savings accounts blocked, their telephone lines cut, and were denied passports and restricted from traveling within Iraq.[2]

When the Ba'ath Party came into power that summer, it implemented these restrictions with sadistic zeal. The government began rounding up, imprisoning, and torturing Jews on phony allegations of spying for Israel—and then hanging nine of them publicly on January 27, 1969, in an incident that drew world attention, if not action. At that point, everyone in the Jewish community knew they had no choice but to leave. Thus for virtually all the remaining Jews in Iraq—an estimated 3,350 in 1968[3]—the overriding question that gripped their lives was not whether to leave, but when and, above all, how.

In this section, we'll hear from several Jews who describe their own imprisonment or the imprisonment of loved ones in the Ba'ath Party's infamous prison, Kasr al Nahaya, "The Prison of the End," named to signal the end of the monarchy, where subhuman conditions prevailed and where Saddam oversaw the torture of Jews and others. First, there is Saeed Herdoon, who spent six months inside its walls; Ronit Dangour, who describes her father's incarceration—one of the harshest documented cases of Jews tortured at the hands of the Ba'ath Party; Zuhair Sassoon, the grandson of Iraq's last chief rabbi, who details his father's symbolic imprisonment; and Oddil Dallall, who tells the story of her husband's imprisonment and hanging in 1969.

Extreme circumstances called for extreme action, and in their accounts Saeed Herdoon and Linda Hakim detail their daring and perilous escapes from Iraq.

Some became experts at helping others to escape. Mayer Attar described to us how his brother Youssif and his late father, Naim, smuggled some 100 families to Iran via Basra in the late 1960s. In mid-1971, Naim smuggled more than 850 Jews to Iran through the north—a journey of more than 20 hours by train and car to the border followed by more than 20 hours by bus to Tehran.

For those left behind, it was a lonely time as the community thinned out to a mere 250-odd families by the mid-1970s. Aida Zelouf describes how she and her family held on until 1974 because her father, Meir Basri, the community's last leader and an Iraqi patriot to the core, felt a great sense of responsibility to the remaining Jews.

Finally, Richard Obadiah describes his childhood in this tense atmosphere and recounts the moment when his father, the last headmaster of the last Jewish school in Iraq, shut and locked its doors. It was a sad and symbolic moment. A 2,500-year chapter had come to an irrefutable end.

* * *

In the wake of the public hangings of nine Jews on January 27, 1969, and earlier anti-Jewish legislation, Jews faced severe persecution and most of the remaining Jews fled Iraq. In his account, Saeed Herdoon, born in 1936 in Baghdad, details his six-month imprisonment that year beneath the royal palace of the young Saddam Hussein, Kasr al Nahaya, and his escape across the Iranian border a year later with the help of Kurdish smugglers.

I was 15 years old at the end of 1951, by which time most of the Jews in Iraq had left. I felt like I had witnessed the end of the world. My father wanted to stay on because of his business. When winter school recess ended, I and one other student were the only ones left in the class. The principal came to our classroom and said, "Go home." We didn't go to school for the rest of the year. Walking home, I noticed that the street where I lived in Betaween, which was 90 percent Jewish, was suddenly empty and silent. I got home and said to my parents, "I want to leave." I cried, shouted, screamed. My father said, "We'll go soon, I promise. But if you want to go ahead of us, I will send you if you want." That was just a tranquilizer for the moment. We left 20 years later.

After Ezra and Nehemiah, only one Jewish school remained in existence, the Frank Iny School.[4] My parents transferred me there and it was full. Life got back to normal again for the Jews. I graduated and went to work in 1955. I remember fondly the period from 1958 to 1963 during the regime of Abd Al-Karim Qassem—it was a very good time for the Jews. The Muslims even began referring to Jews as brothers. The Jews were free to work and do whatever they pleased. It was the real golden age of Iraqi Jews. In fact, I never had any problems with ordinary Iraqi Muslims throughout my life—they were my friends, neighbors, business associates. It was the government that created problems for us and forced a wedge between Muslim and Jew.

But the Six Day War changed everything. On the first day of the war, I was outside the office with a Muslim client. I was working for a company that imported fabrics from Japan and China. While I was showing him samples and getting his orders I heard his radio, which was tuned to a station from Cairo. The announcers were saying that Israel started an aggressive war against the Arabs and Israel was bombing Cairo and the entire country. I asked my client, "Abu Hasan, did you hear it?" He said, "Yeah, I heard it. Let's continue." I said, "What do mean, 'continue?'" I said, "I can't, I can't. My hands are shaking now. I don't know what we will face now. It means a war and we are very small minority of Jews in Iraq and we will be blamed." I walked into the office and another Muslim client was sitting there with some other people. I told everyone there the news. This man said, "Don't worry. Everything will be okay within a week or ten days." But he meant that the Arabs would finish off Israel. I didn't react.

We were conflicted during the war because we cared about Israel and wanted Israel to win but on the other hand we wanted peace and quiet for our Jewish community and knew that if Israel won, it would get worse for us. I went home and a son of one of those clients called me and said, "Saeed, I want you and your family to come now and stay with us in my house." And I said, "Thank you very much. Why should I do that? I am Iraqi like you." He said, "No, no. I want you to come." I said, "I won't come." So he said, "Okay, so I will come to stay with you." I said, "If you come as a guest, you are most welcome, but if you are coming to guard me, no thank you." I didn't want to be guarded in my own country. Then we agreed that if I needed anything, I would call him and he would be there in a minute.

The war changed even the best of those Muslim-Jewish friendships. My very close Muslim friend in Iraq, Rasan, was a very educated person who got into the best universities in the U.S. and Europe. His father was the Iraqi ambassador in

London, Madrid, and Washington, DC. Just after the war, I was sitting and eating with Rasan and a Jewish friend of ours. We were always very frank with each other because we knew each other so well. He was angry, nervous, and upset because the Arabs had accepted a cease-fire with Israel after only six days of war. So I said, "Rasan, what other alternative did they have? The Egyptian army was destroyed! Syria's destroyed! The West Bank was invaded! Jordan was pushed away!" He said, "I wouldn't have accepted a cease-fire." He said he hated Gamel Abdel Nasser and all the Arab leaders. He felt humiliated and cursed them because they accepted a ceasefire. He said, "If all my weapons were destroyed, I would fight with my hands, with sticks, with stones!" I said, "Rasan, think about what you are saying. Now everyone in the world fights with sophisticated technology—everything is done by pushing buttons. And you want to fight with knives and stones?" That is how much the Arabs hated Israel.

During the war of attrition, in December, 1968, the Iraqi army was in Jordan along the border with Israel and the Iraqi units fired on Israel. The Israeli air force retaliated and killed many Iraqi soldiers, though Iraq only admitted to five or six dead. The government brought the bodies to Baghdad and paraded them around the presidential palace in a military jeep, their bodies covered with the Iraqi flag. Then the president, Ahmed Hassan al-Bakr, gave a speech swearing to leave alive no Israeli spy in the land of Iraq, and everybody understood that the spies meant the Jews. The same night, the police started rounding up Jews and non-Jews thought to be "cooperating" with the Israelis, whatever that meant. On December 14, 1968, 20 people were charged with suspicion of spying for the U.S. and Israel. On January 27, 15 people were hanged. Nine of them were Jews. The government shipped in people by army trucks from all over Iraq and 500,000 people sang and danced around the bodies in celebration.[5]

On that day, I was making my way from home to my office downtown, so I had to cross through that square [Liberation Square]. Typically on my way to the office I used to stop at the commercial embassy of Hungary to pick up our mail which it collected for us. During that period the government had stopped delivering mail and telegrams to Jews, and because we imported goods from Hungary we had a good relationship with the embassy. The attaché asked me, "Did you hear?" I said, "Hear what?" He said, "There were 15 people hanged in the square." I went to my relatives to tell them to stay home.

I knew some of the people who were hanged that day. One was a neighbor, Charles Horesh. One of those who was hanged was a boy about 16 years old, Da'ud Dallal, whose family I knew. A policeman had gone to the family's house and asked for his older brother. The mother told him that her son was studying in London, where he had been for the last few years. The police heard the sound of a radio in the house and asked, "Who's here?" She said, "My younger boy." He said, "Could we see him? Could we talk with him?" Shaking with fear, she called him. They grabbed him and left, saying that they were taking him for questioning. She went everywhere across the city to find out what had happened to her son: to the Ministry of Defense, the courts, the police stations, every single place she could think of to help track him down. Finally, one of the officers told her, "Miss, go back home and tomorrow your son will be with you." She walked home, nearly crossing Liberation Square where the hangings were taking place that day. They came to her the next day with the body in a bag. He was underage for hanging according to Iraqi law, but in court they claimed that he was 18.

Inside the "Prison of the End"

At Passover in 1969 I was arrested and imprisoned for nearly six months. I was in my office in the central business district. Three of Saddam's men barged into the office and began to collect the identity cards of everyone there. They separated the Jews from the non-Jews, then gave back the cards of the non-Jews and escorted them out. Five of us, all Jewish men, were left inside. The officers confiscated files and typewriters which they forced us to carry outside and into their cars. They blindfolded us and put us in the car. We remained covered with those same dirty blindfolds for the next two weeks.

We were taken to a police station, guided upstairs, and seated on the floor next to ten others and ordered not to talk. We waited all day and slept at night on the concrete floor. We were given some bread and tea and taken in groups of two to the bathroom. It tore me apart knowing that my family was certainly in agony worrying about me and my brother-in-law, Joseph Zilkha, one of the co-owners of the business who was arrested as well, leaving behind my sister and their three small children. One night I bribed a guard—with a very big sum equal to three months of his salary—to take a personal item I had in my pocket to my family so they would know I was alive. He returned with a note in my sister's handwriting that read, "We are well and working to help you."

Then they interrogated each one of us individually. Finally my blindfold was removed. The officer told me that I was not the target of the investigation—their targets were the co-owners, Joseph Jangana and Joseph Zilkha. I didn't believe it—it was just a ploy to get me to talk. They were after our company's connections abroad: if the company held any foreign accounts that the state was not aware of, the authorities could convict us of betraying the nation. He threatened me by alluding to the torture devices in the room, iron chains, and machines that were used to pull limbs from bodies. I was given a pen and paper and told to write a personal statement. I wrote and wrote but the officer found nothing in there that he was looking for, gave up, blindfolded me again and sent me back to the room with the other men.

After two weeks, we were taken to another location and I was put in a dark six-foot by six-foot cell where two other men were already confined. This became my home for the following months. There were no mattresses and no windows or light of any kind. I learned from one of my cellmates, two Muslim men from Basra, that we were in Saddam's personal prison beneath the amphitheater of the royal palace which the Ba'ath Party named "Prison of the End" to celebrate the end of the monarchy. That cellmate had been there for three months and was a source of reassurance for me. I had nothing to do with my time but worry about my fate and in particular about my younger brother, because if he were arrested, my parents would be left without further protection. I was terrified knowing that nine Jewish men had been publicly hanged only a few months before. I also knew that newspapers often ran front-page stories in which government officials announced that a prisoner had "escaped" but in truth we in the Jewish community knew that he had been killed. We had heard rumors that sulfuric acid was used to dissolve the bodies quickly in order to leave no trace of wrongdoing.

We were allowed to use the bathrooms once a day in the morning. To try to explain the stench that welcomed us there is impossible. The toilets would not flush, so they remained overflowing with urine and feces for months. Finally the guards had to put bricks on the ground around the toilet so we could stand on them when we used the toilet.

We were not allowed to speak, and those who broke the rules suffered harsh consequences, so we were terrified to communicate with one another. Soon after I arrived I learned that Yitzhak Dallall, an acquaintance of mine, was in the cell next to me. I saw him in the mornings during our trips to the bathroom, but he looked at me as if ready to say something, yet stayed silent. Finally, after three weeks, he managed to ask me whether I knew anything about his family's well-being. He had been taken four months earlier and was agonizing about whether they were alive or dead. It took me two weeks until I was able to answer him: I told him that they were all right and working towards his release. [Months later, days after Herdoon's release, Dallall was hanged. See personal account of his widow, Oddil Dallall.]

My other cellmate was a 14-year-old Bedouin shepherd from the desert. He told me he had been taken prisoner because of fears that he had witnessed a guard disposing of a body. A few weeks after I arrived, he was taken for questioning and it was decided that he would be released. Upon hearing this news, he stood in the hallway and yelled out, "God bless you all! I hope all of you will join me!" In doing that, he broke the rule prohibiting speaking, and was killed the same night.

Each man in the prison had his own tragic story, and although we were not allowed to speak, we managed to find ways to communicate and thus learn about each other. One story that I recall vividly is of a man who had been a successful doctor and had recently built a house for his young wife and newborn infant. The house happened to be in a place where Saddam was planning to confiscate all properties around his palace [now the area in the "Green Zone"]. Just as the house was completed, he was approached by one of Saddam's men who asked him to move. The man refused to sell his house. Soon after, guards broke into the doctor's home in the middle of the night and took him, his wife, and their baby and put them in a car. They were driven to a remote area and as the car sped up, his wife and baby were thrown out of the car to their deaths. He was brought to prison. This educated, cultured man quickly lost his mind: he used to sit in the corner of his cell, shaking back and forth as he recited the details of his tragedy over and over. After a short while, he was found dead in his cell.

Another story I recall is of the right-hand man to the former minister of finance in the previous regime. Anyone with ties to the former regime was imprisoned after the 1968 Ba'ath Party coup. He had been incredibly loyal to his boss, so no means of torture could get him to say anything negative about the minister. After being tortured for several days, he was chained to a wall directly across from my cell. Bound and naked, he was forced to drink gallons of water and his penis was tied with a string to prevent him from urinating. For about 36 hours I sat in my cell and listened to his cries of agony and watched him become poisoned by his own urine. He died, but his body revealed no external harm—one of the clever tricks of his torturers.

The stories go on and on. Up to three times a week, Saddam held what became to be known as his "torture parties." Drugged and drunk, Saddam and his thugs randomly selected prisoners in the middle of the night and brought them to a room where they tortured the prisoners until the brink of death. Saddam and his men put electric shocks on their eyelids, pulled out their teeth, and hung them from the ceiling by their hands, which were tied behind their backs. When the prisoners were brought back to their cells, they were barely alive, bloodied and unable to stand. One man used a metal can to cut off large pieces of flesh that were left dangling from his legs. Some of the prisoners died shortly after their ordeal.

The food was horrendous. The guards served it out of buckets and there were no utensils or cups so we had to find our own ways of consuming the meager and disgusting fare unless we wanted the guards to serve us with their dirty hands. I refused to eat most of the time, and my weight dropped dramatically in these months—by thirty pounds.

One day, guards circulated throughout the prison and took notes on each prisoner. When they got to me, they asked me what school I had attended and I told them Frank Iny. The officer turned to his partner and said, "That school graduates all the spies who spy against Iraq!" I worried that if the guard wrote down "spy" next to my name, that would spell my death. I in Saddam's crazy legal system, even if I were given a court hearing and were able to protest the accusation, the judge would look down on the paper and say, "But it says right here that you *are* a spy!" But by a twist of fate, I never had my day in court.

After many long months like this, I and 14 others from what they called the "merchant group" were taken into another part of the palace. At first I was terrified that we were being taken for interrogation, but it turned out that we were put in more comfortable quarters, allowed to speak freely, could finally shower, and were fed half-decent food. We could even order food and receive packages from our families. My first package contained a change of clothing. Then I realized how much weight I had lost because my pants practically fell right off me. We were allowed to get our first exercise in months by walking around our room. Yet I was still suspicious.

One day an officer came with a note from my sister saying the family is fine and they were praying for our well-being [of Herdoon and Joseph Zilkha]. Apparently, after months of standing outside the Ministry of Defense building, she managed to talk to a high-ranking officer who agreed to send the note to us. The officer then asked me if I wanted to talk to her. I didn't know how to react at first but followed him into his enormous office inside the luxurious royal palace, which was filled with paintings of Saddam. He asked for my sister's phone number, but I told him we had no phone because after the Six Day War all the telephones in Jewish homes had been disconnected. I gave him the number of the Muslim Shiite family across the street from my home and he dialed. No one answered. One night the next week he took me and Joseph to try again, and my neighbor answered. The neighbor ran across the street in his pajamas and woke up my parents, who rushed over to speak with us. We were only allowed to say hello and to let them know we were alive and well. After our call, other prisoners were allowed to make calls but few succeeded in making contact because of the phone confiscations.

Since I had been given the daily task to water the dusty yard around the prison cells, I often overheard other inmates' conversations. In the cell next to mine, the former head of Iraq's military academy was being held. Saddam's men often interrogated and tortured this man at night and brought him back to his cell on a stretcher in the morning. Ironically, the same men who did this were officers this man had trained himself, so they would salute him out of habit in the morning and bring buckets of water to relieve his pain. And the strange pattern continued like that.

One day when I mustered up the courage to ask a guard if I could call home again, he asked me, "Do you want to call or would you rather go home?" He told me and some others including Joseph that we would be going home the next day. Anxious and stimulated, we couldn't sleep that night and the next morning the head of the prison, who we met then for the first time, told us, "You are going home. But you didn't see anything, you don't know where you were, you didn't hear anything, and you will never tell anyone what happened here. If you do, it will be your end." They drove us to another building where we saw many other Jewish men whom we knew and were told we had to arrange a 5,000 dinar bail—an amount equivalent to a modern four-bedroom house in Baghdad. But no Jew could post such a bail because the government wouldn't accept bail from a Jew. We sat there for days not knowing what to do. During this time our family visited us. The meeting was an incredibly difficult moment for all of us: one of happiness but great uncertainty and fear that we would never return home after all. My family succeeded in arranging bail for the two of us with the help of several lawyers who took a 10 percent cut.

In this manner many of us were released. We arrived home in September, 1969, haggard, thin, and weak, but alive.⁶

A Decision to Go

The government had confiscated the business and after my experience I knew we had to leave Iraq—that we had no future here. So I spent the following months planning our escape. It was hard work convincing my parents to leave, especially my father. He said, "Why don't you go and I'll come after you in a little while. I have things to finish here." I said, "No! We are all going together."

On March 17, 1970, there was a cease-fire between the Kurds and the Iraqis in a war that had been going on for nine years. In the summer, people started traveling again to the north, the beautiful, mountainous Kurdish area. I went there by taxi to look for someone who could help smuggle us out. I spent some nights there and arranged with a Kurdish man to help us and we settled on a date and agreed on a fee equivalent to $5,000. Ten days later, I went back to meet him again to discuss the final arrangements, set the departure date, and bring him some gifts.

On the day on which we were supposed to leave, a friend who also happened to be in touch with the same smuggler came to my mother and left a message for me from the smuggler. The message was: "Don't come. It's too dangerous now." But we were already prepared to go and couldn't imagine staying another day. I was afraid we'd miss the opportunity to leave altogether. So we decided to go, rent a room in a hotel, and stay there until we found a way out, even with another smuggler if need be.

A friend of mine, Eli Dannoos, came with us. Eli had moved from Iraq to London but had come back to Iraq to visit his sick father. He was sitting in the office of his friend and my neighbor Charles Horesh when the authorities came to arrest Charles. Just because Eli was there, they took Eli too. The two of them and many others were put in Kasr al Nayaha, accused of spying for Israel. The Iraqis set up mock trials for the men, including Charles, which were broadcast on TV and radio for the whole nation to watch. Eli was released. His release, I believe, was meant to show that the Iraqi judicial system was just. Those other nine men were the ones who were hanged on January 27. But Eli meanwhile had witnessed and experienced all the torture and investigations. More than a year after his release, he was still suffering from the psychological trauma of what had happened to him.

He came to visit me at my house on the morning we planned to escape. He was visibly shaken and perpetually looking over his shoulders. We were sitting in the garden and my mother was serving coffee. He asked me with tears of desperation in his eyes if there was a way for him to escape from Iraq. Although we were preparing to go at that moment we were afraid to tell anyone that we were leaving. The Jews always kept their travel plans a secret, even from friends and relatives; a person didn't tell his own brother about his plans if the brother wasn't coming along. But Eli was so sad and hopeless that I decided to tell him about my plans to escape that night. I said, "Eli, are you ready to leave today?" He looked at me and said, "What do you mean?" I repeated my question. He suddenly understood. "Yes," he answered. I said, "Go find a Kurdish taxi driver and arrange with him to take you to the north." I told him where to find such a driver and designated a point at which to meet us in the north. Eli had a girlfriend whom he wanted to marry, so he ran to get her and find a rabbi. He took the two of them to his father's bedside and Eli and his girlfriend got married right then.

We left at midnight with just a few small bags in hand, locked the door to the house, and left quietly in a taxi. We weren't able to liquidate our assets or ship our belongings. My sister and her husband, Joseph, and their three children were in one car; his business partner and his wife and their children in another; and other relatives, my parents and I in other cars. It was a long caravan. We met Eli and his wife on the way to the north. At one point we had to pass a security checkpoint and a guard stopped us and took all of our identity cards. Because Joseph and I had been released from jail on a big bail we were probably listed as having been imprisoned, and our names were identifiably Jewish, so we thought: "This is the end. We're going to be arrested again, and now with the whole family." The soldier went to make a call and kept his eyes on us at the same time. Miraculously, he returned and gave the cards back to us and let us go. Forty-eight hours later, after we arrived in Tehran, we heard that a group of Jews were caught at the same checkpoint and sent back to Baghdad.

For our safety, we did not talk with each other, only when absolutely necessary with our immediate families. We pretended we didn't know each other because we didn't want to bring attention to our large group and raise eyebrows about why such a large group was on vacation together. We were drinking coffee in a coffee shop when suddenly three Land Rover jeeps stopped nearby. Several Kurds stepped out and started asking us if we were ready to leave to cross over to Iran. Just like that! We were shaking. We didn't know whether we should trust them. We looked at each other warily. It felt like a dream, not reality. And then one man nearby, also a Jew from Baghdad, said that these were the people with whom he had arranged to escape, so we mustn't fear. We breathed a sigh of relief—until the Kurdish man said, "Ok, we'll take the women and the children first." To give them the women and the children! It was very scary. But this Jewish man swore to us that we were in good hands. So the women and children left in the jeeps. After about twenty very long minutes, the Kurds came back and took the rest of us in several trips. I was in the last group. They took us to a mountainous area and we began walking—49 people, including children and elderly.

Eventually we were brought to a tent and told to sit and rest on a carpet. Several Kurds began serving us in a way that we couldn't believe. They brought each of us a towel and water to wash our faces, cold water to drink, tea, and coffee. It was unbelievable, surreal. For each one of us, they brought a tray with chicken, meat, and vegetables. I didn't know why they were being so gracious; none of us could figure it out. We ate and thanked them, and again they came with towels and water and tea, and when it was about 11 o'clock at night, they said, "It's time for you to go." They took us from that area in the Land Rovers to a building made out of mud with many rooms lit with lanterns.

They divided us up into the rooms. We were sitting on the floor covered with carpets when suddenly about eight Kurdish "freedom fighters" came in—they called them *pishmorga*, which means in their language "to fight until death." They fought the government for years for Kurdish freedom from Iraqi rule. The apparent leader of the group said, *Salaam alechum* (Hello) and sat down. We didn't know who he was. He talked with us so nicely, and it was clear that he was a very highly educated person. "Are there more Jews like you in Baghdad who wish to escape from Iraq?" he asked. By that point, we all trusted him and his friends. You didn't have to probe to figure out whether to trust a Kurd or not. They were honest and friendly with the Jews. So we began giving him the names and addresses of whomever we knew, though none had telephone service. He talked for more than a half hour with us.

Then he asked, "Are you going to Israel?" We all became silent and grew pale. It was, for all intents and purposes, forbidden to say aloud the word "Israel" at that time. Even though we trusted him, we hesitated. We were in shock and didn't know how to answer. I finally looked at him and said, "Yes," and waited for his reaction. He didn't say anything. He just stood up and started shaking all our hands. He said it was time to go and that we were close to the border. Then he asked us: "Did any one of us"—he meant the Kurds—"ask you for a fee to help you? Because if so I will cut off his head." He continued, "I ask because in every nation, there are some weak, cheap people." Nobody admitted to paying any smugglers.

Then I stood up to shake his hand and thanked him, and he clenched my hand and said, "There is no reason to thank me. Israel gave us training, arms, medicine, and any kind of help that we needed in our war against the Iraqis. If Israel had merely publicized the news about our war and our mission, it would have been enough for us, but they did so much more. So we are very grateful to Israel, to the Jewish people. What we are doing now for you is the least we can do to reciprocate." And then I understood that this was Idris al-Barazani, the son of the head of the Kurds [Moustafa al-Barazani]. It was a wonderful fluke that I met this great person.

Soon after he left, we met Oddil Dallall, the widow of Yitzhak Dallall who had been with me in prison and was executed. She suddenly appeared in our room in this building—she had gotten there independently. She came to me shaking. She was worried that Iraqi intelligence officers were following her. So I promised her that we would not leave without her but until then she must pretend that she didn't know us so that we wouldn't be caught if she were caught by one of these officers.

But in the end I realized there were no intelligence officers—she was just traumatized by what happened to Yitzhak and had become paranoid.

We climbed into the jeeps. The drivers gave a signal with a flashlight to the Iranian border guards who opened the gate and we crossed. On the Iranian side we stayed at a small motel. Early in the morning a bus belonging to the Jewish Agency picked us up. We had a 12-hour bus journey followed by a 12-hour train ride to Tehran. Oddil still believed that she was being followed and couldn't fall asleep and was still shaking. So I gave her a tranquilizer—valium. I sat next to the door of the rail car and told her to go to sleep and that I would protect her. She didn't react. So I put my leg on the seat and said, "Sit on my leg. If I move from here, you will wake up." That worked.

We arrived at a hotel in Tehran at which the Jewish Agency had organized for us to stay and there we met some of our friends who had crossed over from Iraq before us. It was a big reunion in addition to relief and joy. We stayed in Tehran for about three weeks. I met relatives there who had been living in Tehran for years whom I didn't know I had and who had heard that we were there and came to visit us at the hotel. From there we went to Israel.

Saeed Herdoon arrived in Israel at age 34, married, and lived there for 10 years. His parents, who came with him, never learned Hebrew and lived among other Iraqi Jews until their deaths. Herdoon moved to America in 1980, where he lived in Merrick, New York. He died in April, 2007, 10 months after giving this interview.

* * *

Oddil Dallall describes her younger years from the 1940s to the 1960s—decades of comfortable living punctuated by bullets and bombs—and how she raised her children during her husband's imprisonment and execution.

I was born Oddil Eliahou in Baghdad on Yom Kippur in 1932. My earliest recollections are days of fear. I was nine years old when the Farhoud happened. A few days before the Farhoud, we had left our own house when an Arab youth organization called Kaitab al Shabab took hold of a Jewish school next door to us in our neighborhood of Sinak and made our lives unbearable. Thus by sheer luck we had escaped our deaths: our house was looted and some of the walls were torn down by looters hoping to find hidden jewelry. My father's menswear and shoe shop, one of the best on Rashid Street, the main thoroughfare in Baghdad, was left a wreck.

The whole night long on June 1 I sat trembling at my grandparents' house with two pillows pushed against my ears, trying to keep out the sounds of agony on the streets outside: of men being killed, women being raped, children crying for their parents, and bullets whizzing overhead. The whole sky was ablaze. Mixed with all those sounds were the cries of joy of some of our Arab neighbors as they looted Jewish homes and shops.

The next morning, we received the first news of the night's events. The milkman, an Assyrian Christian, advised my mother to stay inside and said, "Jews have been killed and slaughtered like sheep" and that he had seen many dead on his way to us. He offered to buy us bread to last us for the next few days. Eventually, things got back to normal. My mother began to wear an *abaya* in order to pass outside unrecognized as a Jew, and my parents briefly considered leaving Iraq.

Yet in so many ways, my childhood was wonderful. I was the oldest of three children. I remember my grandparents with fondness: my grandfather, Baba Alika, a rich landowner, was a very imposing personality and used to wear a *zboon*, a long, off-white robe with a sash, a light brown *abaya* thrown over his shoulders, and a red fez to cover his head. He used a cane to steady his walk and always had a string of amber beads in his fingers. When he read his books, he often took a break by looking at his waist-watch, opening a small silver tobacco box, licking his fingers, and rolling a cigarette. He used a hand-made straw pen to write. My grandmother, Nana Aziza, taught me all the Hebrew prayers.

I went to the Laura Kadoorie School for Girls (Alliance) and studied for two years at London University by correspondence. My mother and father, who were first cousins, also went to Alliance. We studied in three languages at the same time: most subjects—not just the languages themselves—were taught in Arabic, English, and French. So, for instance, in history, when we studied the French Revolution and the royalty in France and so on, we were taught about it in French. We had reverence and respect for our teachers. When I came to Israel, I was shocked by the difference: once, my son came home from kindergarten and said, "Rachel wants to see you." I asked, "Who is Rachel?" He said, "My teacher." I asked, "You call her by her first name?!" In Iraq, we always used "Miss" or "Madame" or something of the like and their last names.

My otherwise happy childhood was pockmarked with moments of fear and frustration. At a French exam that was held at another school, a nun who supervised the exam stood behind me while I was writing an essay and I overheard her mutter, "She writes very well. Pity she is a Jew." On my way to school one day, I saw two Arabs squabbling over the equivalent of a quarter of a dollar. They were shouting loudly and then suddenly one took an axe and brought it crashing down on the other one's head. Until today, I think of this incident when I think about making peace with the Arabs: how can they make peace with us if they have the capacity to kill each other for less than a shilling? As children, we never had any relationships with Arabs. A few Arabs were friendly with my grandfather and he met them at the coffee shop and drank tea and played *sheshbesh* [backgammon] with them. But that was the older generation, not ours.

The anniversary of the Balfour Declaration[7] was often a day of riots and we always stayed inside our home. Once, the windows of my father's shop were smashed to pieces. After the declaration of the State of Israel, bombs were thrown at the Laura Kadoorie Club and I was there when one of them went off. When we listened to the news from Israel in Arabic on Kol Yisrael, our hearts filled with pride. Some of my friends joined the *Tnu'a*, the Zionist movement. Then our houses were searched for any shred of evidence to accuse us of Zionism, so we cleansed our houses of Stars of David, prayer books and other religious items.

The government's anti-Communist wave came in 1949, and on my way to school one day I came face-to-face with the sight of five executed men, Communists, hanging by their necks in the main square of Baghdad. I was still in school in 1950 when most of the Jews registered to leave, and I wanted to go to Israel but couldn't unless I went with my family because I was not yet 18. My mother had been prepared to go: she had already sold the silverware, the Persian carpets, all our valuables. But we never went. After the mass aliyah, we were given yellow identity cards stating that we were Jewish, with our photos and thumbprints. When I received my card I felt like a convict.

A Couple's Tragedy

I met my husband for the first time at my friend's house and later learned we were second cousins. I was 22. We danced, we talked. We were engaged six months later, on October 30, 1956. It was exactly a day after the Israeli invasion of Sinai.[8] On October 31, I went into the city to shop and saw demonstrations everywhere: Rashid Street was mobbed with angry men. My father's shop was on that street and he closed it for the day. I went to Yitzhak's brother's pharmacy a few steps from there and called Yitzhak to come get me.

Our wedding, held at the Meir Tweig Synagogue, was a very simple celebration. We went by train to Basra for our honeymoon. We took a boat ride with the mayor of Basra, who was friendly with the Jews, to Mehamera, on the Iranian side of the Shaat al Arab [the river separating Iraq from Iran]. I always recall that moment, thinking that had we stayed in Iran, our lives would have turned out so differently.

Yitzhak was a very sociable and liberal man. He pushed me to take driving lessons and get my license. We were continually invited out and we threw parties. His electronics business thrived. As co-owner of the Toshiba agency in Iraq, he imported radios and TVs, as well as other products like fans and batteries. He also had two factories separate from that business, one for chocolate and biscuits and one for perfumes. We lived very comfortably. I had everything I desired.

Our peace of mind ended abruptly on July 14, 1958, when the coup d'etat happened.[9] We packed our bags and went to stay at Yitzhak's brother's house, which was in a safer neighborhood. We learned that the army had slaughtered the royal family during the early hours of the morning. On our way there, we saw mobs demonstrating everywhere, many holding posters of Gamal Abdul Nasser [then

Egyptian president] and calling for the death of Arab dictators everywhere. Our means of receiving news was via the gardener and Kol Yisrael, the only trustworthy news source. The Jews, miraculously, were left untouched. We spent two weeks there until we felt it was safe enough to return home.

Times were good for the Jews during Qassem's regime: we were accepted at universities, allowed to leave the country like all other citizens, and buy and sell property freely. Yitzhak became the agent of another Japanese company and an Indian company. Still, many Jews left during his time because they faced no restrictions in attaining passports and traveling abroad. Nearly all of my family was still in Baghdad, so there was no one outside the country who was telling us to leave. So we stayed.

After the first Ba'ath Party coup in 1963, Yitzhak was arrested and led to the Ministry of Defense. I sought help from a neighbor, a very influential sheik, and he was released later that day. The authorities had wanted to know whether Yitzhak and his partner possessed a particular medical substance which was banned because it lacked a certificate of origin—a certificate which was imposed to ensure no article made in Israel would be imported to Iraq via a third country.

The same month that Yitzhak was arrested I got pregnant with our first son, Elias, and he was born in 1965. Three years later, our son Vico was born.

On June 5, 1967, when the Six Day War broke out, all the shops and offices were closed, and Jews and Arabs alike were rushing to get home safely. During the war we sat in a closed room to hear the news from Israel in Arabic, which we kept very low. But in fact if you went into the street you could hear the same broadcast playing loudly from homes of Muslims and Christians. Many of them listened to the news from Israel because they knew they would hear the real story, not the propaganda and lies that the media in the Arab countries spew out. Radio Baghdad boasted about so-called victories over Israel—fictitious. Even after Israel's victory, Radio Baghdad continued to broadcast its lies and didn't even mention the Arab defeat. With Israel's victory, I felt twice as tall, incredibly proud.

A few days later, the Iraqis learned the truth and turned on us: articles in the press named Jewish merchants as Israeli spies, our club memberships were cancelled, our phones were disconnected, and a wave of arrests began. Jews were fired from their jobs; only doctors were allowed to continue their practice—probably because the Arabs depended on them too much to force them to stop working. Luckily, Yitzhak had an Arab partner, Al-Hilfi, whom we trusted. They had been together for 30 years. So our bank accounts were put under Al-Hilfi's name so we were able to access our money.

A reign of terror began to take shape around us after the Ba'ath Party was reinstated in July, 1968. When the government arrested 20 people in December, 1968, and then put them on trial for spying for Israel, Yitzhak was still at home. On January 4, 1969, the trial of the first nine detainees was broadcasted on TV. We were at home readying for dinner at 6 o'clock when the doorbell rang. I opened the door and saw a man with very frightening eyes—a very piercing look—and Al-Hilfi was with him, his face white as a sheet. The stranger asked, "Is Yitzhak Dallall here?" I said, "Yes." To this day, I regret not having answered in the negative. He asked, "Can we have a word with him outside?" Yitzhak came to the door and went outside. He closed the door behind him. I never saw my husband again.

When 10 minutes passed and he didn't come back in, I opened the door to the pitch darkness. There was no sign of him. I realized he'd been taken by the Ba'ath regime. I took the car and drove to one of his factories—he wasn't there. I went to his brother, Ya'acov, and told him that it seemed that Yitzhak had been arrested. I went to the police, but it was not the police who had arrested him. It was the Ba'ath, and they worked differently—arbitrarily. I went to three detention centers, and at the third, when the jailer realized the man in question was a Jew, he yelled at me to leave.

At 10:30 that night, there was another knock on the door. Seven men were standing there. One of them said, "We need to inspect the place," and they held a search warrant. He wanted to see the children's room and he came with a gun. I said, "Excuse me. Leave the gun outside. The children are asleep and there is no one to threaten you here." I wasn't afraid of him.

He put the gun down and he and his men continued the search. He went to the maid's room and pointed up at two cupboards filled with toys. It was locked. He said, "Your husband said that you have arms hidden in the house." I said, "If he told you this, why didn't you ask him where we keep them? Because I don't know of anything here." I gave him the keys to the cupboard but it didn't open. So I said, "Maybe the arms you are looking for are in here." I was being aggressive, and Bertha, my sister-in-law, was horrified that I was answering him like this. He took two steps backwards—he was suddenly afraid because he never expected me to act this way. So he said, "You are doing wrong to your husband by behaving this way." I tried the key again. It worked and all the toys fell down in front of him. The men left the house in a hurry.

For the next seven and a half months I went from one place to the other looking for Yitzhak or some information about him. After a few weeks, I learned that he was in Kasr al Nahaya. Though it was named to show triumph over the monarchy, for many Iraqis who ended up there it had a parallel meaning: once you were in that prison, you were very likely going to meet your end.

I visited an influential Arab lawyer who promised to help and I asked many others for help. Early on January 27, my mother came to tell me that nine of the Jews who had stood trial had been executed. I collapsed onto the nearest chair. I turned on the TV and switched it off immediately as soon as I saw the bodies hanging like sacks from the scaffolds, surrounded by a crowd reveling at the sight. After hearing the list of the victims' names, I was left thinking of Charles Horesh's wife—Charles was the only one of the nine I knew personally—who was expecting a baby at the time, and he now would never see his child. I was too afraid to think of Yitzhak and what this spelled for his fate. I went to visit our neighbor and friend, an Arab sheik who I assumed would be sympathetic to the Jews. He was watching the event on TV with his family when I entered and I could not believe my eyes: they were actually enjoying this barbaric act. I excused myself and left.

I went to see Yitzhak's brother. "What will become of Yitzhak?" I asked. "We are all finished," he said. "If they can hang innocent men without anyone lifting a finger of protest, we are all finished."

After the hangings, fear gripped all Iraqis and the Arabs I had asked for help were too afraid to do anything. The Arab lawyer I had contacted a week before turned down the case. I went to see the wife of a man who I had heard was a moderate member of the Ba'ath Party and had opposed the executions. She served me tea and I told her about my husband. She wrote down his name and went to the phone presumably to call her husband. Suddenly, her expression changed and she came back to tell me she couldn't help me.

Yitzhak's businesses kept going temporarily because his Arab partner's nephew took over the operation. He gave me some money to keep me going for a while. But within a few months the Ba'ath Party confiscated all of Yitzhak's businesses.

Meanwhile, the regime had convinced most Iraqis that all the Jews were spies for Israel, so Jews were ostracized by everyone. Just after the executions, the Ba'ath took reporters on a tour of the Frank Iny School and a synagogue, accompanied by party officials, to interview students and other Jews in order to show how the Jews were ostensibly faring just splendidly! Of course, everyone who was interviewed was too frightened to tell the truth about the persecution the community was facing. At the school, one clever reporter said he had forgotten his camera in the secretary's office. Once inside the secretary's room, he unbuttoned his coat, under which he had a tape recorder. He told her to tell the whole true story in a hurry. Yitzhak's nephew was also present (which is how I know this story) and he passed the reporter a piece of paper listing the names of all the Jews who were detained in Kasr al Nahaya. Until today, I don't know whether this piece of information had a positive effect or not. We do know that somehow the truth did get out.

I was faced with the task of hiding the truth of Yitzhak's absence from Elie, who was three. I told him first that he was in England and would soon return. But Elie was intelligent and I could see that he knew I was fibbing. I was consoled by Vico's innocence—as a baby, he was the only one who was unaffected by Yitzhak's absence. Meanwhile, my own brother had been detained as well, but he was in a "five star hotel" in comparison to where Yitzhak was. I filled my time cooking food to take to my brother every day and to Yitzhak once a month—though I don't know if it ever got to him—and caring for the boys.

My emotions were like a rollercoaster whenever I heard news about other prisoners. A second one of Yitzhak's Arab partners who had been arrested was released, then re-detained a few days later. A group of Jewish prisoners were set free and told me they had seen Yitzhak inside the prison. I had moments of hope followed by moments of great disappointment and despair.

But the atmosphere in Iraq got worse. On August 21, an Australian tried to set fire to the Al Aqsa Mosque in Jerusalem and for two days military music was broadcast over the radio and TV and tension began to build.[10]

On August 24, the parcel I had just delivered for Yitzhak was returned on the pretext that he was not there. I was not too worried because that had happened before. His brother told me several days earlier that Al-Hilfi's nephew informed him that he got word from the authorities to visit his uncle before his execution—but it turned out that the execution didn't happen that day. The one piece of good news was that my brother was released the same day.

That day I went to see our friend Saleh Basri who worked at the French embassy. When he opened the door for me I saw his face was deathly white. He said that it had just been announced over the radio that Yitzhak's execution was planned for 7:30 that evening. It was already 7:00. I asked for a glass of water and poured it over my head. I knew that was the end.

I went to Ya'acov's house. Then there was another radio announcement. One of the other people who was also supposed to be executed with Yitzhak was a Christian. But because August 24 fell on a Sunday, Christians protested that he not be killed on his holy day. So their execution was postponed until the next morning.

I stood vigil at Ya'acov's house the whole night, waiting for Yitzhak to die. We sat in the darkness in the garden. I couldn't say a word. My mind was blank, and my sister-in-law kept on repeating, "Please God, give him patience." But I was losing my faith in God. I searched up in the stars for something to anchor me in God's stead. I thought of Yitzhak suffering, deprived of holding his children for the last time. I was numb—I couldn't even cry. Bertha was with me all night long, and eventually she tired of praying. When I heard a distant *Allahu Akbar*! from a nearby mosque, a call to prayer, I knew it was morning and that Yitzhak was no longer among the living. I went home.

When I got home, my mother was with the children and she was crying. Ya'acov brought the morning paper, and it had Yitzhak's face on it with the news of the execution.[11] He looked haggard, thin, and had a beard. Visitors came to see us and I escaped into the children's room. I sent Elie off to be taken care of by a friend. Yitzhak's brother called the rabbi and the rabbi asked whether we'd like to see the body before the funeral. I said no: I would have gone crazy. I was angry with God and the powerless rabbi, so I told him, "Please just go." I stayed home with the women while the men went to the cemetery. Traditionally, women didn't go to the cemetery, only men. It was a Muslim tradition but the Jews in Iraq followed it. The men returned shortly after, saying the gravediggers had buried Yitzhak before they were able to get to the cemetery. The men recited the *Kaddish* at our home and left.

I was all alone and it was time to go to sleep. Because it was summer, when we usually slept on the roof, I took Elie upstairs and did something that I will never,

never forgive myself for, but at the time it seemed logical because he was the only one who could share completely in my grief. I told him that his father was not coming back. And he asked, "Why?" I said, "God called him and he is in heaven now. He won't be with us anymore." He said, "Mommy, let's get a ladder and go up to see him. I want to see him." I said, "We can't. We can't go with a ladder because only God can call us to heaven. Whenever he calls us, we will go." And he said, "I don't like this God."

After we came to Israel a year later, Elie came to me—he was five and a half—and said, "Mommy, you know, I think the God here in Israel is much better than the one in Iraq." When I wrote down all the events of my life in Iraq years later, I entitled the manuscript *A Better God* because of what he said.

Yitzhak had been in jail for 234 days. And the strange thing is that by chance the number on his grave 234. The Jewish graves were numbered consecutively, and his name is on it. In 2005 Mordechai Ben Porat sent someone to Iraq to take photos of the Jewish graves and brought back a map of the cemetery. I showed them which one was Yitzhak's. At the time, Ben Porat wanted to have some of the graves of the executed Jews transferred to Israel but the situation now in Iraq has made this too difficult.

When I think about all the opportunities I had to leave Iraq earlier—which would have prevented this terrible tragedy from happening—all I can conclude is that it was fate that we stayed. We all die sooner or later. But what I can't grasp is why Yitzhak had to die in such a cruel way. I've asked myself this question many, many times. There is no answer. Why? Why such a horrible death?

We escaped Iraq through the Kurdish area in the north a year later, on September 7, 1970. Three days later we were in Tehran. From Tehran, we took a plane to Israel. In Israel, the Israeli authorities at the airport wanted to change my name from Oddil to Yudith which I refused to do because I couldn't imagine being anything else but Oddil. I received special treatment at the airport because I was so exhausted and traumatized, and officers took me to the exit door for the prime minister and other dignitaries. When I got to the hotel many people were waiting for me, mostly relatives and friends who had escaped before us.

I had been used to so many luxuries in Iraq, so life in Israel, where I had to fend for myself, was somewhat of a shock. I was given 500 lira at the airport and went and blew it on bathing suits for me and the boys and a taxi ride to relatives in Netanya from Bat Yam [south of Tel Aviv], where we were given an apartment, because in Iraq we went everywhere in taxis. When we reached Netanya, we had no money left. My relatives couldn't believe I had taken a taxi for such a long distance. The next day I called the social worker who had given us the money. I said, "I need money." She said, "But we just gave you!" I said, "Yes, but it's already gone." "What did you do?" She asked. I told her. As a result, she came and moved us to Ramat Aviv, because she understood that we were used to a pretty luxurious lifestyle and would have difficulty in Bat Yam, a poor neighborhood.

The only thing I took with me from Iraq was a film of Elie's third birthday when Vico was a month old, and Yitzhak is in it. That is the only hard evidence for Vico that he had a father. When Vico was 10 years old he came home one day from a friend's party and said, "Mommy, you know what? My friend's father took us and threw us in the air and it was so much fun." You could see his eyes were just wide with amazement, and I said to myself that while I was trying to be both a father and a mother to my boys, I couldn't do all the things a father was supposed to do—all the things Yitzhak would have done.

Oddil Dallall never remarried. In Israel, she toured the country delivering lectures about the Jews of Iraq. The Israeli government also sent her to the United States, Canada, France, and England to lecture. She lived for three decades in Ramat Aviv and currently resides in Even Yehuda.

* * *

Zuhair Sassoon is the grandson of Rabbi Sassoon Khedouri, the last spiritual leader of the Jewish community of Iraq and its president for 37 years. Zuhair was born in 1938 in Baghdad. In his account, he recalls memories of his grandfather, who died in 1971 at age 91. The Hakham Bashi [chief rabbi] also served as the community president. His grandfather presided over a community in peril as it diminished to fewer than 3,000 at his death from nearly 140,000 before the mass exodus at mid-century. Zuhair details some of his family's most trying years including the mass exodus in the early 1950s and the period following the Six Day War in 1967, when Zuhair's father spent a year in Kasr al Nahaya. Zuhair also describes a revealing encounter with Saddam Hussein.

Hakham Sasson Khedouri was chief rabbi between 1928 and 1930, head of the Jewish religious court, and the head of the Jewish community of Iraq from 1933 to 1949, when, after mass arrests of Jews involved in Zionist and Communist activity, he resigned as president when community members protested that he was not doing enough to protect his constituency. Yehezkel Shemtob took his place but Khedouri resumed his leadership role in 1954 until his death in 1971.

I grew up in Salhya, a neighborhood of Baghdad where many Jews lived, though most Jews lived on the other side of the Tigris. I did my elementary schooling at the Alliance and high school studies at the Jesuit American school called Baghdad College. I graduated in 1957 and then left to study at the American University of Beirut. I returned to Baghdad in the middle of my studies in 1958 but I couldn't go back to Beirut to finish because the Iraqi government at that point allowed Jews to leave the country only if they were leaving permanently. During the revolution in 1958 [of Abd Al-Karim Qassem], I was able to enter the engineering college in Baghdad. I graduated as a civil engineer in 1962, and I was involved in many engineering projects in Iraq. I worked until the end of 1969. That year, Jews were thrown out of their jobs and life became a struggle for survival and a quest to escape.

The turbulent political events throughout the years marred so many aspects of our lives. My bar mitzvah was a terrible event. It was 1951 and the atmosphere was chaotic because most of the Jews were leaving and the anti-Jewish sentiment was strong. We did the bar mitzvah on our rooftop, afraid of making a visible event in the house. It was a small and quiet ceremony with my grandfather, my parents, and a couple of Christian friends. Worse than that was the brit milah of my son, Ari. It was August, 1969. We did it in a small room, with only my grandfather, my father-in-law, my mother, my mother-in-law, my wife, and I in attendance. We didn't invite anybody because my father was in prison and Jews were being imprisoned and killed. The mood was somber.

Yet my wedding, in 1965, was like it was out of a fairytale. My wife, Joyce David, was the daughter of an influential rabbi in Baghdad, Hakham Daoud, grandson of Hakham Yosef Haim who was also known as Ben Ish Hai,[12] and her father and my grandfather were at odds with each other over religious issues. So it was a Romeo and Juliet romance. The whole love affair and the emotions involved because of the conflict between our families was really tense, but ultimately both sides agreed to the marriage. My grandfather did so immediately, but, he added, "It also depends on her father. If he doesn't agree, you can't marry each other." My father-in-law agreed.

Many people attended our wedding—Jews, Muslims, and Christians. There was no place big enough to hold everyone who wanted to come. It was held at the Frank Iny School where people were standing in rows upon rows on both sides of me and my family to shake our hands. After the wedding, the tradition was for the bride and groom to give sweets to their invited guests, so we spent days delivering plates of sweets to people at their houses.

Most of my family left Iraq between 1950 and 1952. My grandfather couldn't leave then because of his position. In fact, he continued working until his death, for he felt obligated to care for the Jews who remained in Iraq. My grandfather was esteemed and respected by every government that came to power in Iraq. For the last three years of his life, he used to work nonstop from his offices in the center of Baghdad or from his home in the Karrada district. He would receive visitors or petitioners from his community—people who needed his help or his advice—night and day. He had a library filled with religious books and when he was asked for advice or received a letter inquiring about a religious problem, he used to point to a specific book to be brought to him, then open it to a certain page and cite the answer.

He taught himself to read and write Arabic because he didn't have formal schooling. He learned Hebrew, Torah, and Talmud from the Beit Midrash [yeshiva]. My grandmother, his wife, died before I was born. He never remarried. My great-grandmother took care of him and his children and was over a hundred years old at the time of her death in 1958.

My grandfather's period of service to his community was replete with problems as the community endured the severe persecution that ultimately led to its demise. Problems began in the 1920s when a group of his opponents within the Jewish community tried to deprive him of the title of Hakham, demonstrated against him, and tried to incite people to cause him harm in the streets and in the synagogue.[13] Eventually, they admitted their accusations were wrong and apologized to him. After the Farhoud, he met with ministers and dignitaries to secure the release of the bodies of many of the slain Jews and he ensured their burial in the proper tradition. He also spent weeks and months meeting with family members of the dead and missing to console and assist them.

In 1961, when President Qassem ordered the unearthing and transfer of the Jewish cemetery of Baghdad within six months so he could use the land for his own needs, my grandfather objected.[14] He met with Qassem and when he realized that his objections were in vain, he told the president that six months was not enough time to ensure the careful transfer of thousands of bodies buried there. My grandfather lost this battle.

One of his most difficult periods was leading up to the mass aliyah, when in 1949 he was forced to resign. He was in an incredibly difficult place then: on the one hand, the community needed his help in preparing for the aliyah and in extracting the hundreds of Jewish prisoners from jail who were imprisoned that year, following Israel's independence and the Iraqi government's repression of the Zionist movement. On the other hand, he felt he couldn't give the government the impression that he was pro-Israel, because that would have further compromised the safety of the community. He always said publicly that he was a loyal Iraqi.

As a kid in school, I fought constantly to defend my grandfather with people who thought he was anti-Zionist because he didn't want them to leave, and because he repeatedly made statements about the loyalty of the community to Iraq.[15] He was only doing his job: protecting the community and doing his best to make life in Iraq bearable for them so they wouldn't feel compelled to leave. There was a love-hate syndrome between the Jewish community and the Iraqi government. My grandfather understood that and spent years trying to delicately manage that schizophrenic attitude and protect his community. Meanwhile, at Alliance, I fought my Jewish friends to defend my grandfather. Walking home from school, I fought the Arabs, who taunted me because I was a Jew. Life was hard for me.

Behind Bars: The Rabbi's Son

My wife Joyce and I lived with my parents in Mansoor, an affluent neighborhood of Baghdad. At about 3 o'clock in the morning on November 11, 1968, our house was broken into, searched by about a dozen security people, and my father, Shaul Sassoon, was taken away. He was accused of being the ringleader of a group of

Jewish spies against Iraq. He was held in Kasr al Nahaya for a year, at the end of which he was tried in court, found innocent, and released.

How he stayed alive I really don't know. The conditions were wretched and he was severely tortured. Saddam himself used to sit and watch while his henchmen tortured my father, sometimes ordering his people where and how hard to beat him. Saddam would often direct the henchmen to tie my father's hands behind his back and whip him on his knees, and my father's knees were ruined as a result of the torture sessions. He was imprisoned with the group of Jews who were hanged in January, 1969, and probably would have been among them if—this is my interpretation—he had not been such a high-profile case. He wasn't hanged, I believe, because there would have been an international outcry against the government of Iraq. But it was precisely because he was such a high-profile person, as the son of the chief rabbi, that he was thrown in prison: to signal to all Iraqi Jews that no one was immune from punishment. My father later wrote about his experiences in prison in his book *Three Hundred and Sixty Five Days in the Hell of Saddam Hussein.*

On January 27, 1969, I was driving to work and saw hordes of people on their way to Liberation Square. Unaware of what was happening, I parked and joined them. When we reached the square, I had the shock of my life. Bodies of the hanged men were on display, tied to electrical poles. People all around them were dancing, clapping, and beating drums. Not knowing whether my father was among them, I kept looking for him among the dead and all of a sudden I noticed his shoes on the feet of one of the bodies. My father had been taken to prison wearing his black Bally shoes. This shoe was rather rare in Iraq and I didn't know anyone else who wore it. It took me a few seconds to look up at the dead man's face, though for me those seconds felt like an eternity. I saw that the victim was a young Jewish man—not my father.

A year later, after my father's release, he explained to me the story of his shoes. The basement cells of Kasr al Nayaha where my father and the other prisoners were held had concrete floors that were damp and cold. Because the prisoners had no beds they were forced to sleep on the floor and they used their shoes as pillows. Therefore, with the passage of time their shoes became shapeless and useless. My father, however, continued to wear his shoes rather than use them as a pillow because, he told me later, he preferred to have warm feet instead of a warm head. On the morning of January 27, a young Jewish man who used to sleep near my father had been told that he was being called to trial, and he asked my father to lend him his shoes because he was told to look presentable for the event. The man was hanged that day with my father's shoes on his feet.

Following the hanging, a story appeared in the *Iraqi Post*, a daily English language newspaper, saying that my father was among the hanged Jews. When I arrived at work that day, my colleagues, Italian engineers, came to me and shook my hands and gave me their condolences. Until that moment I had not heard any news about my father, so they brought me the newspaper and I read the article. I left the office and went to a Jewish friend who lived in the vicinity and asked her whether my father was indeed hanged. She said that she heard the names of those Jews who were hanged, which were broadcast on the radio, and that my father's name was not among them.

My father was released a year later, in 1970. When I saw him for the first time after he was released he wasn't wearing his own eyeglasses—he was wearing a different pair. I asked him whether he had been checked by an optician during his imprisonment. He smiled and said, "There are no opticians or any other kind of doctors in Kasr al Nahaya." Then he told me the story about his glasses. At the end of his interrogations by Saddam's security officers, he was asked to sign a statement written by them. He told them that in order to sign it he must read it and without his glasses he couldn't read. His own glasses had been broken on the first day of his imprisonment when he was beaten by his jailers. So they took him to a room filled with eyeglasses taken from prisoners. He chose a pair and read the statement, which accused him of being a spy, but refused to sign it, as doing so would have meant that he was admitting to the charges. The security officers threatened to beat and even kill him if he didn't sign, but he held firm.

My grandfather died a few months after father's release. We sat shivah at the Frank Iny School, and hundreds came. Saddam sent two of his ministers to give his condolences. Saddam asked one of the ministers to ask my father for my grandfather's traditional clothes and hat. This was the priestly outfit that he designed himself and always wore in public. It was totally unique. The minister asked us to personally bring the garment to Saddam, who wanted to put it in his museum.

We didn't want to give him the original, so we took a similar garment to Saddam's presidential palace. We were received by him in a huge reception room. The original garment is exhibited at the Israel Museum in Jerusalem. I went with my father, my grandfather's secretary the Mr. Naji Chachak, and Meir Basri [who became the community president after Khedouri's death]. I handed the clothing to Saddam and he thanked us, and my father and Saddam smiled at each other. It was an extremely surreal moment because my father had just been released from jail and, as I said, Saddam himself used to sit and watch as his henchmen tortured my father. Saddam of course recognized my father. He knew exactly who he was.

One thing that I began to understand about Saddam, and felt in that interaction with him, was that he had an exceptionally high IQ. He was charismatic, bright, and naturally cruel. His attitude reflected the government's warped attitude towards the Jews, whom it regarded as a fifth column from the moment that Israel was born. But at that time, it also needed the Jewish community, which was prosperous and educated and was part of the very inner workings of the economy and society. So on one hand, Saddam imprisoned and tortured my father and on the other hand Saddam's wish to put on display my grandfather's clothes meant to me that he wanted to show off his "good" relations with the Jews and showcase the

Jewish community's prosperity in Iraq for his own needs. Perhaps, on some level, he even respected my grandfather. Such was the complicated and confusing Iraqi mentality. I don't understand it and I cannot explain it.

My grandfather is buried in Baghdad. Mordechai Ben Porat recently brought me a video of his tomb and I authenticated it for him. But when the Americans came [in 2003] they went into the Jewish cemetery and accidentally destroyed some of the tombs with their tanks and the marble was stolen by locals. My grandfather's grave was one of only a handful of graves that have been identified in the Jewish cemetery since the invasion.

After Sasson Khedouri's death in 1971, the position of chief rabbi was terminated. In addition to his account of his time in prison, Shaul Sassoon wrote a biography about his father. Zuhair and Joyce live in Ramat Gan, Israel, and have two children.

* * *

Meir and Victoria Ovadia lived a carefree and comfortable life in Baghdad with their seven children until the day the secret police knocked on their door and arrested Meir in January, 1968. In her account, their daughter Ronit Dangour describes that day and the tumultuous months of her father's detention that followed, when her persistent mother made her way from jail to jail in a desperate attempt to find her husband and his brother, Sasson, who had been arrested with him. After locating their whereabouts and being referred to Saddam Hussein himself, Victoria managed to meet the dictator face-to-face multiple times over the course of several months to plead for her husband's release. At the same time, she happened to witness a fateful period in Saddam's life: his transformation from an unpretentious power broker to terrorizing dictator. The torture of Meir and Sasson Ovadia is widely known as one of the most extreme cases among the many Jews imprisoned by the Ba'ath Party.

I grew up in Masbach, an upper middle-class neighborhood in Baghdad, in a fancy three-storey house with beautiful gardens at 35 Mahad Al-Amel Street. I was born in 1946 and was one of seven children. My name was Suad, which means "happiness," so I chose the comparable name, Ronit, when I came to Israel. Our family name was Abda in Iraq, which we changed to Ovadia after making aliyah. We had a very good life in Iraq for many years which was the reason my parents didn't leave in 1950. We had two houses: one was a summer house on the river. We went to a wonderful Jewish school, Menachem Daniel, and Frank Iny. We had sports clubs where we met for social events and beautiful synagogues. My father owned real estate and did business with government ministers. Both of my parents went to the Alliance school. We traveled to Beirut and Hamdun[16] for vacations, and my parents traveled to Turkey and to London. We had close relationships with Arabs and we went to their weddings and celebrations and they came to ours.

It was a splendid life, until 1967—to be precise, until Monday, June 5, 1967, at 10 p.m. At that moment, a Muslim woman who was a neighbor and very friendly with my mother, Victoria, called and told her, "There is a war." We hadn't known: we had exams and were busy, and we weren't listening to the radio. She told my mother, "For every Muslim that is killed in Palestine, we will kill ten Jews in Baghdad." She had turned on a dime. It was hard to believe that that same morning, mother made her *sambusak* [Iraqi dumpling] and brought it over and the woman had said, "Thank you. It's delicious." I tried to call my grandfather but there was no line. The phone was disconnected.

We spent the week listening to the news. On Friday afternoon, father returned from synagogue, ate, and was resting when suddenly there was a knock on the door. A police officer arrested him and went to the home of my uncle, Sasson, and arrested him too. They were returned a few days later.

They were arrested again on January 9, 1968. Four officers from the *Tichbarat*, the secret police, burst into our house. They asked for my father and pulled him out of bed where he was taking a nap. When he had been arrested in June, it was by the *Amin*, the regular police. But because this time it was the *Tichbarat*, we knew his arrest was going to be much, much more serious and it would be very difficult to reach him. They beat him in front of all of us and I screamed, "Why are you beating my father?"

They turned the house upside down—breaking doors and satchels of rice and sugar, knocking over plants—while they searched for all kinds of so-called evidence. They said our rice in a jute sack was a bomb and they opened it up. Of course they didn't find anything. Except a Jew. They found a Jew. That's all they were looking for. They just wanted a pretext, an excuse, though even if they didn't find one, it didn't matter. My mother stood with the seven of us as they took him away by force. On his way out the door, in order to calm us, my father said, "I'll be back soon." It rained hard that night, and I remember crying and thinking that the heavens were crying with me. Again, my uncle was arrested on the same day from his house and taken with my father—both blindfolded—as was a group from Basra, and all were accused of spying against the country. Radio Baghdad announced that day, "We captured Jewish spies."

My mother searched for my father everywhere. She went from detention center to detention center, from jail to jail, from minister to minister, from clerk to clerk, searching out every possibility. She bribed the guards to get information on them. I went with her many times. She asked the chief rabbi, Sasson Khedouri, for help, but he failed.

We eventually learned that my father and uncle were taken to the Ministry of Defense. They were imprisoned for six months and six days, then sent elsewhere. No lawyer wanted to touch their case because they knew they would be dealing with the Ba'ath Party's inner circle. She bribed the guard to see them and that guard was later arrested for taking a bribe. After eight months of searching, she managed to see them both. She cried when she saw them. Father looked like Saddam looked after he was taken out of hiding [in December, 2004]. They had been tortured terribly virtually every day, we learned later. They were imprisoned in dark solitary cells and used their shoes as pillows. They were starved and prevented from using the toilet at times. Every day they ate no more than a plate of rice. They became extremely thin. Their fingernails were extracted. They were shoved down a well filled with water. In the winter, my father was stripped of his clothes so he would suffer in the cold. They were flogged with hoses day after day. And throughout all this time, they were prevented from seeing each other.

I believe that my father had been tortured more than many others because he was successful and wealthy. His brother was treated better because he wasn't so well off. That's our theory, anyway. The officers and guards were jealous because my father worked with all the ministers. He built their homes. He invested their money. And he made a lot of money as a result. But we also know that he argued with the guards and his torturers and didn't admit to anything they were demanding of him. He was asked to sign documents admitting to communicating with Israel, for instance. And he wouldn't admit to anything. Although we couldn't secure their release, we were at least relieved to know they were alive.

The two of them were among many people who went missing at that time—mostly Jews but some Muslims and Christians too, if they were suspected of being collaborators with or aiding Jews suspected of working with Israel. Suddenly one man was taken and didn't return, then another didn't return, then another was killed. We had a Jewish neighbor named David Zbeida who was taken in the morning and three days later the authorities threw his body back into his garden—he was strangled with a jute sack over his head. Between 1967 and 1969, when the hangings occurred, many things happened. Many people didn't return. Life was torture for many people, and certainly for us.

With my father gone, we had no income. My mother had no choice but to dismiss the gardener, the cook, and the cleaner. She wasn't allowed to touch the money and property we had in the bank because it was in my father's name. At one point, she was able to access some money and she paid a lawyer 15,000 dinars (then about $75,000) to find my father and bring him home. He took our money but my father didn't come home.

On May 15, 1968, father and Sasson were taken from the Ministry of Defense to Muasker Al-Rashid, a military camp, where they stayed for seven months. On December 15, they were taken to Kasr al Nahaya. There, their conditions only worsened. They were forced to sit in the feces and urine of other prisoners and were freezing cold. They were tortured brutally again, every six hours, all over their bodies. They were strung up in the air upside down on a ceiling fan and were spun around. Once, they were strung up by their hands and remained in that position for four days and four nights. At one point, the prison officers took my father to the Yarmuk Hospital for treatment—they wanted to amputate his leg which had been slammed with rusty nails and had become mangled and infected—and on the way they repeatedly struck his head with an iron bar. My father opened the car door and threw himself onto the ground in an attempt to commit suicide. He was pulled back in, and at the hospital he refused to have his leg amputated.

In fact, both brothers tried several times to commit suicide during their imprisonment. My father made six attempts: other than the car episode, he swallowed a key, broke his eyeglasses and swallowed them, stole a razor blade from the barber and then broke it into pieces and swallowed them, put his fingers in an electric socket while shaving, and attempted to throw himself off the prison roof when he was taken there to use the bathroom.

Sitting with Saddam

One day in the summer of 1968, in the midst of the military coup of Hasan al-Bakr, my mother went to the Revolutionary Council. She brought a letter with her requesting my father's pardon. She was told, "If you want help, you must go to Saddam Hussein al-Tikriti. He's the man who can help you." She asked him, "Who is he?" The man answered, "He's omnipotent. He can help you in whatever you want." She asked, "Is he against the Jews?" The man answered, "No."

She returned home and the next morning she set out with one of my brothers to find Saddam's house, which was on the other side of the Tigris next to the El-Yarmuch mosque, on Hai Dra'ar Street. The house was simple and the garden neglected, and a young boy was playing naked in the sand in front of the house. It didn't look at all like the house of a powerful government official. There was no security guard, and a pregnant woman—his wife Sajida—opened the door for her. Inside, simple furniture was covered with blankets. Saddam appeared.

Saddam was wearing a blue *galabyia*—the Iraqi pajamas that people wore casually during the day—and worn slippers. He asked my mother, "What do you want?" She said to him, "I want to talk to you about my husband. No one can save him except for God and you," and she began telling him about my father's arrest and imprisonment. "Write down on a note why your husband was arrested," he said. She wrote that he was arrested even though he was innocent of any wrongdoing. Then she told him what she wrote. He asked her, "How do you know that he is innocent?" She told him, "I'm his wife. I know everything about him." He responded, "Women don't know anything. I created this entire revolution and my wife didn't know anything about it until it was over."

He left the room and returned shortly afterwards. He told her to come back the following week and in the meantime he would check into the case. She came back the next week and Saddam wasn't there—only Sajida. Sajida called him and he asked to speak to my mother. He told my mother that he hadn't gotten a chance to inspect the file and that she should come back in another week. My mother kept coming back over and over again—I accompanied her on many of those visits—and I remember that we would sit, chat, and sip tea with Sajida and Saddam's sister Suhad, and each time my mother was told that Saddam didn't have an answer for her. At one point, Sajida gave birth and my mother brought her a gift for the new baby: a gold anklet with bells.

On one visit, Mother saw the director of a prison where my father had been jailed briefly. He and my mother recognized each other because she had once spoken to him about releasing my father. He couldn't believe she had persisted so far, until making her way into Saddam's house. He was too fearful to enter the house—and meanwhile my mother was making herself at home there day after day!

The final visit was a month later. The experience was altogether different. I went with my mother, as usual, and we immediately saw that the house was fixed up. Several cars were parked and army tents were pitched on the lawn and two tanks were standing guard on the street. Saddam was wearing a suit and tie and although he didn't have an official role in the government, he looked like the leader of the country. Later, when he overthrew his uncle, my mother said she wasn't surprised. He and his wife looked different, spoke differently—with dignity and stature—but his eyes were angry.

Saddam said to my mother, "I took a look at your husband's file, but he is not clean." My mother objected, saying that he was innocent. He said, "I will investigate the matter. But anyone who spies against this country will be hanged!" He then told her not to come back to see him again. Around the same time, the radio announced that a spy ring was caught and my father was the ringleader.

My father's luck was this: his file had been in a pile with the nine other Jews who were ultimately hanged on January 27. While Saddam extracted my father's file from the pile to review it, that same evening the authorities took the remainder of the pile and hanged all those people. In other words, if it weren't for Saddam, my father would have been hanged that day. Whether it was a fluke or purposeful on Saddam's part, we didn't know. However, eventually my mother decided that Saddam had no intention of helping—rather, he wanted to investigate the case himself, and it was just pure chance that the file was separated from the others.

Many of the nine who were hanged that day were my husband's friends, though I didn't know my husband at the time. My husband, Nissim, who was from Basra, frequently came to Baghdad to buy kosher meat. He happened to be in Baghdad at the kosher butcher on January 27, and when he entered the store he saw that people were wailing. He asked, "What has happened?" He was told, "Nine Jews were hanged." He rushed off to the central square to see for himself. And then he saw his friends, dead, hanging from nooses. He saw their faces and he was in shock. I recall watching the trial of these Jews on television. It was very scary. The Jews were represented by a lawyer, but the lawyer stood up and said, "I'm ashamed to defend these criminal spies." He didn't defend them—he was put there so the government could say there had been a lawyer. It was all a show.

One day in 1969, I was at the university and when I returned home my family told me that the newspaper reported that my father and his brother Sasson were spies for Israel and that they were to be hanged. I realized that some of my friends at the university—many of them were Muslims and Christians—must have known but didn't tell me or ask me about it. To me that was a sign of our friendship: they didn't act differently to me because of what my father was being accused of. I actually only have good things to say about the university. We weren't kicked out as Jews. But I left Iraq before I was able to graduate.

My father and uncle were kept in prison and tortured for seven more months, until the end of August, 1969. Then, they were taken to the Revolutionary Court and the military prosecutor charged them with spying for Israel and demanded their executions. But their lives were spared once again. This is how it happened. Attendants used to sit beside the doors to the courthouses in Iraq, and a newspaper reporter asked one of the attendants, "Is there something new going on in there?" The attendant told him, "I think there are two Jews on trial who are going to be hanged." The reporter published the story in his newspaper—a very small article, and it was an Iraqi newspaper. Because the hangings of two Jews on August 25 had just occurred, the government knew the whole world was watching and waiting to see what would happen next. So instead, they were given a trial—if you could call it that. It was only because of that article that we learned there was a trial and that my father and uncle would need a lawyer to represent them. The journalist, who was not Jewish, was hanged, accused of revealing state secrets.

Mother searched and searched for a lawyer who would take the case. Most lawyers wouldn't touch the case because it involved defending Jews. Those who were willing to defend Jews knew they would pay the price with Saddam so they declined. She finally found a lawyer who she thought was strong and could withstand the government pressure, and who had friends within the government.

She paid him 5,000 dinars ($25,000)—enough money to buy a house in those days. Not only was he paid this sum, but the lawyer entered our house before the trial began and demanded many gifts for himself. He walked around the house selecting from our things. My mother gave him whatever he requested because she had no choice. He took two valuable Persian carpets which were hanging on the wall. He acted like a king. We knew that the trial would be a sham, and it was. But what was important for us was that father would come out alive. That, for us, would be a victory.

In the end, my father and his brother were sentenced to five years in prison, though they only had to serve an additional three because they had already served two before the trial. The moment he was put in jail he was better off. In jail, the conditions were terrible but at least he wasn't tortured anymore and he knew that he just had to count the days.

All along, he refused to sign any documents admitting guilt of any kind. He knew he was innocent, and he stuck to it throughout all the pain and suffering, amazingly. Among the nine Jews who had been hanged in January, 1969, some had signed because they were told that if they signed they would get a lighter punishment. But later on, their admissions were used against them. My father didn't know this because he was imprisoned during that period, but he just determined by himself that he wouldn't admit to something he didn't do.

Meanwhile, because of my mother's efforts to save my father's life, she became known as being very brave—she is still known as the Iraqi Avital Sharanksy.[17] She wasn't afraid, even though as a young Jewish woman it was very dangerous to go around to all the places she went to. She endangered her own life. And she did that with seven children at home. All of her children admire her greatly for what she did.

I made aliyah in the middle of the trial. Some of my other siblings began to leave too. Mother didn't tell us to run away. We decided on our own that if we wanted a life, it was clear we couldn't continue to stay in Iraq. When we told her we planned to leave, she didn't refuse. She had to cope alone with seven children during the most difficult years, and it got harder, not easier, that we all gradually began to leave her and come to Israel, except for the youngest ones who stayed.

I escaped alone through Persia. I disguised myself as a Kurd and my mother cut a dinar in half, giving one half to me and keeping the other half for herself. The plan was that if the escape went okay, the Kurdish smuggler would bring my half back to her. We were very nervous, because at the time another group of Jews had been caught in the north. A Persian man took me over the border on a horse with my Kurdish smuggler as the Persians had no great love for Iraqis and were ready to assist us. In fact, the animosity between Iraqis and Persians was so strong that when we studied history in Iraq, we were told that the most contemptible people were Jews and then Persians, and that a Jew and a Persian dog carry the same value. It was December, before Hanukah, at the end of 1972. I was 26 years old.

I met my husband, Nissim, in a hostel as I was traveling from the border to Tehran. It happened like this: I saw a man with a Jewish face and we started talking. It turned out that he was escaping from Iraq, and he was with his family. His family couldn't believe that I had come on my own. So I traveled with them the rest of the way to Tehran. There, I met up with my brother, who had left shortly before me. In fact, many of my school friends were there—it was a huge reunion—and they were all waiting for the next plane to take them out. I was put up at the nicest hotels. It was like Paris! The hotels were filled with young men my age. Like Nissim and me, many couples met in Tehran or on the way there from the border. I had run away only with the clothes I was wearing—not even any food—so the Jewish Agency gave me a little money. Once in Israel I didn't have the difficult aliyah that those who came in the '50s had. I already had family in Israel, and an uncle from Ramat Gan who had fled in 1950 took me and my brother in. Nissim and I got married soon after.

My father and his brother were released from jail on January 11, 1971. They had only been allowed to change their clothes once in all those years. My father was in a horrible physical and mental state. His leg still needed to be amputated but he continued to refuse. He said, "If you take my leg, you might as well kill me, because I don't want to be without a leg." Both of their bank accounts had disappeared and their property was confiscated. In addition, all of my father's property—cash, land, assets, everything, was nationalized. We lost everything. They couldn't sell our houses and mother had spent whatever money they did have on lawyers and bribes. Both brothers were stripped of their passports. On July 23, 1973, father and mother fled Iraq for Israel with the rest of my siblings, also through Persia with the help of Kurdish smugglers.

Life in Israel was initially very difficult for my parents because they were not young and didn't know Hebrew, and my father was in no condition to work. Mother was 48 and father was 52. So they did volunteer work. My father had the status of "Prisoner of Zion," which enabled him to a monthly stipend from the government. He limped and lived with the pain in his leg until he died in 2001. He refused to use a wheelchair—just a cane. He shook uncontrollably and was a broken man the rest of his life, physically and emotionally. However, when he talked about his days in prison, he laughed at the brutality—he never cried. He was not a whiner. He was very defiant and never caved in, which is part of the reason the guards tortured him so much.

The irony is that despite the horror that my father endured, my mother, until today, has a soft spot in her heart for Saddam for sparing my father's life. Before he was hanged, when she saw him on television, she felt that she knew him.[18] She prayed that God would give him strength so that he would see the natural end of his days. She misses Iraq—misses the kind of high life she had there—and a big part of her yearns to go back despite the sorrow and pain.

Ronit and Nissim live in Ramat Gan. Ronit was a high school Arabic teacher and is now retired. The couple has one daughter. Ronit's mother Victoria died in June, 2007, soon after taking part in Ronit's interview.

* * *

Linda Masri Hakim was born in 1948 in Baghdad. She describes the good life in Iraq: her family lived on Baghdad's fanciest street and many of her family members were among the country's most influential citizens. The small, close-knit Jewish community she knew in Iraq left her with many happy and quirky memories—like when her father, frustrated at the lack of cleanliness at the last remaining kosher butcher, defiantly began slaughtering his own sheep, nearly causing havoc in the community. Masri Hakim and her family fled Iraq in 1972.

When members of my family spoke about their ancestors, they often spoke with great affection for a woman referred to simply as Bibi, a great-great auntie on my father's side who initiated a major positive change in the legal rights of widows in Iraq. Bibi, who was born in the mid-1800s and died in the 1920s, had been married to one of Menachem Daniel's brothers.[19] She was widowed at an early age and didn't have any children. At the time, Islamic law dictated that a widow could not receive any compensation from her husband's estate if she had no children. So Bibi fought through the courts with the support of her family. The man who changed the law as a result of her initiative was a Jewish judge and a law professor, Da'ud Samra.[20] He enacted new legislation declaring that a widow, regardless of whether she had any offspring, was eligible to receive a third of her husband's wealth, and when she died, that wealth would be distributed to her own family. My grandmother was one of the people who benefited from Bibi's wealth as a result of the change of the law and many people in my family had ownership of valuable land in Iraq because Bibi's husband's family were major landowners.

Bibi was also beloved by all the children in the family because she had a big swan as a pet which always sat on her lap. Whenever visitors came to her house—she had a big, beautiful house—the children used to congregate around her and the swan. For generations, everybody in the family remembered the swan.

At the turn of the century, my grandfather and his brothers founded the Masri Synagogue, which was dedicated to their father Nissim Masri. The government confiscated it when it wanted to build a road there. All the prayer books and the *sifrei torah* [Torah scrolls] were distributed to various synagogues. When we left Iraq in 1972, my father asked Meir Basri [then president of the Jewish community], who was married to his cousin, if we could take with us a *sefer torah* that belonged to the community because we had passports—we were one of the lucky ones who left Iraq by passport—so the trip would be smooth, by airplane. But Meir was worried that my father might be stopped at the airport by customs and searched and if they found the *sefer torah* we'd be turned around and possibly punished. That was a likely scenario, and an ironic one: the Iraqis did everything to destroy the Jewish community but it would recognize a Torah scroll as a precious item not to be removed from the country. I remember the two of them had an argument and my father told him, "I can tell the authorities if they ask that I pray with it every morning—that it's my prayer book." Meir didn't budge. In the end, nobody did search our suitcases. But I understand Meir's position: in those days we were all concerned about our safety first, not about any treasures or wealth or land or homes. We just wanted to leave.

My ancestors had a great life during the Ottoman Empire. My grandmother, who lived during that time, used to tell me that on Shabbat they used to go picnicking on the grounds of a mosque on the far bank of the Tigris River and she experienced total respect between themselves and the Muslims at moments like those. But when the British occupied the country, they caused divisions between the religions—a philosophy of divide and rule. I always say that I wish the Ottomans had never entered World War I. Then we would all still be under the Ottoman Empire. No Palestine, no Israel, no Iraq, and no Jordan—and perhaps greater tranquility.

I was born in August, 1948. The '50s were good days. We had a beautiful house and were very comfortable but my father nevertheless wanted to leave Iraq as well in 1951 and go to England, to join my maternal grandparents who had moved there in the '40s. But unfortunately the British government didn't give him a visa. Part of the reason for that was that British government didn't want any immigrants in those days, particularly any Jewish immigrants. My father then tried to go to Israel. But my aunty in Israel, his sister, told him "Don't come to Israel. Things are really bad here. Stay in Iraq." He said, "We'll come to Israel and wait there for a visa to England." And she said, "No, don't come at all." A few months later everybody forgot about the *taksin* [partition of Palestine in 1948] and normal life resumed again in Iraq.

My father had many opportunities to leave Iraq from 1950 until we finally left in 1972, but he didn't take them because he was happy and he was making a good living. He was a textile merchant, a wholesaler who imported men's clothing and sold it to shops, and we had property and a lifestyle that we knew we probably couldn't have anywhere else. Furthermore, we lived close to family in a tight-knit community. The house was always full of visitors—particularly on Jewish holidays, when the entire extended family gathered together. One day we'd go to one branch of the family and the next day the whole family would come to us. We used to sit all day long with the drinks and sweets, ready for people to come and knock at our door and visit. We looked forward to it immensely and used to really feel the holiday.

Because there were hardly any synagogues left in Baghdad during my childhood, for Rosh Hashana we used to go to a big garden with a tent and the men used to sit inside and pray and we children used to have a fantastic time playing in the garden. We called it the Alwiya Synagogue though it wasn't really a synagogue.

Modernity came late to Iraq—like refrigeration. Typically, the milkman would bring milk bottles to people's homes in the mornings, but my father knew that the milkmen often cheated by adding water. So when I was a child the milkman used to come every day with his own two cows and he used to milk the cows in front of the maid because my father worried that if the maid didn't watch him he might mix the milk with water. We had a tap in front of the house and when the milkman arrived the maids made sure he washed his hands properly and provided him with a white bucket for the milk.

One day my father went to the kosher butcher in the morning and he saw a rat in the store, and that was the end of my father buying his meat from that butcher. But there were no other kosher butchers anymore in Baghdad, so he and his cousin decided to take matters into their own hands. They began to go once a week to a farm in the area of New Baghdad to buy a sheep, and they brought *shochet* [kosher slaughterer] to our garden where he slaughtered the sheep. They also brought a man whose task was to examine that the *shochet* did his job properly—that the slaughtered sheep was indeed kosher. Then my father and his cousin divided the meat between the two families, and the next week they did the same thing again.

Then, on the third week, they brought the sheep and the *shochet* slaughtered it but the examiner announced, "This sheep is not kosher." The examiner took the sheep away with him because we were not allowed to eat it. The same thing happened the next week. My father and his cousin knew there was something funny going on between the *shochet* and the butcher and the examiner. They realized that the butcher, who worked with the examiner, worried that if my father was doing this, every other Jewish family would start to do the same and it would destroy the butcher's business.

So my father went to plan B. The next week, they brought another sheep home. I should add that we would slaughter them within the first 24 hours, otherwise we grew attached to them and they became pets and we couldn't bear to slaughter them. We did keep pet sheep in our garden and as kids we used to feed them. Anyway, this time they brought only the *shochet* (who was not Jewish), without the examiner. But my grandmother, who lived with us, was very religious so my father pretended that the sheep had been examined and was kosher.

Two days later our doorbell rang. I answered the door—it was the male servant of the chief rabbi, Sasson Khedouri. He said, "Hakham wants to speak to your father. Can your father come and see him?" I ran to tell my father and he wondered aloud, "What does the Hakham want from me?" The Hakham lived on our street and he was a good friend of the family.

My father went to see him and the rabbi said, "What are you trying to do? Are you trying to close down our butcher? Stop this nonsense immediately." So my father told him, "I saw a rat in his store. I refuse to buy meat from that butcher unless he improves the cleanliness. Otherwise I'm going to buy non-kosher meat." My father didn't want to create a big problem by continuing to boycott the butcher, so he started going back there. I think later on the butcher sort of improved the place.

Life on the Best Street in Baghdad

In my parents' generation, all the marriages were arranged. Only very rarely would you hear a story about a man and a woman falling in love and getting married. The upper class always intermarried with the upper class, the middle with the middle, and the lower with the lower. A matchmaker would set up a couple who would meet in a department store in the afternoon and if they liked each other, the matchmaker would bring a rabbi in the evening and they would all go to go to the girl's house and hold a simple engagement party. Then the couple would distribute sugar almonds and Turkish Delight to the houses of family and friends and announce the wedding.

Simple as that. The wedding was usually a very plain affair. A half-hour ceremony would take place at a synagogue—no speeches, nothing. The big affair was the henna, two or three days before the wedding, when the whole community would be invited. There would be a lavish party at night that was the equivalent of a wedding party today. There would be belly dancers and singers and a beautiful dinner.

Marriages stayed together better than they do now. Nobody divorced, and if the husband or wife was unhappy, they had to live with it and get on with life. My parents were set up with each other. My mother told me that when she was of marrying age, her parents tried to marry her off to a businessman and my dad fit the bill. They never considered professionals like doctors or lawyers or engineers or accountants because they didn't make enough money. My parents were married for over 50 years until my father died. I call that a good marriage.

My mother didn't have to cook or clean: we had cooks and maids and nannies and other servants. In mother's youth everybody had Jewish maids. But all of the Jewish maids left in 1951 for Israel so everybody who stayed had no choice but to hire non-Jews. So as a child, I had non-Jewish servants, mostly Christians from the north of Iraq. They were all good, honest people who worked hard. My grandmother used to stay with them in the kitchen and trained them to make Iraqi Jewish food and they were very good at it. We also had a woman come to wash the clothes because we didn't have a washing machine and it was a long process including walking up 72 steps to the roof to hang the clothes to dry. We had drivers and servants who did our shopping. When she got to England, my mother had been so spoiled that when my father brought home a chicken for her to cook she asked him, "There are only two legs here. Where are the other two legs?"

In our household my father was a very strict man. While he used to work with Muslims in his office, he never mixed business with pleasure and we never had Muslim or Christian guests in the house. Likewise, we usually weren't invited to their homes. However, we weren't really typical: many of my Jewish friends had Muslim friends and used to go to their houses to visit them, and vice versa.

My house was next door to the French embassy. It was the fanciest residential street in Baghdad, which everyone used to refer to as "the street of the Lawee house." The Lawee family built a big palace there, which, unfortunately, they hardly lived in because they left after the Farhoud and immigrated to Canada. They left it to the French embassy. We were separated from the Lawee house by one house. I was inside it several times as a little girl. It was a palace, a magnificent place. The Lawee house was so well known that what I got into a taxi to go home I didn't tell the driver my home address—instead I just said, "Take me to the Lawee street."

In between our house and the Lawee house were the Pashas. The Pashas were Muslims from Turkey who came to Iraq when King Faisal I was installed so the head of the family would serve as his mentor. Pasha meant "king" in Turkish and Persian and it was a title given to generals and governors. The Pashas maintained a close friendship with the royal family and when I was a child, King Faisal II used to visit them frequently. Sometimes, when they ran out of tea cups, the Pashas would come and borrow teacups from our house to serve tea to the king. Jewish homes always had the best silver and china, and everyone knew that.

The Pashas were the only Muslims who were allowed in our house. The wife of the governor often visited our house and she was a great friend of my grandmother's. She used to bring two handbags with her: one with money and the other with all the keys to her cupboards because when she left the house she used to lock up everything and nobody, not even her servants, was allowed to open the cupboards.

We had nice memories of the Pashas, but they left before the revolution in 1958. Had they been there then, they would have been killed along with the king because they were close associates of the royal family.[21] When the Pashas left, their house also became part of the French embassy so then we were living next door to the embassy. That wasn't always a good thing. After the Six Day War, there was a lot of security around the embassy and I was even too scared to go to the balcony of our house because security men were all over the street and they used to sit outside our front door. They were Saddam's henchmen, not French security, and they were there just in case some of us, Jews, would go to the embassy and report the persecution of the Jewish community. So we were terrified to even look at the embassy lest they think we were even thinking about going in. We turned our heads in a different direction when we passed by it. All the spies roaming around all over the place outside knew everything about each one of my family members, and that was scary.

We probably had one of the most valuable houses in Baghdad at the time but we never tried to get restitution for our house and other property. My husband filled in property restitutions forms for his family's property, but I have never bothered because I know it's a waste of time. No one will fulfill the Jews' claims. We are just a minority that most Iraqis still hate. I'll tell you something about the Iraqi Jews—in fact, probably about Jews in general. We never look back. We always look forward. I'm not going to go back and claim a house which used to be mine 40 or 50 years ago. I really couldn't care less. I live for the future. The European Jews were the same way after the Holocaust. If you look back, you never go forward.

When I was a child, we had the freedom to travel abroad, but there was still so much anti-Semitism. I recall that when I was five years old, my brother was in diapers when we went to Europe. Before we boarded the plane at the Baghdad airport, the officers undid his diaper to check whether my mother had hidden money or jewelry inside—just because we were Jews. Whenever we went abroad, they used to take my coat off and search the hems and the hems of my dresses for valuables too.

Qassem, a socialist, abolished all these practices when he came into power. He expressed the view that Jews were equal to everyone else in the population. Many Jews took advantage of that period and left Iraq. That's the irony, of course. And some people who forgot about all their miseries and whose business flourished then—my father was among them—stayed. But the wise people sold their houses and property, took their money and belongings and left. There were still limits on the amount of money one could take out of the country, but people were able to smuggle out money with ease.

When I was young, there were only two Jewish schools, and I went to both: Menachem Daniel and Frank Iny. Menachem Daniel had a fantastic nursery and kindergarten. We used to have British teachers to teach us English and French teachers from France and Lebanon teach us French. It was in large part because the Jews experienced persecution for so long at the hands of the Arabs that the Jewish community made multilingualism a high priority. We knew that we must prepare ourselves for living outside of Iraq. I remember when I got sick and my mother would keep me at home for the day I used to cry. It was that nice. We learned French, English, and Arabic starting at the age of five.

I have good and bad memories of the Frank Iny School. Bad memories because it was such a strict school with a strict headmaster, but the educational level was very high. Also, things were changing in Iraq and nobody was in the mood to study. We were concerned with our safety and I became preoccupied with leaving Iraq. So I was never happy there. But in 1963 when the Ba'ath Party briefly came into power, President Aref[22] wouldn't allow the Jews to travel. We were held as prisoners in our own country. And this is how I grew up starting from the age of 13, chained to a country I desperately wanted to leave.

The End of Tranquility

I was 18 when I took my high school matriculation exams, which began on the first day of the Six Day War. The woman who came to monitor the series of exams was a Muslim. All of us Jewish girls were sitting next to each other and we were all light-skinned, some blonde, some pretty, and all of us were clever. This woman used to tell the other monitors, who were also Muslim, "What a shame she is Jewish," pointing to one of the girls. "What a shame she is Jewish," pointing to me, as if I were invisible and deaf. To them, a Jew was a dog, a monkey, a donkey, and lots of Jewish girls used to hear the words this monitor said repeated in other settings. The monitor said to me several times, "Why don't you become a Muslim? I have a brother whom you can marry. What a shame you are a Jew!" This is how they used to look at us. Our headmaster, Abdullah Obadiah, heard about the monitors' comments and he sent us a message through his daughter, who was also taking the exams, not to respond to them. This is why my father never wanted me to mix or mingle with the Muslims. He was always fearful of them. And whenever there was a coup or a revolution or turmoil in the government, he would tell us all to sleep with our clothes on, ready to leave if need be, because of his bad memories of the Farhoud.

On our last day of our exam [Egyptian President Gamel Abdel] Nasser resigned.[23] The news sparked massive demonstrations against his resignation across Baghdad but the biggest mob gathered in Sahdi Tahrir, Liberation Square. We were taking our exams on the balcony of Rahbad, a prestigious Christian government-run school which overlooked the river and the square. As we tried to concentrate on our exams, we saw people were congregating by the thousands in Sahdi Tahrir. As usual in any mass protest in Iraq in my lifetime, the mob began to chant, "Death to Israel!" and "Death to the Jews!"

The Muslim girls didn't want to finish the exams and instead wanted to join the demonstration so they started calling to people from the street to come into the school. The girls teased us and called us names—"You Zionists," "Golda Meir," et cetera. Those girls would have killed us if they could have. The girls and the boys used to take the exams separately so only the girls were there that day, and there were about 16 girls, half of whom were Jewish. But when the hooligans entered the school, the Muslim girls got so caught up in their actions that they forgot to tell them that we were Jews! Only their stupidity saved us. Had the demonstrators known we were Jewish they would have thrown each one of us over the balcony to our deaths. Meanwhile, the demonstrators entered the school like hooligans and destroyed everything—the chairs, the desks, our exam papers. They tore up our exams and anything they could get their hands on.

We took advantage of a moment when they were not paying attention to us and quickly ran out of the school. We mixed among the demonstrators and then met somewhere and all of the sudden we saw Abdullah Obadiah, our headmaster. He had anticipated a problem and was waiting for us in his Volkswagen Beetle, that small car that seats only three or four people. I don't know how many girls got into that car but we certainly beat the Guinness Book of World Records' record for the number of people to squeeze into a Beetle! He took each one of us to our own houses. Meanwhile, the demonstrators destroyed Rahbad.

If it were not for the voices of Golda Meir, Aba Eban, and Gideon Rafael I do not believe that I would have survived to tell my story today. I remember huddling up by the radio with my family to hear these Israeli figures standing up for us and insisting the world recognize our plight. It was their voices that gave us hope in those dark days and kept us going despite the attempts of the Iraqi government to stop us from listening to the Voice of Israel radio in Arabic by constantly interfering with the radio frequency.

It was then that my family began to consider leaving Iraq. My father closed his business when his license was confiscated and hid away at home, out of sight, fearing that he would be jailed. He spent day after day in the house—he was too scared to venture out. Many of his Jewish colleagues who continued to try to work were arrested and jailed. After the war, when I walked in the street, the Muslims would call me "Golda Meir." Every woman, every girl, was Golda Meir. And every man was Moshe Dayan. We used to hear the same pathetic mantra from the Arabs around us: "Israel, that tiny, illegitimate country! All the Arabs will unite and take it back just like that. In a half hour we can conquer it and we can take our land back!"

After passing my matriculation exams, I graduated from Frank Iny, and that year Jews weren't allowed to go to university. So we stayed at home and I studied by correspondence with the Sorbonne University in Paris. Each one of us who graduated that year did something just to occupy him or herself. And then the Jewish schools couldn't get any more teachers from abroad and funds were running short too because the government confiscated a big chunk of the money in the community trust that used to provide for the schools. So Abdullah Obadiah asked all of us who graduated that year to teach. I taught French to the primary school children. Some of my friends taught physics, others chemistry, and so on.

After the hangings of January 27, 1969, it became even clearer to us that we must leave Iraq, as it became clear to all the Jews. The issue, of course, was how. At the time, the Interior Ministry was giving passports only to Jews over 60. So my grandmother left in the summer of 1971. But the community as a whole was growing increasingly desperate. So in December, 1971, some of us decided that a group of 25 women and teenage girls would go to the Interior Ministry to try to get passports for our families. My mum and I went without telling my father—he would have forbidden us to go if he knew our plan, as it was hardly a safe thing to do. In fact, none of the women told their family members. We thought our chances were better if just the women went, and the men wouldn't dare to venture there anyway because they could have quite easily been thrown in jail.

We all had letters in hand asking the minister to grant us passports to leave Iraq. At that point, the treatment of the Jewish community had improved ever so slightly. In fact, we got the sense that they were giving us a little bit of encouragement to do something like this. We told the policeman standing guard that we wished to see the minister. He went in, came back, and said, "Yes, the minister would like to see you." All the women pushed forward to get in. He said, "Hold on, hold on. I can't take everybody." I was chosen to go in along with three other women. One of them kissed the minister's shoes. I stood there a bit stunned—I wasn't going to kiss even his hand! Then, this woman told him, *Saidi* [my master], we want to leave. The minister stood up and said, "I have no objection. I don't care. I will give you all passports. Give me your letters."

He looked at me and said, "My sister, it is fine with us if you want to leave. Even if you want to go to Israel, you can go to Israel." Just like that. He explained that we'd all receive our passports the next day. But of course, how many times had various officials said that to so many Jews and then never followed through? So we thought it was one of their performances. We gave him the letters and thanked him without feeling either excitement or disappointment. He told us that the next day the ministry would publish a list of names of people who could claim their passports which would be posted on a wall outside the ministry.

My mum and I returned home and I immediately told my father what we had done. I was emboldened by the minister's positive response and felt compelled to tell my father what we did because we had come back safely. My father said, "The minister is joking. You know it can't be serious."

But on the following day, we heard that the names of every woman in the group appeared on a list of eligible passport holders outside the ministry, and it meant their families were eligible as well. My father went to the passport office and picked up our passports and within a week, we were gone. We left on January 2, 1972. We didn't want to waste any time because we feared that at any moment the authorities could change their minds and withdraw the passports. I remember hearing a few months later that the government stopped granting passports again.[24]

We came to England on one of the first direct flights from Baghdad to London. It took us four and half hours, compared to the 18 hours it once took me on visits to England as a little girl. I still feel very emotional about that flight. Saddam's guys came up to the airplane as we boarded to look at us one by one, though they were not allowed on the plane because it was a foreign flight. Just to terrify us, they said, "We're going to call some of you to come back down off the plane." Indeed, they called back one young man, who used to be a classmate of mine, though he managed to get out on the same flight the following week. It was just a move meant to shake him up and rattle all of us. After we took off and we saw the desert of Iraq below us, my father told us, "Only when we see the white mountains of Lebanon and Turkey, covered with snow, can we breathe easy and say we are free, because until then they can turn the airplane around and bring us back."

I regret leaving Iraq so late, as did my father. We had a golden opportunity in the '60s when my mother was in England for six months. But only once I moved to England did I realize how comfortable our lives had been in Iraq. My mother couldn't cook and didn't know how to do lots of household things, and we couldn't afford in England the staff that we could in Iraq. It was a big upheaval for us—different social life, friends, environment, climate. It wasn't easy. But I was young at the time, 23, and had an easier adjustment than my parents and my grandmother who had to adapt at late ages. Yet for years after arriving in the UK my heart would race when I would see a policeman because I couldn't rid myself of the fear that the Iraqi secret police had installed in me.

After coming here, I wanted to start a new life, and forget the past, so I didn't speak much about my childhood in Iraq. Only after the fall of Saddam did my husband and I begin to talk about Iraq. Then it became an explosion of expression among many Iraqi Jews. And it was a relief. I, like my other friends, still have nightmares about being stuck in Iraq. When I wake up, I touch my pillow and say, "Thank God I'm not in Iraq." I would like to close the book on our history in Iraq and forget about perpetuating the memory. This is my attitude because we can't go back to Iraq in the same way that the European Jews can go back to Europe after the Holocaust. For us, there is no point in maintaining Arabic and in keeping history alive, because all we have, sadly, is a history we can read about in books. My children can't go back and see where I was born, the school I went to. Everything is destroyed, everything is gone forever.

Linda's husband Ramzi Hakim emigrated from Iraq to England alone as a 12-year-old, when he was sent to boarding school by his father who saw no future for him in Iraq. Ramzi was reunited with his parents at age 23, when they finally were able to join him in London. Linda and Ramzi were classmates at the Menachem Daniel School. They live in London and have three children.

* * *

Aida Zelouf is the daughter of Meir Basri, the last official head of the Jewish community in Iraq. In her account, Zelouf describes her father—eminent businessman, author and poet, community leader, and family man—who was born in 1911 and died in 2006 in London at the age of 94. Zelouf recalls the waning days of the community. She was one of a few hundred Jews who remained after the second large exodus in the years following the Six Day War.

After graduating from the Alliance school for boys in 1928, Meir Basri worked as secretary to the Foreign Ministry and Chief of Protocol. When Nazism began to infiltrate the country in the early 1930s, Jewish loyalty became suspect and he was transferred to a lesser post in the Ministry of Post and Telegraph. Later, he became deputy supervisor of the Stock Exchange and secretary of the Chamber of Commerce, where he founded and edited the chamber's monthly magazine in Arabic and English. In 1943, he became the director of the Baghdad Chamber of Commerce. During World War II he was appointed to the post of secretary and member of various government committees concerning commerce and food supply. In 1945, he left the Chamber of Commerce to direct the Eastern Commercial Cooperation, and was elected a member of the General District Committee and of the Administrative Board of the District of Baghdad. After the creation of Israel, Jews were thrown out of public sector jobs but he managed to hold on to several government positions including assistant director general of the Date Association of Iraq, a major commercial role since dates were the country's major export together with oil; and was Director of Commerce and Publicity.[25]

His real love, however, was the written word, and he composed his own poetry and translated famous French, English, and Hebrew writers to Arabic. As a teenager, he composed poetry in French and Hebrew and was influenced by Bialik and Tschernichowsky,[26] *as well as by the French and English romantic poets. He also studied Arabic poetry, and he became one of the leading romantic poets in Iraq. He was the first to introduce the form of the Western sonnet into Arabic poetry, and composed two epics and various lyrical poems. He wrote well over 20 books on a spectrum of subjects, including many biographies of prominent people in art, politics, and literature, as well as his own short stories and poems that received favorable reviews in Arab countries. He also wrote articles for newspapers and magazines, many of which he read on Baghdad radio, and gave talks on the BBC and Israeli radio on current affairs and literature.*[27]

My grandparents on both sides came from very large families and they were able to trace their lineage back hundreds of years. Both sides of my dad's family, the Basris on his dad's side and the Dangoors on his mum's, were descended from pious rabbis. His maternal grandfather was the chief rabbi, Hakham Ezra Ben Reuben Dangoor. There were also many successful merchants among them too, and my paternal grandfather used to import swords, medals, and army uniforms during the Ottoman Empire. He died young and my father, who was 16 years old at the time, together with his brother, began looking after the family: their mother as well as their sisters who were not yet married and two younger brothers.

My dad in his heart was very Iraqi. He loved the language, history, and culture, and this was evident in his poetry and books. He relished the fact that the Jews had over 2,500 years of history in Iraq, and that he could trace his ancestry very far back.

My parents married right after the hanging of Shafiq Adas in October, 1948, so they made it a small affair in my mother's family garden. They didn't think it would have been appropriate to have a big wedding and they didn't want to bring attention to themselves as Jews.

When I was born in 1953, life was simple and easy. I have three sisters and dad's sister lived with us. We had servants, a driver, and a gardener. My mother, Marcelle, cooked, but she didn't have to go shopping herself. We lived very close to my grandparents—there was just one house between us. And we always spent time at my cousins' house. One of my favorite memories of Iraq was the *chagim* [Jewish holidays]. The whole family went from one house to another visiting each other. That was one of those wonderful things that I miss today. At Passover, we used to make everything at home, including the grape juice. We made date syrup from the 12 types of grapes my maternal grandfather grew in his garden. The garden was so massive it was more like a farm. Everything we ate was handmade and home-made, because large extended families lived together so there was always a lot of help. I also miss Purim when we used to play card games like *Dosa* and *Naqish Yehud* and go from one party to another for two days. I miss sleeping on top of the flat roof the whole summer until Succoth, watching the sky, moon, and the stars.

I loved my schools. At the Menachem Daniel primary school, we had a wonderful Armenian headmistress who dedicated her life to the school, which was really amazing because she was not Jewish. I continued my studies at Frank Iny and Shammash.[28] They were both wonderful places but it was sad for us to think that there were once dozens of Jewish schools in Baghdad including yeshivot. When the community dwindled and the other schools, Jewish clubs, and most synagogues shut down, Frank Iny became the center of Jewish life in the '60s. All the Jewish weddings and major community events were held there, and we went there during holidays to play on the beautiful grounds. Our friendships between classmates were so close that we still keep in touch to this day.

My mother's aunt, Masouda Sasson Sehayek, opened a school called Hagouli's Atelier for poor Jewish girls where they learned embroidery, dress-making, and tailoring. The girls did the most beautiful embroidery using real gold thread. When women in the community got married, they used to have their clothes, nightdresses, sheets, and tablecloths custom-made at the *atelier*, which also produced beautiful cases for *ketubot* [Jewish wedding certificates] which were embroidered with gold. They were really gorgeous. But this whole art has been lost.

It was a shock to the community when President Qassem announced his plans to bulldoze the Jewish cemetery which was over 600 years old. My dad once told me the story of how the cemetery was created. It was a tale told through the centuries by the Jews of Baghdad: the Shiite Persians captured Baghdad in 1624 and held it for 14 years, spoiling the city, killing their foes the Sunni Muslims, and desecrating their shrines. When Sultan Murad IV heard in Istanbul that the city had fallen to his loathsome enemies, he came with a large army intending to invade it. Before his attack, in order to assess the size and characteristics of the city, he decided to enter the city gate disguised as a dervish.

He walked through the streets and came to a house in the Jewish ghetto where he smelled fresh bread being baked. He thought that if he were given a whole unbroken loaf it would be a good omen. He knocked on the door. An old woman opened it and invited him to enter. He told her that he was a poor, tired dervish. She welcomed him and gave him a whole loaf of hot bread. She then invited him to stay the night. The next morning he returned to his army and, in a few days time, took Baghdad and expelled the invaders. He returned to the woman's house and revealed his true identity and inquired whether she had any favor to ask of him. She said, "We are poor Jews and have no private cemetery for the community. We would like a cemetery." Murad IV ordered that a spacious area near the city gate be assigned to the Jews for the burial of their dead.

So when Qassem ordered the bones removed and the place bulldozed, it was a horrendous thing for the community. Not all the bones could be salvaged in time, and the remains of hundreds of thousands of our ancestors were destroyed. The period of his presidency was otherwise good for the Jews, but everything changed for us when his government was overthrown in February, 1963. Dad was the managing director of the Chevrolet and Buick franchises in Iraq, and the government nationalized the company. As children, we used to go to his office and everybody adored us: we were the boss' girls. But that month, I remember my mum saying, "Dad is out of a job." Things became horrible. Most Jews were without jobs then, but somehow we managed to carry on. My dad turned to his writing and to assisting the Jewish community in an honorary way.

The Six Day War and its reverberations in Iraq changed our lives completely. The Jewish sports club we went to, which was built by the Daniel family

[Ezra Menachem Daniel Sports Club] was taken over by the government. Telephone lines were cut, Jews were excluded from all clubs and universities, and kicked out of jobs in the public and private sectors. We were excluded from literally everything. My eldest sister was taking her baccalaureate exam in 1967 when her class was attacked by a mob. All the students ran away, scared to death.

Because we could not use our phones we met in groups of families and friends even more frequently to exchange news and socialize. But my memories of these difficult days are bittersweet, not bitter: because the community was so small, it was extremely close, and that was really wonderful. It was nice to spend time with my best friends as we did our dress-making and knitting together, especially during the long summer holidays.

Days of Anguish

I remember all the propaganda on the radio in 1967 when it was announced, "We are killing Israelis! We bombed Israel! We shot down all their airplanes!" We didn't know it was all lies, and we were really petrified because if Iraq wiped out Israel, God forbid, we [the Iraqi Jews] would be next. Then they began to rounded up the Jews and put them in prison, saying, "We're just protecting you." My father-in-law was imprisoned three times and each time was told it was for his own protection. Even very old people were imprisoned, including my dad's uncle, Eliahou Dangoor.

My dad did a great deal for the community, especially in this period when so many people needed help. As chairman of the Jewish Schools Committee, he fought the government when it took hold of the community's trusts and refused to release them. He put a lot of sweat into solving that issue—in the meantime, money was needed to help secure the release of relatives from prison, to feed the poor and to run the schools. Those trusts were critical in the post-1967 years because so many Jews had lost their jobs and began to depend on these trusts which were supported by the richest Jews. My dad, together with the community's secretary Naji Chachak and others, went to see Saddam Hussein or the relevant minister whenever they wanted to plead for the release of imprisoned Jews or imprisoned members of the community or learn the fate of those who had disappeared.

Our most pressing problem became that we couldn't leave: we were denied passports. In increasing numbers, our friends began to leave illegally across the southern border, through Basra, or through the northern Kurdish areas. I would go to school and come home to find friends had packed up and left, and I'd go to school one day with a friend who didn't show up the next day—and I knew he or she was gone. It was terrible for children, especially, to lose their friends that way.

We had a driver who used to take us back and forth to school and starting in the end of 1968, when the arrests of Jews were becoming rampant, we would come home from school and immediately lock the door and close the shutters. We stopped playing outside. We were even scared that people could hear us talking through the windows. It was just terrifying. We used to turn on Israeli radio to hear Ibin Al Rafidain, a Jew who was born in Baghdad and who spoke beautifully in Arabic about the corruption and anti-Semitism of the Iraqi government, teasing the government in a very bad way. Even the Muslims in Iraq used to listen to him. But in this period we stopped listening to him, too, out of fear.

On January 1, 1969, which was a Shabbat, dad was arrested on false accusations of spying and imprisoned for two months—55 days to be exact. On that day, only my mum and I were in the house. I was 14 at the time. The moment we opened the door, the officers said, "We have a warrant to search the house." I'll never forget that day. It is the most horrible memory I have. Loads of men from the secret police came inside. My dad came back home with his sister and my sisters shortly after. The police searched for hours, until 2 o'clock in the morning. They just wanted documents—any kind of evidence—that they could use against dad. They even searched through the rubbish bins for anything "incriminating" we had written down and discarded. They found a photograph of me and some of my friends at a picnic which I had just received that day from a friend. I had stuck a piece of paper on it as I didn't want anyone to see something that was written on the back. But the police saw the picture covered up like that and accused me of trying to hide critical evidence: at the time, the government was using random photographs of Jews as bogus evidence that the people in them were spies against Iraq and then would arrest them.

The police started screaming that they were going to put me in prison too because of that photo. It was very, very frightening. I was screaming at the top of my lungs. Eventually, my dad had to shout at them and say, "Stop! She is really scared. Don't do that to her." They took dad and the picture and said they were going to come back to finish searching the house. Eight months later I heard that the security official who had searched our house was still asking about me and I think it was a miracle that I escaped arrest.

We were only allowed to see dad once a month, on the first of the month. I went with my mum and my eldest sister to the jail where he was being held, the prison of Al Amn. When we saw him for the first time, dad was fraction of his original size. And he was so worried about us—worried how we were faring without him. Every night, he slept on the floor with his shoes as a pillow on the rock-hard floor. Many people around him had been interrogated and tortured but he always told us that he wasn't tortured.

My sisters and I were followed often. One day I was followed so closely that I jumped out of the double-decker bus I was on in order to get home fast, but the man managed to get off behind me. He caught up with me and got hold of me. I tried to escape from his grip and started screaming and nearly got killed crossing the road. He and the others who followed me could have caught me if they really wanted to but I guess their purpose was to scare me more than anything else. I never even told my parents about this incident. Jewish females were generally nervous about being followed because in addition to all the anti-Semitism, there was also lots of harassment of women, and many of the Jewish women were fair and blonde and good-looking, which were sought-after qualities in Iraq.

A month after dad's arrest came the January, 1969, hangings. We were at home that day and watched the hangings on television. We locked everything—doors, windows—and didn't leave the house. We didn't know what would happen next. Thousands of people went to the square to see the bodies, and everyone was cheering wildly, so we feared a pogrom. It was particularly scary because dad was in jail and until we heard the names of the victims we worried that he might be one of them.

During the time dad was in prison, the government compiled a propaganda booklet in English with interviews of many Jews who were imprisoned, which included an interview with him. Each of them said that "life is wonderful," and Jews were living well in Iraq. The purpose of the book was to show that Jews were equal citizens and that only spies for Israel were traitors and were being hanged. Finally, dad was released because a Jewish friend of his had written a poem expressing how much both of them loved Iraq and brought it to one of the government ministers. So one day, just because of his association with the man, some guards called him and said, "Don't you want to leave?" And he said, "Yes, of course."

I believe he was put in prison to shut him up during the time of the hangings because at the same time the son of the Hakham Sasson Khedouri was also imprisoned in Kasr al Nahaya for a whole year and tortured badly. So I suppose the idea was to shut up the Jewish leadership which in turn would make all the Jews too terrified to speak up. Dad was known for always speaking out in defense of the Jews. He continued to do so, even when he got out of prison.

In June, 1971, he was elected honorary president of the community and chairman of the Jewish Council of Iraq following the death of Hakham Khedouri. In that capacity, until our departure, he was often in daily contact with the various authorities to help secure the release of Jews who had been imprisoned and inquire about those who had been kidnapped or killed. He wrote numerous articles in the Iraqi and international press defending their cases and demanding that the government restore the Jews' civil rights, including allowing them to work and travel freely. He defended the Jews as loyal Iraqi citizens and set the record straight in the face of false accusations and assaults against them. He condemned discrimination and hatred against minorities, not only Jews. He said many things that others were afraid to say but his status gave him the ability to say it and be heard by the right people—though clearly the forces of evil ultimately won out.

The Bitter End

After his release, I was desperate to leave. Our lives had become completely paralyzed. In 1971, I was one of 30 Jewish students who had graduated from high school; 29 of them left Iraq during that summer. I was the only one left and I became the only Jewish student to attend university that year. I had Muslim and Christian friends at the university, but I was terribly lonely and sad to have lost all my Jewish friends.

We could not go anywhere or do anything without being followed. The security officer was still following me and asking questions about me, months after dad's release. We were always afraid that undercover police were behind the windows listening to what we were saying. And the police started imprisoning and killing girls. In one of the most horrible incidents of my time, the Kashkush family was killed in their home in April, 1973, the day before their planned journey from the country. They even had their passports and tickets and their bags were packed. One of the daughters in the family, by chance, attended her classes at the university that day and when she returned there was blood all over the house and her family was gone. Their bodies had been taken away—no one ever saw them again. Luckily a woman in the community hid this daughter, and who managed to leave Iraq.

With great difficulties, some Jews managed to get passports starting in 1972 and up till the Yom Kippur War in October, 1973. To do so, you had to go through the channels of security and police—you couldn't simply apply for a passport and leave. My parents-in-law managed to get passports and left for England to be with their children. In 1973, we had passports and applied for a permit to leave, which was granted; however, we were not quick enough to leave and the Yom Kippur War broke out and our window of opportunity disappeared. At that point, the community probably consisted of about 250 people. Dad felt an obligation to them. I think he could not bear the thought of leaving anyone behind.

After the war, my parents used to sit with several other families on Saturday mornings to relax and talk. One day, an elderly woman asked dad, "What happened to your passports? Is it true that we are really not allowed to leave?" My parents told them, "It is true. However, you can tell anybody this, but don't tell Aida." I wasn't there—I learned about this conversation over a month later. One night, after pleading with my parents to leave, my dad told me that we couldn't. I cried until 4 o'clock in the morning. I felt that all the doors were closed in front of me. The next morning I had an exam, which I could not even study for as I was so distraught.

But then one fateful day after travel restrictions had loosened slightly, my dad went with Naji Chachak to a minister's office and while they were waiting to go in, Naji peeked over the shoulder of a clerk who was typing a confidential letter: it turned out it was about my dad aiding Zionists and Israel. The clerk quickly removed the letter from the typewriter and told Naji to go away, explaining that it was a secret letter.

That day, my dad came home and, standing at the kitchen door, announced to my mum, "We are leaving on Tuesday." He didn't tell us about the letter—we learned later that this is what spurred his urgency to leave. My mum said, "No, next week," or something like that. So we stayed another week. We packed the few belongings that we were allowed to take. The few books and family photos had to be stamped by the Ministry of Information. It was Succot. A Muslim girl, a friend of mine from the university, came to visit me and we had to cover all the suitcases with tablecloths and blankets so she wouldn't see them. I was petrified that word would get out that we were leaving and someone would prevent us from doing so at the last minute.

Finally, the day of our departure came. I went to class the day before, then pretended I was ill and returned home. We took a few suitcases, locked up the house, and didn't look back. After we had gone about five of my friends from university came to the house looking for me. I know this piece of the story because after my dad passed away one of my former classmates, a Muslim woman, had read the obituaries about him in an Arabic newspaper and managed to track me down. She said, "I've been looking for you for 31 years." She had left Iraq and was living in Sweden. I asked her, "What happened after I left?" She said, "We went to the house and your neighbors came out and they were crying and told us that your whole family had left with your luggage. And we started crying too."

She left Iraq in 1990 after marrying a Kurd who was in our class and they lived for a long time in Kurdistan before emigrating. As Communists, they were condemned to death and they fled to Sweden. She was only one of my many Muslim and Christian friends, and my dad had many, many more of course. But, unfortunately, when it came to the crunch and he was in prison, none of them wanted to help. They were either scared or pretended they didn't know what had happened to him.

Our plane stopped in Beirut, then again in Greece and we changed planes again in Switzerland. Then we flew to Amsterdam. While we were flying, we were scared that somehow we'd be turned around and forced to go back. When we landed in Switzerland, it felt wonderful—it was our first taste of freedom. I remember very clearly seeing someone wearing a *Magen David* [Star of David, a Jewish symbol]. It felt like a miracle to see one out in the open like that. I exclaimed to my parents: "Look what she is wearing!" So when we arrived in Amsterdam, the first thing I bought was a *Magen David* necklace.

Towards the end of his life, my dad became intent on setting the record straight about why the Jews of Iraq had left: whether it was the creation of Israel, Nazi-influenced anti-Semitism in Iraq, or Arab nationalism. For decades, the familiar Iraqi and Arab account was that Jews lived in peace in Iraq and it was the Zionists that caused the demise of the community by extracting them from their land and bringing them to Israel. Dad spoke vociferously about how it was not a Zionist plot but rather brewing Arab nationalism, exacerbated by Nazi influences, that caused the Jews to leave. The Iraqi government continued to identify its Jewish population with Israel and took out its anger against Israel on the local Jews, and Israeli emissaries who helped the Jews leave in the 1940s and through the end of Operation Ezra and Nehemiah helped a population in distress to leave. His views not only contradicted the classic Iraqi and Arab nonsense, but also the traditional Israeli-Zionist narrative which tends to promote the idea that all the Jews of Iraq were Zionist and the Zionist operatives helped them to fulfill their dreams of aliyah. My dad consistently stuck to his belief that the Jews of Iraq were loyal Iraqi citizens who, because of the persecution they faced, were forced to leave their homeland.

His identification with the people of Iraq was clear to everyone even after his death: his memorial service was attended by as many Muslims and Christians as by Jews. He had helped many Muslims in many ways in Iraq, and continued to do so here in London, in business, academic work, and daily life.

Four Muslims who attended the service, which was conducted in Arabic, gave moving speeches in which they said wonderful things about dad. They praised him, but they also praised the Jews of Iraq—what the community had done and what a loss it was for Iraq to have expelled nearly all its Jewish population. Their regret at the loss of the Jews was obvious. At the service, one Muslim cleric approached my daughter and said, "You know, you were so lucky to have had a grandfather who had such a wealth of knowledge, and he didn't differentiate between Jews and Christians and Muslims. He would sit with us and speak to us like he was one of us."

In an obituary about Meir Basri written by Professor Shmuel Moreh, Moreh called Basri "the last advocate of Jewish Iraqi patriotism." Aida and her husband Freddy Zelouf have three children and live in London.

* * *

Richard Obadiah is the son of Abdullah Obadiah, the last headmaster of the Frank Iny School, the last Jewish school in Iraq. Abdullah was also one of Iraq's most prominent mathematics professors until the 1980s, teaching high government officials in many Iraqi governments.

Richard was born in the Bustan Al Khas neighborhood of Baghdad in 1949 and left Iraq in 1971, and was himself a student at Frank Iny. Richard describes how his father's vision of training Jewish children for future lives in the West and with great academic rigor was at the heart of his management of the school. At the same time, Richard recalls, his father kept the school alive and thriving for more than two decades in large part by utilizing his access to government officials and cleverly finding ways to protect the school and its students from discrimination. Not infrequently, this led to run-ins with a brutal police.

My father, who was born in 1908, only briefly considered leaving Iraq during the major exodus in the early 1950s. He had a purposeful life in Iraq and was well-respected as a mathematician, so he felt no particular urgency to leave other than his affinity towards Israel. Though he experienced the Farhoud, he didn't personally feel singled out for persecution at any time.

A telling story that reflects the changing fortunes of the Jewish community in Iraq and its standing in Iraqi society is something my father recounted to me about a meeting between the chief rabbi, Hakham Sasson Khedouri, and Abdul Rahman Aref, President of Iraq between 1966 and 1968, who, despite also being the Chief of Staff of the army, was a weak leader. My father was not in that meeting, but he was one of the first to be briefed about it. Hakham Sasson went to Aref to air the grievances of the Jewish community because persecution of the Jews was worsening at the time. After the rabbi pled his case, all that Aref uttered in response was to recall his own childhood. He told his visitors, My father used to take me with him to the market and we always used to pass a date seller who sold his dates out of a basket. I always asked my father to buy some dates for me from this man. And every time my father would tell me, *ra'as al-salla lil-Yahud,* meaning, "the top of the basket is for the Jews." What he meant was that the best dates were for the Jews because they could afford it while the older, rotten fruit usually hidden below were for everyone else. Hakham Sasson and his group were in disbelief. What he was saying was, "Don't complain. You were always the top, the cream of the crop, the richest people."

My father graduated from the government schools in Iraq at the top of his class. As a result, he was sent on a government scholarship to the American University of Beirut in the 1930s, where he studied mathematics. Although he always aspired to be an engineer and possibly continue to live abroad, he returned to Iraq after graduation because a condition of the scholarship was that he would become a professor of mathematics and teach in the schools and universities of Iraq.

After his graduation, he assumed professorial positions at various institutions starting with the Central Secondary School in Baghdad and later at the College of Engineering, the Institute of Higher Learning, and other colleges of Baghdad University. These were positions which had a great effect on his stature in Iraq and on his contribution as well, because many students who ultimately assumed high government positions and other high-profile jobs passed through his classes and tutorship. These relationships proved useful in many ways, personally and professionally, and made it easier for him to run Frank Iny. In addition, he was commissioned by the Ministry of Education to co-author some of its mathematics textbooks, and as a result, during the 1940s and the 1950s all the official mathematics books in Iraqi schools were ones that he co-authored. So he was known and respected by Jews and influential non-Jews.

The future head of the Directorate General of National Security of the Ba'ath Party, Nazim Kazzar, was a student of my father's in the early 1960s when Kazzar was in his twenties and was beginning to be clandestinely active in the Ba'ath Party.

At that time, the Ba'ath Party was underground and the regime in power then was always hunting for Kazzar and other antigovernment activists. A janitor at the university, an acquaintance of my father's, used to hide Kazzar in the garbage barrel when the police would come looking for him. Kazzar didn't study hard—he was focused on his political activities. At some point in his studies, he asked my father to give him a passing grade despite the fact that he didn't deserve it. My father resisted. One day the bell rang at our home and I answered the door. Kazzar was standing there with another guy slightly older than him. We received them in our living room and served them the usual refreshments and sweets. Kazzar didn't say anything. The other guy was his advocate, pleading with my father to let Kazzar pass his class. He said, "We are activists, we are nationalists. We are trying to change things in this country and there has to be some consideration for us," and so on. My father listened to him and then launched into a lecture about how they should concentrate on their studies while they were going to school, that they could engage in politics after they graduated from school, and that he was not going to do anything questionable like pass a student who didn't deserve to pass.

The advocate turned out to be Saddam Hussein, we learned later, who was himself enrolled at the university but hardly showed up for class because he was too busy with his underground activities, though he was a nobody then. Eventually, in order not to complicate matters, my father gave Kazzar a grade of 47, which meant that Kazzar had a chance to go before a committee comprised of the dean and several key professors who would decide whether or not to give him the extra three points to get to 50 so that he could pass. The committee passed him, as there were a lot of politics on the university campus and plenty of antigovernment folks. My father had essentially passed it off to the committee because he didn't want to get caught up in a web of politics.

Kazzar continued studying at the university while he remained in the underground until the Ba'ath Party came to power in 1968 when he became the head of the Directorate of National Security. He still hadn't finished his degree, so even at that time he was still coming to classes once a week. Having a university degree was considered very important for one's stature in Iraq, so even if a person was in as plum a position as he was, he would still seek out a degree. Such officials would show up for classes one day a week for several years just to claim that they attended college and graduated. When I used to pick up my father occasionally after his lectures at the university, I often would see Kazzar's bodyguards standing by the classroom, most often a giant of a man named Ja'adan with whom I exchanged greetings after he came to know me as my father's son. Kazzar eventually became nicknamed by Iraqis *Nazim al-Jazzar*—*jazzar* means "butcher"—as he had killed so many people.

Getting a passport in Iraq involved many formalities, key among them obtaining security clearance from Kazzar's department, and many Jews were having difficulty getting passports at the time and were resorting to fleeing to Iran. So when I decided to leave Iraq that year, my father passed on word to him that I was applying for a passport. Every day people would gather in front of the Directorate of National Security and an officer would call out the names of people who were being considered for positive security clearance. I went there every day for a month or two, waiting for my name to be called. One day they finally called me. I entered and there was Ja'adan, the bodyguard.

He said to me, "Come with me and these guys will stamp your passport." He ushered me into an office at the same moment that some officers were taking somebody out of it, and it was immediately obvious to me that they had been interrogating him because blood was gushing out of his head. When I was told to sit down, I glanced down on the bench next to me and saw blood all over it. I found a place to sit on a few clean inches on one side. The officers asked me routine questions, like where my father taught and when I was born. Eventually they gave me the stamp I needed. And that's how I got my passport.

At that time, Nazim Kazzar was perhaps in his early thirties and power was getting to his head. One day, President al-Bakr was coming back from a visit to Romania, and Kazzar and some other ministers conspired to stage a coup. Someone alerted the airport, where according to custom, Iraqi dignitaries were gathered to receive the president, that there was a conspicuous absence of a few ministers and high officials, among them Kazzar. Soon enough the authorities discovered the plot and quickly Saddam and his loyalists foiled the coup. Kazzar and his fellow conspirators began fleeing to Iran. Saddam sent helicopter gunships after them and his henchmen stopped them, forced them out of their cars, and executed them on the spot.

The Last Jewish School in Iraq

In 1950, my father was asked by Frank Iny to become the principal of the school that bore his name when Iny was in the midst of expanding it from a small schoolhouse to a major state-of-the-art facility.[29] When he assumed his position at the school (without leaving his university posts), my father had a clear vision of what he wanted the new generation of kids to be able to do when they graduated: to be accepted by any university in the West—British, French, or American. So with that vision in mind, he organized nearly the entire curriculum around the goal of preparing students for that caliber of university. (In fact, fitting with my father's Western orientation, he and my mother, Rachel, gave me and my sister Linda English names because he planned for us eventually to go to the West.) That made the school incredibly rigorous because in order to qualify to enter French and American and British universities, one had to achieve certain requirements and pass exams particular to each system. The exams required a huge amount of preparation. Most students took the exams which were administered by the respective French, British, and American embassies. The Jews were usually the only ones to take these exams. Of course, this was all in addition to mastering the material required to pass the Iraqi government baccalaureate exams. That meant that students had to be fluent in English, French, and Arabic. And we also studied Hebrew. The government restricted modern Hebrew study but my father managed to get permission to institute Hebrew at the elementary level after arguing that it was needed to learn how to pray to God in our religion.

Several architectural designs for the school were rendered at the time that Frank Iny, the benefactor, decided to build a new school building, including one that almost looked like airplane wings. Ultimately, the design that was used was a beautiful one. The school was built in a lovely Bauhaus style with many balconies overlooking a central garden which was filled with shrubs and flowers and was constantly being cared for by a team of gardeners. One of the most wonderful features of the building was its auditorium, where students gathered for plays or other big events. The school also had science labs, a library, a sports hall, and outdoor tennis, basketball, and volleyball courts—features totally unprecedented for a school in Iraq.

The central lawn was used at the end of the school year for a prize-giving ceremony for the best students. Typically on those occasions my father invited government dignitaries whom he knew such as the minister of education or army officers. He made these invitations because they were good political moves for the school and for the Jewish community.

I saw the school from both sides, from my father's perspective and also as a student. Being the son of the principal may have had its privileges, but it also had its tough moments because whenever I excelled on my own merits, some jealous students would allege that I was given good grades because I was the principal's son. But overall there were probably more privileges, because my father was very well-respected as a fair man by both the teachers and the students. Certainly he had influence over an entire generation: after all, most of the Jewish kids who lived in Iraq after 1950 attended the school from kindergarten to high school.

As headmaster, my father was responsible for everything necessary to run the school: the budget, the selection and hiring of the teachers, the curriculum, and upkeep of the building and grounds. For example, because of all the foreign language curricula, he often had to travel abroad during the summers to recruit English and French teachers. We had French teachers who had come from France and from Lebanon, and English teachers from England and Australia. The teachers were a mix of Jewish, Christian, and Muslim, some Iraqi, some foreign. In fact, the majority were Christians and Muslims.

Frank Iny was established with the idea of being an elementary and intermediate school that would be a continuation of studies for graduates of the Menachem Daniel primary school. But when the student population of Menachem Daniel declined, the school closed and Frank Iny absorbed its students, and thus Frank Iny spanned kindergarten through grade 12. There were also other benefactors who played important roles at the school. For one, the benefactor of the Shammash High School became a benefactor of Frank Iny when Shammash closed, and grades 11 and 12 of the Frank Iny high school were considered the Shammash Secondary High School, so that when students graduated from grade 12 of Frank Iny, they received certificates saying that they graduated from Shammash. In addition, some of the school's prizes were named after other benefactors such as the coveted Nakar Prize, for Ja'izat Nakar. Another benefactor was Ezra Menachem Daniel who also established a sports ground (Mal'ab) for Jewish youths.

Athletics were mostly conducted on the Ezra Menachem Daniel sports grounds, which was essentially an adjunct of the school. It wasn't physically adjacent, but it was not far away, and it was where everybody went to get their physical activity and where Jews of all ages met up with friends and socialized after school, during the evenings and weekends, and all summer long. The life of a young Jewish boy or girl growing up in Baghdad revolved around the school and the sports grounds. The Mal'ab attracted much more government scrutiny as a place of Jewish congregation than the school. From time to time, government officials would allege that it was possibly being used to train Jewish youth to become future Israeli soldiers. At one point government officials showed up at the Mal'ab demanding a list of the names and ages of all the members. My father, who participated in the club's management, gave the officials a short list comprised of very few Jews who actually paid dues, and populated the rest of the list with bogus names of boys and girls mostly below the age of 10. In reality, a few major donors financed the Mal'ab and all Jews were welcome, so registering and paying dues was just voluntary. That trick saved the Mal'ab temporarily, though the government eventually shut it down in the late 1960s.

Frank Iny was more than just a school. It was a center for the Jewish community: weddings, bar mitzvahs, and all sorts of events were held there. Those events provided a source of extra income for the school. No fee was levied and it was left to individual families to donate what they could afford.

There were a few Muslim and Christian students at Frank Iny. They came from very liberal-minded families who had traveled to the West and valued a Western-oriented education. These families valued education to the extent that they were willing to put up with the stigma of sending their kids to a Jewish school. Typically when my father admitted Muslim or Christian students, it was because of their fathers' positions in the government or other connections which, my father expected, might be of political value to the school. Some of the fathers were those government officials who attended the school ceremonies. Whenever the school was subjected to harassment from a low-level inspector from the Ministry of Education, for instance, my father could then call one of these parents and ask for help.

After the Six Day War some of the Muslim teachers resigned. I remember one incident in which a history teacher, Ustath Yahia, who had taught at the school for a long time, told my father that his own children were ridiculing him for teaching at a Jewish school. The children were being bombarded by constant negative propaganda about Jews and were ashamed that their father was teaching Jews. So the man was apologetic to my father but told him he had to resign. Around the same time, the government began to restrict the entry of the school's foreign teachers to Iraq.

Meanwhile, Jewish university graduates couldn't get jobs because no one would employ them, so it became an opportunity for my father to start recruiting recent Jewish college graduates. I was one of them. So after getting my engineering degree, I taught advanced applied mathematics at the high school.

For my father, these were his most difficult years in terms of running the school—he faced so many pressures. But he knew the key to survival in such an environment was to keep a low profile. For example, for the longest time the school had no sign proclaiming the school name. There was a yearly government inspection of the school, and one year a particularly tough inspector demanded that a sign be erected. My father stalled for a while until the inspector came again and asked, "Where is the sign?" Eventually my father commissioned a sign but placed it out of view from passersby. The inspector returned and said, "I can't see it from the street. It needs to be moved to a more conspicuous location." Just as he had cleverly provided the bogus membership list of the Menachem Daniel club to the authorities, my father played a game this time too and moved the sign a little bit so it was just barely visible from the street.

Such were the tactics many Jews in the community used in order to avoid being targets of harassment. For instance, at one point the community decided to begin calling itself *Altai'fa al-Mussawiya,* meaning the "Community of the Followers of Moses," rather than *Altai'fa al-Yahudiah,* the "Jewish Community." This change, the community felt, reduced discrimination slightly because many people were not really sure what *Altai'fa al-Mussawiya* was.

Playing humble and not engaging in fights when instigated, and quietly moving on—that's how we learned to live. On one occasion I went to get some sort of permit at a government agency and I was lined up with lots of people all the way down the corridor. The clerk in charge called my name and as soon as he read in whatever he was reviewing that I was Jewish, he launched into a tirade against the Jews, right there in front of everybody. He said, *Damcum halal!* meaning, "your blood is *halal,*" or, "it's okay to kill Jews." I listened humbly, got his stamp, and got out of there. As a young Jew experiencing this kind of stuff on a daily basis, you had to keep in mind that there was nothing wrong with you—it was they who were the problem.

The sports club was a prime target for Arab kids in the neighborhood who knew the place was a gathering spot for Jewish kids. Therefore, when we left the facility, we tried to go in a group in case some Arab kids were waiting there to taunt us or play a trick on us. Usually they screamed and yelled *Sahioni kather,* "dirty Zionist," or other insults. We would not react and just move on. We adapted our whole lives around being careful and thinking a step ahead when we went out in public.

My father was more than just a headmaster to the students. We were a small community that over time was growing smaller and more tight-knit, so he knew most of the students' families personally and he socialized with them. Because of his role, he was invited to almost every important occasion in the community, from bar mitzvahs to weddings. Moreover, he deeply cared about the education of his students and felt responsible for them. The school became his life and he was very, very dedicated to it and to its well-being. He used his position to advocate for the community and to protect it from the negative external problems caused by discrimination. Being so closely connected to the community also had its challenges, as people were always coming to our house to plead a case for a student son or daughter: to raise his or her grade or allow him or her to cut corners, et cetera. My father handled that by setting particular standards, and in time, people respected them because they knew he was a fair man.

In the early 1970s, when the Jews were escaping to Iran through the Kurdish areas, the emptying out of the community was noticeable at the school. Some days I'd come in and three students in my class wouldn't show up that day, and everyone knew that they were, simply, gone—over the border. This didn't escape the notice of Muslim teachers, as well as the janitors and gardeners, all of whom were Muslim and some of whom were informants recruited by the government security services. My father knew which ones were the informants. Through some of his ex-students within the security services, he was even given the reports filed by these informants, on several occasions. But he never got rid of these people because doing so would have only raised unwarranted suspicion.

As a result, my father was called to the interrogation center of the secret police [a separate entity from the Directorate of National Security], which used to be a Bahai temple that the government had taken over after throwing out the Bahais (whose religion the Ba'ath Party refused to recognize). I remember driving my father there and waiting nervously outside for him. He emerged three or four hours later. He told me he had been ushered into a room and told to sit and wait. They kept him waiting—part of their psychology of intimidation and fear. He guessed that they had a few interrogators observing him as he waited. Eventually they brought him into another room and asked him, "So, you're the headmaster of the Frank Iny School. Where are all your students disappearing to? Are you organizing them to leave? If you tell us the truth nothing will happen to you. If you don't tell us the truth, something bad is going to happen to you." My father was not the type to be intimidated. He gave them a biting lecture about his service and loyalty to the country and threw out a few names of top government officials whom he knew well, some of whom he had taught in the university. Then he told them that they had no right to speak to him in such a threatening and accusatory manner. He wasn't going to be intimidated by what were, in his eyes and in truth, a bunch of thugs—junior thugs, kids. And that was that. They let him go.

He remained headmaster until the school closed in the mid-1970s. It closed not because of government decree but simply because the student population had dwindled so dramatically as more and more Jews escaped. Whereas classes once consisted of 30 or 40 students, by that year there were barely a handful of students in each class—and in some cases an entire class completely emptied out—so it didn't make any sense to continue operating.

Closing the school was a sad moment. It was sad for him because he had invested so much in the school. It was sad for the school, which had really been an exceptional place. But most of all, it was sad because of the historical significance: its closing symbolized the end of the community—the complete and total end. There is an expression in Arabic that refers to the origin of the Jews in Iraq as being the result of *al-sabi al-babili,* the Babylonian exile, when we were brought from Jerusalem to Babylon 2,500 years earlier. The Jews of Iraq had survived for so long, through so many good and terrible regimes, and at the moment when my father shut the front doors and turned the lock for the final time, all of that precious history came to a definitive end.

The building then became a public school and although I was no longer in Iraq myself, I heard that it quickly grew dilapidated, the roof leaked from hundreds of holes, and the gardens dried up and turned to dust.

What worries me today is that while there are still many Muslims who acknowledge the history and the contribution of the Jews in Iraq, the new generation of Iraqis is so anti-Jewish and anti-Israel that we could soon reach a point of the Iraqis' total denial of the historical existence of the Jewish community and its contribution over so many centuries. Given the news we hear these days, I'm afraid that's where Iraq looks to be heading. Iraq is in a sad chapter today. In our days, while the division between Shiite and Sunni was acknowledged, there wasn't physical fighting or even a belligerence of any kind between the two. What's happening now is absolutely shocking. And while it's very sad that the Jewish community of Iraq is gone, can one imagine what the Jews would have faced today if there were still a good-sized Jewish community in the country? I think most Iraqi Jews really had strong feelings for Iraq and great wishes for its prosperity.

When I left in 1971, I had already been admitted to graduate school in Canada, at the University of Toronto. My younger sister followed me a year or two later. My parents couldn't get passports at the time, because they knew that if the whole family tried to get passports at once we would have been under tremendous scrutiny. Throughout the years he was headmaster of Frank Iny, my father was also teaching at the University of Baghdad. So when the school closed, he just continued his teaching at the university until the day he left Iraq to join us, in 1982. My parents never tried to leave or really wished to until then, as my father had a good position at the university and he wasn't sure what he would do if he were to join us in Canada. Eventually, as he got older, the urge to be with his children became stronger and that year my parents moved to Montreal, where my younger sister also got married and settled.

When I arrived in Canada my first thoughts were, "This is a re-birth. This is almost like life starting again." I knew I was free, but several years later as I was relaying some feelings to a Canadian friend, he told me, "Richard, relax. You're free!" And then I realized that all this time that I was in Canada I was physically free but I hadn't been free from the oppressive feeling of restraint and fear that I experienced in Iraq. Yet in spite of the hard times my generation of Jews experienced growing up in Iraq, the more enduring feeling I have is one of the camaraderie between students who shared their lives for 12 years from kindergarten to graduation between the walls of the Frank Iny School.

After Abdullah Obadiah arrived in Montreal, alumni of Frank Iny organized a reunion in New York in his honor. Many reunions have been organized since, in the United States, Canada, and Israel. The former headmaster passed away in 1997 in Montreal, where his wife Rachel lives today as well as their daughter Linda and her family. The epitaph on his grave reads: "A visionary educator who nurtured many to great achievements." In 1979, Richard moved from Toronto to Boston, where he and his wife Patty live today.

Notes

1. From *American Jewish Yearbook*, 1956, p. 518.
2. From Caorle Basri, pp. 685–686.
3. Kazzaz, p. 183. Kazzaz states that in a conversation with Meir Basri, Basri told him that Iraqi Interior Minister Sa'doon Ghaydan told him that figure.
4. It was the high school affiliated with the Menachem Daniel Primary School, which also continued to operate.
5. Figure verified in Carole Basri, p. 688.
6. Many Jews were released from prison after world conscience had been aroused about the 1969 hangings and the imprisonment and persecution of others, according to Herdoon.
7. November 2, 1917.
8. The Suez Crisis, beginning on October 29, 1956, was a military attack by Britain, France, and Israel on Egypt following Egypt's decision to nationalize the Suez Canal.
9. Abd Al-Kareem Qassem took power that day and his government lasted through 1963.
10. The fire, set off by an Australian Christian, Dennis Rohan, caused major damage to the mosque and set off massive demonstrations by Arabs. From Sennott, p. 35.
11. Another Jew, Yehezkel Ya'acov, was hanged that day together with nine Muslims and four Christians. Kazzaz, p. 250.
12. Yosef Haim was best known as author of the work *Halacha Ben Ish Hai*, about Jewish law, and as a result he became known as the Ben Ish Hai.
13. Other rabbis accused him of not being stringent enough on the keeping of mitzvah. From Saadoun, p. 59.
14. Many of the bodies and gravestones in the old Jewish cemetery that existed from early Ottoman times were lost and destroyed in 1961 when President Qassem ordered the cemetery to be bulldozed and for the community to evacuate the land and to transfer the dead. Qassem forced the Jews to move everything from the original 42 dunam-site (10.5 acres) to a new space they were given of six dunams (1.5 acres). Ben Porat.

15. Khedouri issued multiple declarations disassociating himself and the community from Zionist designs on Palestine, Zionism, and later Israel. In one case, in 1936, Jews were attacked on and after the newly declared Palestine Day when the community came under fire from Muslims for Zionist leanings. Hakham Khedouri and a number of other Jewish leaders issued a declaration distancing themselves and the community from Zionism. The chief rabbi made a similar declaration in 1947 after an eruption of Muslim anger in Iraq after the UN partition of Palestine. From Rejwan, pp. 218–219 and p. 237. In another instance, during the Six Day War, Khedouri appeared on Iraqi television to reaffirm the loyalty of his community to Iraq and disassociate it from Israel and Zionism, and announced a donation by the community to the Iraqi army. The statement, which surely came as the result of great pressures by the government, was re-broadcast many times. From *American Jewish Yearbook*, 1968, p. 141.
16. A popular vacation destination in northwestern Iraq.
17. Avital Sharansky worked tirelessly to free her husband, Nathan Sharansky, the Soviet refusnik who is now an Israeli politician, from Soviet prisons in the 1970s and 1980s.
18. This interview was conducted four months before Saddam's execution in December, 2006, and was adjusted here accordingly.
19. Menachem Saleh Daniel (1846–1940) was a member of the Ottoman Baghdadi Council and later represented Jews in the 20-member Senate between 1925 and 1932, when he was replaced by his son, Ezra Menachem Daniel. He and other members of family were major land holders, and their total holdings were said to be worth 400,000 Lires (about $2 million in pre–World War II days). In 1910, he established the Menachem Saleh Daniel Kindergarten and Primary School, which was confiscated in 1976. Ezra Menachem Daniel (1874–1952) replaced his father as Senator in the Iraqi Parliament, until 1952. He established schools and medical clinics in Baghdad, Hilla, and al-Hindiyaa. Rejwan, p. 198, 215, and Meir Basri, Vol. 1, pp. 25–40.
20. Da'ud Samra was appointed in 1923 as a member of the High Court of Appeal, a post he held until his death in 1946. Rejwan, p. 215.
21. Qassem's forces assassinated the royal family and killed Prime Minister Nuri el-Said in 1958. Almog, p. 124.
22. An alliance between nationalists and the Ba'ath Party overthrew Abd Al-Karim Qassem in February, 1963, then assassinated Qassem and his inner circle. President Abd al-Salam Aref became president and the government made efforts between 1963 and 1965 to further the cause of Arab unity. Aref was killed in 1966 in a helicopter crash. Taylor and Francis Group, p. 431.
23. Nasser announced his resignation after the Arab defeat in the Six Day War, but the news caused mass demonstrations in Egypt and throughout the Arab world and he stayed in power for three more years, when he died of a heart attack in 1970. Ibid., p. 287.
24. The Interior Minister was Lieutenant General Sa'doon Ghaydan. As a result of this episode, the Passport Department of the ministry began granting passports to many Jews without restriction, enabling many Jews to leave Iraq (until the next crackdown, at the time of the Yom Kippur War in 1973). Bekhor, p. 287.
25. According to Zelouf; Moreh in "Obituary to Meir Basri."

26. Russian-born writer Haim Nahman Bialik (1873–1934) moved to Tel Aviv in 1924 and frequently wrote about the suffering of the Jewish people. He is considered Israel's national poet even though he didn't live to see the creation of Israel. Shaul Tchernichowsky (1875–1943), also Russian-born, moved to Palestine in 1931. He wrote poetry in Hebrew, frequently describing his idyllic childhood as well as the Jewish struggle for survival. From the Jewish Agency Web site.
27. The lyrical poems were collected in his anthology *Songs of Love and Eternity* (1991), published by the Association of Jewish Academics from Iraq in Jerusalem. His memoirs were published by the same association, as was his collection of biographies of Eminent Jewish men in Iraq and historical information about the community. Zelouf.
28. By this point, Shammash High School had merged with Frank Iny following a dramatic decline in the number of students at Shammash. Zelouf.
29. Frank J. Iny (1894–1976) established the school that bears his name in the Christian quarter of Baghdad in 1949. The school was confiscated by the government in 1973. Meir Basri, pp. 97–98 and Darwish, pp. 52–54.

SECTION FOUR

On the Outside

Introduction

With Iraq behind them, Jewish emigres began to build new lives for themselves in their new homes. Israel, where most settled, was a difficult homeland for some, a welcome one for others. By all accounts, their absorption into Israel in the 1950s was exacting, as Israel, a then-young, poor country faced the formidable challenge of taking in European Jews after the Holocaust and simultaneously Jews from Arab lands.

Nissim Rejwan has written extensively on the community, including his most recent book, *Outsider in the Promised Land* (2006), a semi-autobiographical account of Israel's reception of Iraq's Jews. "This reception, ambivalent and on the whole openly hostile as it was, has proved to be one of the cardinal in a series of fateful mistakes that Israel committed—and continues to commit—which have led to its isolation and alienation and continued rejection by the world surrounding it," he told us.

This attitude toward the Orient and its Jews deeply affected the lives of Iraqi (and other Mizrachi) immigrants, Rejwan said. Perhaps the biggest hardship they faced in Israel upon arrival in the early 1950s was lack of employment. Especially during Israel's first three decades of existence, most work came directly or indirectly from the government, so livelihoods depended almost exclusively on one of the ruling Ashkenazi establishment's centers of power—the government, the Histadrut (General Federation of Labor), the army, local governments, the largely nationalized industrial concerns, the media, or academia. Meanwhile, day-to-day discrimination was a theme commonly repeated by many of those we interviewed. Rejwan recalls that at the start of his studies at Hebrew University in Jerusalem, where he is now a research fellow, a professor told him that all the Iraqi students were considered Communists and also recommended that he change his last name. Later, as a proofreader and writer for the *Jerusalem Post*, Rejwan's editor often referred to him as "that Egyptian Communist," and expected him to be capable of writing only about the Arab world.

Only the term "cultural cleansing," Rejwan said, can describe Israel's handling of the Jews from Arab lands. Rejwan wishes that, instead, Iraqi Jews would have been "seen and treated as being a potential bridge between the ruling elite hailing exclusively from the countries of Eastern Europe and Russia, on the one hand, and the culture of the new state's habitat and its peoples, their way of life and language, on the other."

But from his perch deep within the army and national government, Baruch Levy's view is altogether different, as we learned in an interview with him. Levy came to Israel with his ultra-Zionist family at the age of one in 1934, all six family members making do in a one-room apartment in Tel Aviv. Given Israel's circumstances at the time—when over the course of three years (from 1948 to 1951), the Jewish population in Israel doubled to 1.2 million—he told us the state made enormous efforts to integrate Mizrachi immigrants after the mass aliyah. When he joined the army in 1950, he witnessed the influx of Mizrachi immigrants, and thought, "I'm an Israeli. I'm a native. If not someone like me who comes from that culture, who will help manage all this? Who will integrate them into Israeli society?" he told us.

He was the commanding officer of the Gadna, the youth corps for pre-military training, and of a military academy that prepared youth for army careers. In those jobs, he made special efforts to recruit and assist Mizrachi youth from poor development towns. After the Six Day War, the government began confronting social issues it had mostly ignored in its first two decades while it focused on existential matters. Under Prime Minister Golda Meir and then Yitzhak Rabin in the 1970s, Levy served as chief adviser on underprivileged youth, which then primarily meant children of Mizrachi origin.

The success of Iraqi Jews is evident today, he said. But even early on, Iraqis in particular fared rather well: they left the transition camps faster than most Mizrachi immigrants, which he attributes to the high levels of education among many of them. Many entered the army and moved up into high ranks as early as the 1950s, and played critical roles in the Mossad and Shin Bet (Israel's internal intelligence service).

In the mid-1980s Levy became the chief of the Civil Guard. Today, Iraqi Jews point to Levy and his brothers as proud examples of Iraqis who integrated thoroughly into Israeli culture, having risen to plum positions in what was then an Ashkenazi-dominated army. (His brother Moshe was a Chief of Staff in the 1980s.)

Meanwhile, Levy believes Israel's Western orientation has served the country well. The Ashkenazi pioneers "set the pattern of the way of life, which, in my opinion, was very important, because they created the foundation for a Westernized society," he said. "Later on, when people came from Arab countries, they had to integrate into that society, and rightly so, because I for one would not want this country to be an Oriental country. A Western society offers freedom—freedom of mind, freedom to achieve, and everything that we know today in terms of economics, education, science, democracy, and society. So I think that all those who speak about discrimination do not take into account the value of Israel as a Western society and what it means to integrate into such a society."

We end this section with the stories of Dhiaa Kasim Kashi, from whom we'll hear the perspective of a Shiite Muslim from Iraq. His experiences with Iraqi Jewish friends and his own reflections have led him to advocate for Iraq to recognize that it had expelled its Jewish population and to call for his country to make amends, for the sake of justice and for its own sake.

We begin the section with the words of novelist Eli Amir who tells a life story of profound Muslim-Jewish friendships, mass emigration, and the twists and turns of a Zionist dream.

* * *

Eli Amir, born in 1937 in Baghdad, is a best-selling Israeli author, many of whose novels are part of the Israeli school curriculum. His well-known trilogy of novels, Farewell Baghdad, Scapegoat, *and* Yasmin, *rooted in his personal experiences in Iraq and as a new immigrant in Israel, has contributed to a deeper understanding of relationships between Eastern and Western Jews in Israel, and relationships between Jews and Arabs. In his account, he describes the impetus for and the experiences that underlie his storytelling.*

My novels tell the story of the Iraqi Jews who came to Israel, and my own story. I was born into the Khalastchi family in a Muslim neighborhood in Baghdad called Mad'am. During my early childhood, relations between Muslims and Jews were good. My brothers and I were breastfed by our neighbor, a Muslim woman named Kheria, and my mother breastfed her children as well, when our own mothers had to go to the market or run errands. She and my mother were like sisters. Kheria protected our family during the Farhoud. By that point, we had moved to a Jewish neighborhood, but she came from her neighborhood to help us the moment she heard that there was a massacre in some of the Jewish neighborhoods. So she came to our house and stood in front of the door and yelled at the mob coming towards our house, "You will never touch these people! Jews are our neighbors in life. You will not touch them!" She stood guard there for 48 hours and she cried the whole time. She was in shock. To commemorate her great act, I made Kheria a character in *Farewell Baghdad* (Mafriach Hayonim)[1] and name her as she was in reality. As a result of her courage, my immediate family was untouched by the Farhoud.

One branch of the Khalastchi family was very successful in agriculture in Iraq. Ours was a second branch which managed the region around the tomb of Yehezkel Hanavi [the Prophet Yehezkel in Al Kifl, near Al Hillah]. Jews came from all over Iraq to the tomb on *Shavuot* [Jewish holiday celebrating the spring harvest] to participate in a prayer ceremony. It was a very big place where hundreds of people came and stayed overnight—it was a kind of industry. I went to the tomb as a child and recall that people came there with a feeling that they were coming to a holy place. People asked for God to grant them good health, a good wife, a good husband, good livelihoods, and even success on exams.

At some point my grandfather left this town to come to Baghdad because he wanted his children to attend university. They first went to Kirkuk to work there, separating themselves from the rest of the family, the branch that was in farming. That branch remained in their village and in the 1920s were the first to bring modern agricultural equipment to Iraq—combines, tractors, et cetera. They did very well, and also ran a car company, then left for England. They left Iraq very late—in the 1960s, 1970s, and even 1980s. Today, they are among the most affluent families in London.

My father had a shop: a small factory where he made rubber shoes. He was successful, but he was crazy about coming to Israel. He was a Zionist, as was my uncle (my mother's brother), who was the editor of a daily Jewish newspaper in Iraq named *Al-Barid Al-Yaumi* (The Daily Mail) which defended Jews. He was arrested and thrown into jail along with all intellectuals who were suspected of being Zionists, leftists, or antiregime activists. My father registered to leave Iraq on the first day that the citizenship revocation law was activated. In fact, he was at the registration station at midnight the night before and took me with him. I was 11 years old. He said to me, "We have no future in this country. Our history is finished here. We have to go to our homeland. If we are lucky and are able to go to Eretz Yisrael, I hope that the Jewish people there treat Arabs with equality and dignity, the way we want Muslims to treat us here in Baghdad." This was the moral will of my father, my own moral will all my life, and the moral standing I took in *Yasmin*,[2] my most recent novel, a love story between a Jewish Zionist from Iraq, Nuri, and a Palestinian, Yasmin, after the Six Day War.

That was an extremely exciting day, and one could feel in the air that those were the days of Messiah, the days of redemption. As a child, I had a feeling, a very, very strong one, that I was witnessing a chapter of history, actually the last page of a history: the history of my family and the history of the Jews of Iraq. There was something incredibly moving about witnessing tens of thousands of Jews giving up their past and preparing to leave. They were endangering themselves by the fact that they were relinquishing their identity cards and living as citizens without documentation until the day they were to leave, and in some cases that took a year. It was a very a courageous step to take, especially since the government was not trustworthy and could retract any decision at a moment's notice. Moreover, they didn't know what lives they were coming to in Israel.

I think I was happy then, generally speaking, but in shock as well, because I was witnessing all these major events. When we gave up our citizenship, my father could not work anymore and life became very dangerous. The schools weren't operating as normal because people were beginning to leave and there was unrest. We were quite afraid during that period, not knowing what the future held for us. In the final years, perhaps my greatest semblance of normalcy was as a student in the Frank Iny School. I was in the first group of students who attended the school.

Meanwhile, my mother did not want to come to Israel. She knew it wasn't the land of milk and honey: we had heard about the difficult life in transition camps, the unemployment, and the *Fidayoun*—the Palestinians who were attacking Israelis. In fact, many women didn't want to come because their chief concern was to feed and clothe their children, and they worried about taking chances with the family's livelihood. We were a family of six children at the time, so her worry was real. But my father convinced her. We all left together in May, 1950, on one of the first flights.

Farewell Baghdad deals with this period, the last chapter of the Jews in Iraq—the community on the eve of its immigration to Israel in 1950—through the character of a 16-year-old boy named Kabi (a nickname for Jacob). He tells us about his family, his school, about Muslim and Jewish friends. Other chapters are narrated by a 50-year-old, who tells the story in perspective 35 years later. The book deals with the Iraqi Jewish immigrants' dreams of the paradise they would find in Israel, and the collapse of those dreams. The book is also about the Zionist dream, the Communist dream, religion, Arab nationalism in Iraq, and how all these dreams—really, the instability they created—came together in the 1940s to instigate a turning point in the history of Iraq, especially among the Jews of Iraq.

The book begins with the story of Shafiq Adas. Adas was an assimilated Jew and not even Iraqi—he was from Syria. He was friendly with the prime minister and all the highest officials in the government, whom he hosted at his home. In 1948, a journalist who wanted to extort money from Adas published an article accusing him of selling ammunition to Israel during the War of Independence. Iraq's crown prince did not sign the verdict for a couple of days because he knew Adas and knew that he was innocent and patriotic, and that the article was a lie. Then the prime minister came to him and said, "It's your head or his." And he signed. After this incident, Jews knew that if something like this could happen to Shafiq Adas, it could and would happen to other Jews. So this is the event I used at the beginning of the book because it gets the reader hooked immediately. And later on, I use my personal memory of the Farhoud from when I was four years old to tell Kabi's story. I also used my memories of what Baghdad was like when Jews and Muslims coexisted there. After reading *Farewell Baghdad*, the fifth president of Israel, Yitzhak Navon, said, "This is the last word about the Jews in Iraq. No book of that level will ever be able to better describe the last chapter of the community."

When I came to Israel I found that those who absorbed us and who took care of us knew nothing about us. They thought to us as Arabs, and Arabs were Israel's enemies. So they didn't know how to handle us—didn't know what preconceived category to put us in. Arabs were considered primitive, defeated. Their language was considered stagnant, their music monotonic and primitive. Israelis looked down upon them because they had no modern literature and no culture to admire. Also because of their colonization by either the British or French, the Arabs were seen as not independent enough to take care of themselves, without modern technology or modern educational institutions. So a Jew who came from such a country was immediately considered one of them. We were labeled in the opposite way in which an immigrant from America was labeled: you might be stupid, primitive, zero, poor, nothing, but if you're from America, you're a shining star!

In Iraq, I had grown up like a prince in my family. I was the oldest sibling and came from a good family, and was an excellent pupil. But all of the sudden after arriving Israel I felt like dust. My father lost everything, and we started from nothing. I was in a *ma'abara* for seven months; my family for seven years. The *ma'abarot* were unorganized, neglected, dusty, dirty. The people in them walked and behaved like shadows of themselves. They had lost everything they had: their money, property, status. Their clothes were ridiculous. Most people wore their best suits when coming to Israel because we were allowed only a small suitcase each on the flights. And our outfits were the most modern style in England because at the time as Iraq was so heavily influenced by the British and the Jews' second culture and language was English. In Iraq, we used to have English tea in the afternoon, and our education was either British- or French-oriented. So it was the most unbelievable sight to see Iraqi immigrants walking around the transition camps in fancy English suits—though they quickly became dirty and worn. Meanwhile, in Israel at the time, a tie and fancy clothing were things to be ashamed of: the ideal was the khaki clothes of the tough farmer.

I was eager to be literate in Hebrew right away, but it wasn't easy to get newspapers and books in the camp. I started with scraps of newspapers because we didn't have money to buy newspapers, so I used to go to towns nearby, Hadera and Pardes Hanna, to rummage though the garbage for a newspaper and bring the scraps I found back to our tent.

I tell the story of how the dreams of the Iraqi Jews fell to pieces upon coming to Israel in *Scapegoat* (Tarnegol Kapparot), my first novel.[3] The Zionists won the battle in that they brought the Jews here, but failed in the way they absorbed and integrated them in Israel. The book tells the story of Nuri, a Youth Aliya pupil, and my alter ego (and the protagonist in *Yasmin*). The whole novel is loosely based on my own first years in Israel. Nuri's story is bittersweet: an Iraqi immigrant boy who is torn between the world he knew and loved in the old country and the new one he must adopt. Through his eyes, we see what I witnessed as an adolescent in Israel, the many ways in which European and Middle Eastern Jewish culture clashed. The great success of this novel was that it brought into national consciousness this painful social and cultural conflict, which shapes Israeli society still today. In *Scapegoat*, I describe all the major conflicts of the 1950s: interethnic strife, the growing religious-secular divide, the struggle between socialism and capitalism, East versus West. Its two central characters, Nuri and Nili, are ambitious and talented and symbolize hope for the future of Israel.

Everything the immigrants came with here was nothing, zero. Even the names once revered within the community were rendered meaningless. The Ashkenazis pronounced my name, Khalastchi, in 11 ways and wrote it 11 different ways. Every office clerk wrote it the way he heard it. He did not pay attention to how you told him it should be spelled. In fact, I was almost put into prison when I was a soldier after my commander made a joke out of my name and I got angry at him.

Eventually I changed my family name to Amir. Why Amir? I was able to get out of the *ma'abarot* quickly because I entered the Youth Aliya and went to live on the kibbutz, Mishmar Ha'emeq, for three years. Every group of children on the kibbutz had its own name. Our group was an Iraqi one, with 40 children, and the children competed to come up with a name for the group. About 20 names were suggested. I came up with Amir, which means a bundle of wheat. So that had metaphorical meaning as a group of children working the land, but the name was also an acronym created out of the Hebrew letters *ayin*, which is the first letter in the word "Iraqi"; *mem*, the first letter of our teacher's name, Menachem; *yud*, the first letter of the group's housekeeper's name, Yocheved; and *resh*, for Rivka, the group's counselor. These three people worked for us and we liked them.

I did not change my name until later, however. I left the kibbutz in 1954 and I used Khalastchi until 1960. In 1960, I finished the army and when I came to Hebrew University I didn't want to start the same laborious experience of explaining my name and correcting its spelling and pronunciation a thousand times. And I wanted to date girls! I didn't want to start conversations with them by spending time explaining my name. So at that point I began using the name we gave our group on the kibbutz, and my brothers and sisters followed me. My parents did not.

I established myself in Jerusalem so that my family could leave the camp and join me. When that day came, we moved to an area of slums in the Katamon neighborhood. Before attending university, I studied at night to finish my high school matriculation exams and during the day I worked as a messenger boy in the prime minister's office. My dream was to become adviser to the prime minister on Arab affairs, which I became. Some of these experiences are in *Yasmin*, which is the story of the Six Day War through two narratives, Israeli and Palestinian.[4] I consider *Yasmin* the final book in my trilogy [following *Farewell Baghdad* and *Scapegoat*] because in telling the story of Israel itself, it completes the story of the Jews of Iraq and their transition to Israel, a place where Arab and Jew, again, must also coexist. It was my dream to bring peace to this country, like many other naive people here from the eastern countries—Arabic-speaking people who thought that they should be given the opportunity to make peace with the Arabs. But that was the sentiment after the Six Day War, when Iraqi Jews did not yet have any influence in Israeli society and nobody listened to what we had to say.

A major part of Israel's problem is that we—its government and citizenry—don't speak to our Arab neighbors—we don't try to articulate what we do and why we do it. And that neglect is purely derived out of an arrogance that we are part of the West so we are on another level. We just throw our hands up in the air and say, "These people know only the language of force, so why should we explain anything to them?" We could be using our many Arabic speakers who also understand Arab culture in this country to explain ourselves to the Arab world, but we don't.

But the talents of the Iraqi Jews eventually did come out in Israel. We are paid attention to because we became important people, even celebrities. We succeeded in all aspects of life in Israel and have made major contributions to Israeli society. The Iraqis channeled themselves into two occupations, generally speaking: either working with Arabs, teaching Arabic, translating, or working in the Shin Bet or the Mossad; or into professions as accountants, bankers, or businessmen. I rebelled a little and didn't want to take either of these paths, and desperately wanted to belong to Israeli society—a conclusion I came to at age 28. I could have become a career soldier, but by then it was too late. So I decided to work in the absorption business, something which was fundamental for the country.

When I became director general of Youth Aliya for the Jewish Agency, I was the first Mizrachi Jew in that job and was responsible for all the youngsters who came into the country. Since those days, Israel has corrected many of the mistakes it has made in terms of absorbing immigrants, but something fundamentally problematic still today is the question of how to ensure that immigrants feel that they belong and are really integrated into the broader society, rather than isolating themselves in their own communities. I also feel that mastering the language is critical for all immigrants, though I find myself still struggling with it at times.

I believe that my work has helped make known the story of the Iraqi Jews. I think that Iraqi writers and poets have done a superior job explaining the community and its roots to other Israelis. We have made the Iraqi characters likeable and accessible to many and have made them come alive for the ordinary Israeli. This success has proven to me that if you want to become known and familiar in this society of immigrants, literature, poetry, and music—the arts—are the three major vehicles that will pave the way for you, because they reach everyone.

But the story of the Iraqi Jews, and of Mizrachi Jews in general, is not understood in the United States, in the West, and my books have not been published in English[5] which is a symptom of this problem. The West doesn't want to deepen its understanding of the Islamic world. It views the East as exotic, and doesn't invest any substantial efforts in getting to know that world. The West will pay an enormous price because of its failure in this respect, as we see in the current war in Iraq.

I recently had a very eye-opening experience which showed me how the Arabs have buried and forgotten the story of the Jews of Arab countries. The most popular weekly magazine in Egypt had translated four chapters of *Yasmin* and published them over the course of month. I was then invited to Egypt and given a public forum. A number of prominent Egyptians came including friends of President [Hosni] Mubarak. As I spoke to them they realized that they were talking to somebody who spoke their language, who was very familiar with their culture, and who came in peace. One of the members of the audience said, "You are not a typical Israeli. We've never met an Israeli like you." I said, "How many Israelis have you met?" He said, "Not many, but you are so familiar with our culture. You are one of us! You are an Arab Jew." I said, "I am a Zionist Jew, an Israeli. I write in Hebrew. Israel is my home, and I have no other place in the world." I don't like the term Arab Jew because I consider myself foremost a Zionist and an Israeli, I will never go back to Iraq, and I never want to live in an Arab country. So the term was perhaps once meaningful, but no longer.

And there was, surprisingly, applause. That's because, I think, I did not hide anything. Others were so curious about how I could have written this book because they said it seemed to be written "from the sprit of an Arab" with my portrayal of the Palestinian character. So I said, "My dream is that an Arab writer, be it Egyptian, Syrian, Palestinian, will write his own *Yasmin*, telling a love story between an Arab and a Jew. When that happens, it will be the first step to understanding each other. If I internalize you and try to identify with you, even though you are my enemy, it means I have the capacity to live with you. It is a great loss between our two peoples that we haven't reached that first step yet."

The main lesson of my life is as follows: I came as a refugee from Iraq. The Jews of Arab lands are the real refugees of the Middle East. The Jews of Iraq did not fight Iraq. We did not harm the country of our birth. On the contrary, we made enormous contributions in every aspect of life in Iraq. Nevertheless, they ousted us. The Muslims took everything that we had, and we came to Israel with the clothes on our back. But the Israel that welcomed us was a poor country and couldn't supply us with the basics—shelter and food. Although we went through terrible absorption difficulties including discrimination, we overcame all such obstacles and succeeded over the course of 20 years to achieve everything we wanted—to touch the sky.

Meanwhile, Arab countries hold the Palestinian refugees of 1948 as political prisoners in refugee camps in miserable conditions, haven't granted them citizenship, and otherwise discriminate against them in a myriad of ways. These countries have doomed their Palestinian populations to a terrible life just so that they would become a breeding ground for hatred against Israel and thus a threat against Israel. These refugees are hostages in the countries in which they live, and are endangering any possibility to settle the Israeli-Palestinian problem.

Eli Amir served as executive director of the American Sephardic Federation in the mid-1970s. He won the Yigal Alon prize for outstanding pioneering service to Israeli society in 1993. He and his wife Lilian live in Jerusalem and have three children.

* * *

Dhiaa Kasim Kashi is a Shiite Muslim born in 1952 in Baghdad. He describes his family's relationships with Jews in Iraq and his friendships with Iraqi Jews in London, where he lives today. Kashi traveled to Israel twice in 1998 to meet with Iraqi Jews and helped to found the now defunct Israeli-Iraqi Friendship Committee. He laments the community's demise and has become a vocal advocate pushing for Iraq to acknowledge its treatment of its Jewish population, which he often compares to the Ba'ath Party's decades-long discrimination against Shiites and other minorities.

I left Iraq in 1980 just before the Iran-Iraq War because my family had faced years of persecution by the regime. We were persecuted against as Shia generally and also as a wealthy family, because the regime felt threatened by the Shia majority and in particular by the richer Shia families—all this despite the fact that we didn't have any political ambitions. I lost 19 members of my family who were either executed or disappeared and whose whereabouts are still a mystery to us today. We certainly lost many more distant relatives as well whom I didn't know. But this was the norm in Iraq under the Ba'ath Party. I don't think there is a family in Iraq that hasn't been affected by that brutal regime, even Sunnis. I had the chance to escape with my wife, and we didn't have any children at that time so the two of us just picked up and left everything behind. Our families followed later.

The Iraqi regime was typically in the hands of the Sunni minority even prior to the rule of the Ba'ath Party so the Shia and other minorities—Christians, Jews, and Iraq's 17 or so other religions—were oppressed by various governments throughout the last century, but with greater severity starting with the Ba'ath Party coup in 1963. In a period of 10 months in which the Ba'ath Party ruled before it was overthrown, it killed about 100,000 Iraqis, mostly leftist political opponents. The brutality began again after the party overthrew the nationalists in 1968. The Ba'athists killed people just to control the society with fear so no one would threaten the regime. It killed just for the sake of killing. Some of the victims were young university students or adults whom it accused of being members of the *Hizbil Dawa* Party—an Islamic, mainly Shia Party—or the Communist Party. Some victims were members of the Ba'ath Party itself and who were accused of being traitors.

I was born into a secular Muslim family. As Shiites, we were told by the regime that we were not originally Iraqis but rather that we were of Iranian origin. By the time I was born in 1952 most of Iraq's Jews had left the country, so as I was growing up I didn't get to know a lot of Jews personally. Many of the Jews who were still in Iraq when I was young kept their identities quiet as they were afraid of persecution and harassment from the government, the police, and the *Muhabarat*.

I consider myself lucky that I was born in the part of Baghdad that used to be a wealthy Jewish quarter, Betaween, near the commercial center of Baghdad. In fact, the house in which I was born and lived all my life until I left Iraq had previously belonged to a Jewish family who had been my grandfather's friends. The head of the family had begged my grandfather to buy his house when he left Iraq with his family in 1950. My grandfather didn't like the idea of buying Jewish property because he knew the Jews were experiencing persecution and were being forced to leave and forced to sell—if they could sell. So he didn't feel right taking over their property. But the Jewish friend insisted, saying that he wanted my grandfather to own the house because he thought of him like a brother and therefore felt that that he wouldn't really be losing the house.

The year my grandfather purchased the house, which was two years before I was born, was the year most of the Iraqi Jews left the country, though I consider what happened to them expulsion. I don't believe it was their choice to leave, although the law enabling them to leave was worded as if the Jews were being given a choice. But it wasn't like that. They were forced to leave and some of them escaped for their lives.

The Jewish owner used to own several houses on our street, and his own house was the one next to our family's original house. The house was built in a Jewish architectural style, the kind of house in which many Jews in Baghdad lived. It was designed smartly for the Baghdad climate: a courtyard in the middle which kept the house ventilated and cool, rooms with high roofs to let the heat rise, and two rooms that were built slightly deeper into the ground, making them cooler than the other rooms in the hot summer months.

In 1981, at the beginning of Iraq-Iran War, when the regime was still wealthy, it drew up a plan to demolish a large section of Betaween beside the river in order to turn it into a sprawling green park and entertainment area for tourists. All the homes were to be bulldozed down. But a government committee chose one house—our house—to be kept standing as an example of clever Jewish architecture in Baghdad. The government offered to buy the house for one million dinars, which was about $3 million at the time. But the plan for the park never came to fruition because the war drained the government's wealth and Iraq was left a poor country after those eight terrible years. Although all of my family has left Iraq, the house is still registered in my grandfather's name.

A few Jews still lived in our neighborhood during my childhood. Our house was on the street where the prominent Rabbi Daoud Hayim lived. When I was very young, my grandmother, who was a devoted Muslim, used to send me every Saturday to help the Hakham's family turn on the lights or the stove because it was Shabbat and the family couldn't light a fire on Shabbat. I did this for other Jewish families in our neighborhood as well. So I felt like I was part of one big family spread throughout the neighborhood and which included Jews and Muslims alike.

I mostly played with Christian or other Muslim children in the street, and a few Jewish kids, though we lost the Jewish friends over time as they left Iraq. Mostly, my knowledge about Jews in Iraq is from my older family members—my parents and grandparents and others in their generation—who used to tell me wonderful stories about their Jewish friends. They showed me photos of these friends and tried to trigger my memory of them, asking me, "Do you remember Mr. So-and-So, Mrs. So-and-So, who were our friends, our neighbors, and used to come sometimes to our house and stay overnight?" They spoke about their Jewish friends and business partners with admiration and wistfulness. I recall hearing from my parents and grandparents only positive stories about the Jews. They told me stories about how good, how trustworthy they were. For example, in the days when there were no banks in Iraq and a Muslim wanted to hide his money or gold in a safe place, he entrusted a Jewish friend with it because Muslims knew that Jews would never betray them while they feared that their own Muslim friends and relatives would.

For instance, a friend of mine in London is the nephew of the former Mufti of Baghdad [the highest Sunni religious authority in Iraq, a government appointee]. When this man's father died, his mother gave full power of attorney to the Jewish neighbor, a friend of theirs, despite the fact that her brother was the Mufti, a prominent and thus supposedly reliable man. So as a child my friend asked his mother, "Why do you trust our neighbor over your own brother, the Mufti?" She told him, "Well, my son, you are too young to understand now, but when you grow up you will understand." And in fact, my friend told me, years later, he saw that she had been smart as the Jewish neighbor never betrayed them, while the Mufti was considered untrustworthy. I also heard stories from Muslims who lived in Basra and Mosul about their good friends, Jews, whom they trusted with their lives, their money, and their family. In fact, I believe that anybody who wishes to learn about what it was to be trustworthy and good has only to look to the Jews of Iraq.

The Jews were so central to commercial life in Iraq that business across the country used to shut down on Saturdays because it was the Jewish Shabbat. They were the most prominent members of every elite profession—bankers, doctors, lawyers, professors, engineers, teachers, et cetera. In 1925, the parliament issued a law to change the official rest day from Saturday to Friday when all commerce was to be closed, but everyone ignored the law because Jews dominated the marketplace and much of the commerce and they continued to shut down on Saturdays.

All of Iraq's famous musicians and composers were Jewish, and Iraqi art and music in general was preserved by Jews because Muslims were restricted by Islamic law from practicing most types of art and music. It is a tremendous shame for Iraqi culture that the country lost these people. The country suffered a big shock when the Jews left [at mid-century]: it took a decade or more to reestablish music culture, and I can't say that it has even really been reestablished. Today, 60 years after the Jews left, 90 percent of the songs Iraqis sing are ones composed and sung by Iraqi Jews. Iraqis don't realize that this is the case because the government has covered up the facts. Whenever you hear a song played on Iraqi radio that is identified as having been written by "an unknown composer" or that it is "too old to know who wrote it" those are signs that the songs were written by a Jew.

Whenever someone from the older generation talks today about the golden days of Iraq and mentions a famous math or physics teacher, or a successful businessman, or a famous doctor, or an author, they were almost always Jews. Of course, this doesn't characterize all the Jews of Iraq, and there were many quarters in Baghdad that used to be well-known as Jewish areas and they were the poorest in the city. But the icons of Iraqi society were its Jews. And that made the Sunni leadership resent them and want to get rid of them, while instead the leaders would have been better off admitting that other Iraqis should learn and benefit from, and work side by side with, the Jews. Getting rid of the Jews was totally self-defeating for Iraqi society.

The effect of Hitler and the Nazis in Iraqi society was strong, and this played a major role in Iraq's persecution of its Jews. Before that and even during the period of Nazi influence, Muslims were very happy to have neighbors or business partners who were Jews. It was the politicians who wanted the support of the Nazis in order to oppose the British occupiers and force them to leave Iraq, and so the government took on the Nazi ideology. When the Nazi era ended, the Iraqi government wanted the support of the wider Muslim Sunni community throughout the Arab countries to bolster its own minority rule in Iraq. So the regime maintained the same ideas that it took on during the Nazi era, which then became integrated into the Arab nationalist political ideas. And that, not only the creation of Israel, is how anti-Jewish sentiment has continued to pervade the Arab nationalist ideology. Thus the anti-Jewish feelings in Iraq originated with politics and only evolved into religious hatred.

Greed and jealousy on the part of the Sunni leadership was also at the heart of its treatment of the Jews. And just as the Jews were persecuted largely out of jealousy by the Sunni leadership, the wealthy Shia were similarly persecuted, had their property confiscated, and were killed or thrown out of the country. My belief is that this practice of property confiscation originates in the strong Bedouin culture that was pervasive in Iraq which viewed property confiscation as permissible in appropriate circumstances.

Jews and Muslim Shia were both persecuted by the continuous chain of Sunni leadership in the twentieth century. There's a huge similarity between the persecution of Jews and the persecution of Shia, which came later, starting in the 1960s and until Saddam's overthrow. The Shia suffered greater persecution than the Jews did but the Jews were the group on which Saddam sharpened the knives he used later on the Shia and other minorities including the Kurds (who are mostly Sunni).

Memories and Dreams

When I was about nine years old—around 1960 or 1961, in the middle of Qassem's regime, which was a honeymoon period for Iraqi minorities—I used to go with my uncle every day in the summer at about 3 or 4 o'clock in the morning, when it was still dark and the air was still cool, to swim in the river Euphrates, which we called Dijla. We lived very close to Dijla. When we arrived, we would see many people, over 100 or 200 families, swimming on the other side of the river. My uncle used to tell me, "Those are Jews, and many, many more of them used to swim in the river every day in the early mornings in years past. Now there are only a few left." There were a few Muslims amongst them: the boat owners and the swim teachers. I recall vividly mulling over the fact that I was not able to notice any difference between that group of human beings and ourselves. They were enjoying themselves just as we did, and I could hear the children's noises and laughs. I remember those days as the golden days. But it looked and felt like the end of the golden days.

I distinctly remember January 27, 1969, the day 15 Iraqis, mostly Jews, were hanged in Liberation Square. We lived five minutes from the square. I was 17 years old at the time. I heard about the hanging and wanted to see if the news was true, so I walked out to the square and saw the bodies with my own eyes. Many ignorant people were gathered around the bodies, chanting and dancing. I looked into the eyes of some of the celebrators and saw that some of them looked afraid too, but appeared to be acting that way in case the authorities were watching to see how they reacted. Others were genuinely celebrating. A feeling of disgust came over me, and then of fear—fear of the horrendous brutality of the regime. I didn't know if those who were hanged were innocent or not, but regardless, the way in which they were killed and publicly hanged shocked and angered me. I had a feeling that this was the beginning of a new era of control by fear. People had been hanged many times before in Iraq, but usually inside prisons. With these public hangings, the regime was giving a message to the Iraqi people that it is okay to kill others and no one will stop them.

The regime ceased public hangings after that in response to international condemnation. However in the late 1980s, Saddam's eldest son, Uday, who was even more brutal than his father, established the group *Fedayeen Saddam* which killed people in the streets by cutting out people's tongues, then beheading them. They left the bodies hanging on the door of their homes for a week or two—though Islamic law requires bodies to be buried as soon as possible—and they prevented families from any kind of religious mourning.

When the persecution of political opponents and Jews began in the 1960s and 1970s, some Iraqi Jews hid their religious identities, gave their children Muslim names and even told their children that they were Muslims in order to protect them. In one instance, a Jewish boy who fought in the Iraq-Iran War was hailed at his death as a good Muslim—yet his mother was Jewish and had hidden her Jewish identity from her three sons. Later, when her husband died, she left the country with her two other sons. I believe there are some people living in Iraq today as Muslims who are in fact Jewish and do not even know it.

During the 1960s when I was a teenager, the nationalists and the Ba'athists directed the media against the Jews because of the Israeli-Palestinian issue. I grew up in a culture which was prejudiced against all minorities but especially against the Jews. We were taught in school about the Jews and Israel and the Palestinians from the government textbooks, which, we eventually discovered, were full of lies. We knew the textbooks spewed lies about the Shia and we began to suspect the tales about the Jews were lies as well, especially since in many of the more sophisticated Shia homes children got a different—positive and truthful—story about the Jews. In the 1960s and '70s, we were bombarded with propaganda against Jews that was politically, not religiously, motivated. The powers that be consistently used the Jews as scapegoats, calling them spies and thieves, people without morals and an evil force that was opposed to all that was good in Iraqi society. That was the official line in society, in school, and in the media, and it continues until today. We see this, of course, throughout the Arab and Muslim media.

My first friend in London was a Kurdish man who introduced me to my first Iraqi Jewish friends there and I have become very close to them ever since. I look forward to many years ahead of friendships with Iraqi Jews. These first Jewish friends of mine were extremely supportive people who were ready to help any new Iraqi newcomer in London. After that initial experience I started making more and more Jewish friends and I started to feel as if these relationships were a continuation of my parents' and grandparents' friendships with Jews in Iraq. I feel as if I knew my Jewish friends from my previous life in Iraq because we talk about their memories and my memories of Iraq, and they are the same memories: both happy and sad ones. I have many close friends in the Jewish community, such as the late Meir Basri, Daoud Khalastchy, the late Shaul Sassoon, and Edwin Shuker. At least once a week, we gather together—Muslim, Christian, and Jewish friends from Iraq—in one of our houses for tea and Iraqi food and we celebrate our friendship. I have found that Iraqi Jews still love Iraq and the people of Iraq probably more than any other Iraqi community does. That is quite incredible, given the persecution they faced.

As a result of these friendships I determined that I must do my bit to highlight this injustice and to bring the Jewish community back into the fold of Iraqi society in the Diaspora. If there were peace in Iraq today, my aim would be to bring Iraqi Jews back to Iraq to reestablish the community. But because that appears impossible, I'd like, at least, to integrate them into Iraqi communities around the world because other Iraqis don't know their Jewish brothers anymore, as it has been so long since they lived together. Only politics has driven them apart. I believe we have a chance of accomplishing this dream because we live in democracies and in the West. In fact, this dream to bring Iraqi Jews together with other Iraqis has become my main aim in life.

As part of that quest, I went twice to Israel, in 1998, to meet Iraqi Jews and to learn more about them. I went to help establish a formal organization, together with a group of prominent Iraqi Jews in Israel—including Sami Michael, Sasson Somekh, David Sassoon, and Dr. Shaul Sidqua— dedicated to reestablishing Iraqi-Israeli relations at the grassroots level. I was the only Iraqi Muslim involved in these meetings. We called the group the Israeli-Iraqi Friendship Committee, but the Israeli government rejected our request to register it as a nonprofit, saying it might be a cover for Saddam's agents. This was seven years after the first Gulf War and in the midst of a flare-up with Saddam that year. We applied first under Likud and then under Labor governments but both rejected it. It was a big disappointment.

Still, my six-day trip to Israel was an unbelievable experience. My schedule was booked well in advance, for breakfast, lunch, and dinner, at homes throughout the country—from north to south. Whenever I entered a house for a meal, I saw that the family had invited all their friends to meet me, and people greeted me with hugs and kisses. Many repeated the warm Iraqi saying, *Ashtem reehat Baghdad*, which means "I smell Baghdad when I hug you." But literally speaking, these people loved Baghdad so much that they remembered how it smelled 50 years later. During my visit I videotaped and chronicled the daily life of Israelis of Iraqi origin and their longing for Iraq. I sat with the other members of the committee to discuss how to achieve our objective, which was to reestablish ties between Iraqi Jews and other Iraqis throughout the world, and to communicate to the Israeli people that the Iraqi people are distinct from the brutal regime.

I returned to London on a high from my visit and wrote about my trip and our objectives in *Al Hayat* [the London-based Arab newspaper]. I received hundreds of e-mails, letters, and phone calls from many Muslim friends and strangers in support of our efforts, and many of them were disappointed with the refusal of the Israeli government to approve the committee. Some of the nationalists in the Iraqi opposition accused me of claiming to be the representative of the Iraqi opposition, angry that I was making what they perceived to be a bold statement in their name by going to Israel and appearing on Israeli TV and radio and in newspapers. Since then, I have written many articles and made presentations to Arab groups in England about my visit to Israel and the need to bring the Jewish community into the fold.

Many Iraqis, and I am one of them, feel that if the Jews had stayed in Iraq, we wouldn't be in the situation we are now and might not have experienced all the atrocities we have in the last 50 years. That is because if the Jews had been allowed to stay in their positions of power, as the elite of society, they would have managed the country far better than it was indeed managed. They would have been a moderating influence on society. Second, if the conditions had been right for them to stay in the country in the first place, that would have meant that we wouldn't have had to experience this extreme brand of Arab nationalism. I feel strongly that if we hadn't lost the Jews, Iraq wouldn't be in its current terrible state, which is the result of decades under Saddam.

I would like to do whatever I can to highlight the injustice against the Jews of Iraq. I feel that it is our duty—as Muslims, Arabs, Iraqis, and as Shia—to do this because we are the majority. It is also our duty to our friends and brothers of the Jewish community in Iraq to help them reclaim the property that is rightfully theirs. And it is in the best interests of Iraq society to recognize the persecution it caused to Iraqi Jews, to recognize the rights of the Iraqi Jews, and even—eventually—to try to get them to come back to Iraq, because doing so will mean we will have entered a new era for a new Iraq, which we are all hoping for.

I implore the Jews of Iraq not to allow the culture and contribution of your community to disappear in this generation and to ensure that you transmit as much of it as possible to your children and grandchildren. After all, Iraq was originally your country—Jews were there long before the Muslims set foot on its soil. Even if most of you have no intention of returning to the motherland, you owe it to your ancestors, those pillars who helped shape Iraq and its history, to perpetuate in exile, at least, your glorious past.

Dhiaa Kashi and his wife Nadhiaa live in London. They have two children.

Notes

1. *Farewell Baghdad* (1992, Am Oved Publishers) has not been published in English.
2. Am Oved Publishers, 2005.
3. *Scapegoat* (1983, Am Oved Publishers).
4. Also loosely based on Amir's own experiences. In the novel, Nuri becomes an adviser on East Jerusalem affairs to the minister in charge of the occupied territories, a position Eli Amir himself held.
5. Only *Scapegoat* has been published in English, in the United Kingdom.

Conclusion

This collection of personal histories has sketched the story of how a vibrant community of nearly 140,000 in the years before the mass exodus with a 2,500-year history in Babylonia lived, struggled against oppression, and finally left, most with almost nothing. At Iraq's birth in the 1920s, the country's Jews helped build the foundations of Iraqi society. They made music, treated the sick, taught in universities, published newspapers, participated in the civilian government, and traded goods. Some ventured to the Far East where they made fortunes and established schools, hospitals, and jobs.

Since the community left Iraq, the number of Iraqi Jews worldwide has more than doubled: counting their offspring, there are now 240,000 Iraqi Jews in Israel. They have integrated into Israeli society and occupy the spectrum of positions professionally and socially in the country. Another 35,500 reside outside of Israel, mainly in the United Kingdom, the United States, Canada, and Australia.[1]

The largest population outside of Israel is in the United States, where about 13,000 Iraqi Jews live today.[2] Iraqi Jews began to immigrate to the United States and Canada at the turn of the twentieth century, when about 20 families settled in New York. After the breakup of the Ottoman Empire following World War I (1914–1918), more settled in the United States and continued to come over the next two decades, in particular those seeking education and business opportunities. Meanwhile, other Jewish immigrants of Iraqi ancestry from the Far East (Bombay, Shanghai, Rangoon, Hong Kong, and other cities) settled in Southern California in the early 1920s; after the turmoil of World War II most of those communities in the Orient emptied out completely and the majority of their members left for America.[3]

Iraqi Jews also made their way to Canada beginning in the early 1950s, many of them following educations in England when that country declined to renew their visas. Their destination was typically Montreal, where an estimated 2–3,000 Iraqi Jews currently live. Iraqis comprise the bulk of the members of Montreal's Spanish and Portuguese Synagogue, the Iraqi community's largest congregation in Canada.[4] An estimated 8,000 Iraqi Jews live in Canada today.[5]

The tightly-knit United Kingdom community, which also numbers about 8,000, has its roots in the nineteenth century when Iraqi Jews were active in a textile trading network that included Manchester.[6]

Since the American invasion into Iraq in 2003, Israel has helped most of the few remaining Iraqi Jews to emigrate. Today, less than a dozen Jews live in Iraq, though others have intermarried or converted to Islam.[7]

* * *

Many might celebrate the fact that the Iraqi Jews are no longer a community within Iraq: Zionists who believe all Jews should settle in Israel; Arab nationalists who have been infected by a virulent anti-Semitism canonized by school and media; and even many of the children of the Iraqi Jewish Diaspora who revel in the freedom, opportunity, and absence of fear offered by the societies to which they have moved. But there is more to this story than the escape of a persecuted people from the hands of their persecutors.

First there is the story of what might have been. Let us recall the words of Dhiaa Kashi, a Shiite: "If the Jews had been allowed to stay in their positions of power, as the elite of society, they would have managed the country far better than it was indeed managed. They would have been a moderating influence on society. Secondly and conversely, if the conditions had been right for them to stay in the country in the first place, that would have meant that we wouldn't have had to experience this extreme brand of Arab nationalism." In this reading, Jews served primarily as the canary in the coal mine. Once arbitrary abuse over Jews became acceptable and commonplace, mass murder of Shiites and Kurds became imaginable. This reading also suggests that the traditional Jewish qualities of education and imagination might have contributed to a better Iraq. After all, it is only logical that when an important community that had been entrenched in a land for hundreds of generations suddenly disappears, the fabric of that society loses in richness and beauty.

Looking ahead, we see the possibility that this community may still constitute part of a bridge for peace. As Eli Amir says: "A major part of Israel's problem is that we—its government and citizenry—don't speak to our Arab neighbors... We could be using our many Arabic speakers who also understand Arab culture in this country to explain ourselves to the Arab world, but we don't."

Thus even though the Jews of Iraq and other Arab lands have mostly left their home countries, they could still, perhaps, play a critical role: to help reconcile Arabs and Israelis in a conflict that an overwhelming majority of all Middle East peoples want to resolve peacefully. Their story of expulsion is relevant to the plight and demands of Palestinian refugees. One reason is that the Jews from Arab lands and the Palestinian refugees from what is now Israel constituted a roughly numerically equal population exchange. Second, and even more important, Jews from Arab lands appreciate many aspects of Arab culture and know that mutual respect and even friendship between the two peoples were once the norm.

Notes

1. Figures from the Babylonian Jewry Heritage Center.
2. Ibid.
3. Shohet.
4. Interview with Lisette Ades.
5. Babylonian Jewry Heritage Center.
6. Ibid.
7. Ibid.

Bibliography

Adler, Marcus N. *The Itinerary of Benjamin of Tudela.* London: Philipp Feldheim, 1907.
Almog, Orna. *Britain, Israel, and the United States, 1955–1958: Beyond Suez.* London and Portland, OR: Frank Cass, 2002.
Al-Sheakh-Ali, Faiq. *Mudhakkirat Warithat al-'Urush* (Memoirs of the Thrones' Heir). London: Dar al-Hikma, 2002.
American Jewish Committee. *American Jewish Yearbook vol. 57.* New York: Jewish Publication Society of America, 1956.
———. *American Jewish Yearbook vol. 69.* New York: Jewish Publication Society of America, 1968.
Amir, Eli. *Farewell, Baghdad.* Tel Aviv: Am Oved Publishers, 1992.
———. *Scapegoat.* Tel Aviv: Am Oved Publishers, 1983.
———. *Yasmin.* Tel Aviv: Am Oved Publishers, 2005.
Azrieli, David. *One Step Ahead.* Israel: Yad Vashem Publishers, 2001.
Babylonian Jewry Heritage Center, Or Yehuda, Israel.
Basri, Carole. "The Jewish Refugees from Arab Countries: An Examination of Legal Rights—A Case Study of the Human Rights Violations of Iraqi Jews." *Fordham Law Journal*, Vol. 26. No. 3, March 2003, pp. 656–720.
Basri, Meir. *Eminent Jewish Men of Modern Iraq, Vols. I & II,* edited by Shmuel Moreh and Nissim Kazzaz. Jerusalem: Association of Jewish Academics from Iraq, 1993.
Bat Ye'or. *The Dhimmi, Jews and Christians under Islam.* New Jersey and London: Associated University Presses, 1985.
———. *Islam and Dhimmitude, Where Civilizations Collide.* New Jersey and London: Associated University Presses, 2002.
Bekhor, Georji. *Fascinating Life and Sensational Death: The Conditions in Iraq Before and After the Six Day War.* Israel: Peli Printing Works, 1990.
Ben-Jacob, Abraham. *Babylonian Jewry in Diaspora.* Jerusalem: Rubin Mass, 1985.
———. *A History of the Jews in Iraq, From the end of the Gaonic Period (1038 CE) to the Present Time.* Jerusalem: Ben-Zvi Institute, 1965.
———. *The Jewish Annual Cycle in Babylon.* Jerusalem: Bne Issakhar Institute, 1993.
Ben Porat, Mordechai. *To Baghdad and Back: The Miraculous 2,000 Year Homecoming of the Iraqi Jews.* (English edition). Jerusalem: Gefen, 1998.
Benjamin of Tudela. *Rihlat Ibn Yona al-Andalusi [Travels].* Translated into Arabic by Ezra Hadda. Beirut: Dar Ibn Zaydun, 1996.
Berg, Nancy. *More and More Equal: The Literary Works of Sami Michael.* Oxford: Lexington Books, 2005.

Cernea, Ruth Fredman. *Almost Englishmen, Baghdadi Jews in British Burma.* London: Lexington Books, 2007.
Cohen, Hayyim, J. "The Anti-Jewish Farhud in Baghdad, 1941." *Middle Eastern Studies,* Vol. 3, No. 1, October, 1966, pp. 2–17.
Cohen, Yayyim J., and Yehuda, Zvi. *Asian and African Jews in the Middle East 1800–1971.* Jerusalem: Ben-Zvi Institute, 1976.
Dabby-Joury, Lilian. "The Writer and Poet Ya'acov Lev (Balbul)." (In English). In *Ya'acov Lev (Balbul), The First Ember & A Mind's Plight, Selected Short Stories and Sonnets in Arabic and Hebrew,* edited by Shmuel Moreh. Jerusalem: Association of Jewish Academics from Iraq, 2006.
Dangoor, Naim. *The Scribe:* www.dangoor.com
Darwish, Salman. *All Quiet in the Surgery.* Revised and annotated by Nissim Kazzaz. Jerusalem: Association of Jewish Academics from Iraq, 1981.
Elias, Flower, and Cooper, Judith Elias. *The Jews of Calcutta, the Autobiography of a Community 1798–1972.* Calcutta: Jewish Association of Calcutta, 1974.
Eppel, Michael. *The Middle East in Our Times, Book 2. Iraq—Monarchy, Republic, Tyranny.* Ra'anana: Open University of Israel, 2005.
Gilbert, Martin. *Israel: A History.* New York: William Morrow and Company, 1998.
———. *Jews from Arab Countries: Their History in Maps.* London: Furnival Press, 1975.
Goitein, S.D. *Jews and Arabs: Their Contacts through the Ages.* New York: Schocken Books, 1955.
Haim Nahman Bialik: http://www.jafi.org.il/education/100/PEOPLE/BIOS/bialik.html
Hillel, Shlomo. *Operation Babylon: The Story of the Rescue of the Jews of Iraq.* New York: Doubleday, 1987.
Jewish Agency Web site. Shaul Tchernichowky: http://www.jafi.org.il/education/100/people/bios/shaul.html
Kazzaz, Nissim. *The End of a Diaspora: The Jews in Iraq during the Twentieth Century.* Jerusalem: Ben-Zvi Institute, 1991.
Kadoorie, E. "The Break between Muslims and Jews in Iraq," In *Jews among Arabs,* edited by M.R. Cohen and A.L. Udovitch. Princeton: Darwin Press, 1989, pp. 21–63.
Kojaman, Yehezkel. *The Maqam Tradition of Iraq.* London: Author, 2001.
Kranzler, David. *Japanese, Nazis & Jews, the Jewish Refugee Community of Shanghai, 1938–1945.* New York: Yeshiva University Press, 1976.
Longrigg, Stephen H. *Iraq 1900 to 1950: A Political, Social, and Economic History.* London: Oxford University Press, 1953.
Louis, William Roger. *The British Empire in the Middle East, 1941–1951: Arab Nationalism, the United States, and Postwar Imperialism.* Oxford: Clarendon Press, 1984.
Meir, Esther. *Zionism and the Jews in Iraq, 1941–1950.* Tel Aviv: Am Oved Publishers, 1993
Meir, Golda. *My Life.* New York: Putnam, 1975.
Meir, Yosef. *The Silent Wireless Connection in an Arab Land.* Tel Aviv: Shlomo Levi, 2005.
———. *Socio-Cultural Development of Iraqi Jews since 1830.* Tel Aviv: Naharayim, 1989.
Michael, Sami. *Equal and More Equal.* Israel: Bustan, 1974.
———. *Handful of Fog.* Tel Aviv: Am Oved Publishers, 1979.
———. *A Storm among the Palms.* Tel Aviv: Am Oved Publishers, 1975.
———. *Tin Shacks and Dreams.* Tel Aviv: Am Oved Publishers, 1979.
———. *Victoria.* Tel Aviv: Am Oved Publishers, 1993.

———. *Water Kissing Water.* Tel Aviv: Am Oved Publishers, 2001.
Moreh, Shmuel. *Arabic Works by Jewish Writers.* Jerusalem: Ben-Zvi Institute, 1973.
———. "The Farhud in the Literary Works of Jews from Iraq." In *Misgav Yerushalayim Studies in Jewish Literature.* Jerusalem: Misgav Yerushalayim, 1987.
———. "Obituary to Meir Basri." *The Scribe,* No. 78, January, 2006: www.dangoor.com/issue78/articles/78026.htm
———. "The Role of the Palestinians in Incitement to the Farhud Massacre in Iraq and the Attitude of the Arab Intellectuals to the Farhud." In *Zion and Zionism.* Jerusalem: Misgav Yerushalayim, 2002, pp. 419–441.
———. "The Writer and Poet Ya'acov Lev (Balbul)." (In Hebrew and Arabic). *Ya'acov Lev (Balbul), The First Ember & A Mind's Plight, Selected Short Stories and Sonnets in Arabic and Hebrew,* edited by Shmuel Moreh. Jerusalem: Association of Jewish Academics from Iraq, 2006.
Moreh, Shmuel, and Yehuda, Zvi. *Hatred of Jews and the Farhud in Iraq.* Or-Yehuda: Babylonian Jewry Heritage Center, 1992.
Raphael, Chaim. *The Road from Babylon: The Story of Sephardi and Oriental Jews.* London: Weidenfeld and Nicolson, 1985.
Rejwan, Nissim. *The Jews of Iraq: 3,000 Years of History and Culture.* London: Weidenfeld and Nicolson, 1985.
Roth, Cecil. *A Short History of the Jews.* London: East and West Library, 1953.
Saadoun, Haim. (Ed.) *Jewish Communities in the East in the 19th and 20th Centuries, Iraq.* Jerusalem: Ben Zvi Institute, 2002.
Sachar, Howard M. *A History of Israel: From the Rise of Zionism to Our Time,* 2nd ed. New York: Alfred A. Knopf, 2003.
Sassoon, Shaul Hakham. *A Leader and His Community: A Biography of the Late Hakham Sassoon Khedouri,* edited by Shmuel Moreh and Nissim Kazzaz. Jerusalem: Association of Jewish Academics from Iraq, 1999.
Sehayik, Shaul. *Parasha Aluma (An Unknown Episode: The History of an Encounter of Thousands of Polish Jewish Soldiers with the Jews of Iraq and Iran in 1942–3).* Israel: Author, 2003.
Sennott, Charles M. *The Body and the Blood: The Middle East's Vanishing Christians and the Possibility for Peace.* New York: Perseus, 2003.
Shaul, Anwar. *The Story of my Life in Mesopotamia (Memoirs).* Jerusalem: Association of Jewish Academics from Iraq, 1980.
Shiblak, Abbas. *Iraqi Jews: A History of a Mass Exodus.* London: Saqi Books, 2005.
Shimoni, Yaacov. *Biographical Dictionary of the Middle East.* New York: Facts on File, 1991;
———. *Political Dictionary of the Arab World.* New York: Macmillan, 1987. Shohet, Maurice. "Iraqi Jews in the USA," 1999: www.iraqijews.org/usa.html
Speiser, E.A. (Ed.). *The World History of the Jewish People, Series I, Vol. I: "At the Dawn of Civilization"* Jerusalem: Rutgers University Press/Jewish History Publications, 1964.
Stillman, Norman A. *The Jews of Arab Lands: A History and Source Book.* Philadelphia: Jewish Publication Society of America, 1979.
———. *The Jews of Arab Lands in Modern Times.* Philadelphia: Jewish Publication Society of America, 2003.
Taylor and Francis Group. *Regional Surveys of the World: The Middle East and North Africa 2003,* 49th ed. London and New York: Europa Publications, 2003.

Twena, Abraham Hayim. *Jewry of Iraq, Dispersion & Liberation*, Parts 1–7. Ramla: Geoula Synagogue Committee, 1979.

Zilkha, Ezra. *From Baghdad to Boardrooms: My Family's Odyssey.* Arlington, MA: Author, 1999.

Other Sources

Ades, Lisette. *Personal Interview*, June 6, 2007. Ades is an active member of the Iraqi Jewish community in Montreal since her escape from Iraq in 1970.

Index

Note: There is a Timeline provided at the end of the book after the index.

Adas, Shafiq   7, 74, 79, 169, 195, 216; *see also timeline*, 2
Africa   41, 94
Agriculture   65, 193
Al-Gilani, Rashid Ali   6, 44
Al-Hilfi   141, 142, 144
Aleppo   26, 112
Alliance Israelite Universelle   3, 37, 60; *see also timeline*, 1
Almog, Orna   186, 213
Amir, Eli   193ff, 197, 199, 207, 213
Arab Jew   198, 199
Arab Lands   9, 215
Armstrong, Richard   92, 93
Ashkelon   25, 95
Assyrian Christians   81, 88, 89, 139
Australia   24, 180, 209
Azar, Raya   80
Azrieli, David   108, 123

Ba'ath   142, 143, 152, 199
Babylonian Talmud   xi, xiii, 2
Balbul, Ya'acov Lev   214, 215
Balfour Declaration   66, 139
Bank Zilkha   25, 57
Barnett, Ronnie   91, 92, 120
Bashi, Louise   27, 33
Basri, Carole   10, 185
Bat Ye'or   9, 213
Begin, Menachem   75, 121
Ben Gurion, David   92, 123
Ben Ish Hai   147

Ben Porat, Mordechai   7, 8, 14, 79, 97, 99, 100, 110ff, 121, 122, 123, 145, 151, 185, 213
Berg, Nancy   75, 213
Bialik, Haim Nahman   187, 214

Calcutta   3, 214
Caliphate   2, 5
Carmil, Moshe   87, 92
Chachak, Naji   150, 171, 174
Chalghy Baghdad   20, 51
China   129, 163
Communists   2, 13, 47, 48, 63, 67, 68, 70, 72, 90, 113, 140, 175, 191; Ashkenazi-dominated Communist Party   1, 63; Communism   1, 14, 46, 48, 66, 67, 68, 69, 70, 71; Communism-changing Iraq   1, 14; Communist Jews   1, 90; Communist Party   1, 15, 42, 46, 47, 48, 49, 63, 65, 67, 68, 69, 70, 72, 200; Egyptian Communist   1, 191; Iraqi Communist   1, 65, 70; Iraqi Communist Party   1, 41, 69; Iraqi Jewish Communists   1, 69, 72; Iraqi-born Marduch-a Communist   1, 72; Jewish Communists   1, 6, 14, 41, 47, 68, 70; *see also timeline*, 2
Cyprus   93, 96

Dabby-Joury, Lilian   10, 214
Dallall, Oddil   138ff, 145
Dangoor, Eliahou   171
Dangoor, Hakham Ezra   3
Dangoor, Naim   9, 214

Dangour, Ronit   128, 151ff, 158
Daniel, Ezra Menachem   181, 186
Dayan, Moshe   107, 123, 165
Depression   29, 36, 63
Dhimmitude   9, 213
Diaspora   46, 121, 205, 213

El Al   93, 97
El-Kevity, Shlomo   14ff
El-Kuwaity, Daoud   15, 16, 17, 20, 21, 22, 25
El-Kuwaity, Salah   14, 15, 16, 17, 20, 21, 22, 24, 25
El-Suweidi, Tawfiq   91, 115
Elias, Meir   4, 40, 127
Equal and More Equal   72, 73
Eshkol, Levi   92, 122

Faisal I   4, 5, 81; *see also* King Faisal I
Far East   6, 27, 80, 209
Farewell Baghdad   193, 195, 197
Farhoud   ix, xiii, 6, 7, 9, 10, 14, 34, 39, 41, 45, 66, 79, 80, 82, 102, 103, 111, 112, 138, 148, 162, 164, 176, 193, 195; *see also timeline*, 2
Fattal, Salim   14, 41ff, 49

Galbak Sachar Jalmud   16, 17, 24
Germans   13, 67, 88
Gilbert, Martin   10, 214
Glasberg, Abbe   88, 89
Gulf War   73, 205

Haganah   86, 122
Hakham Sasson Khedouri   3, 173, 177, 186
Hakim, Linda Masri   158ff
Halahmy, Oded   49ff, 57
Halifa, Salim   103, 104
Handful of Frog   64
Hanging Gardens of Baghdad   96, 123
Hebrew University   121, 191
Herdoon, Saeed   128ff, 134, 138, 185
Herut   70, 75
Herzliya Gymnasium   81, 82
Hillel, Shlomo   80ff, 94
Hitler   67, 202

Holocaust   ix, 69, 82, 83, 87, 88, 91, 163, 167, 191
Horesh, Charles   130, 135
Hungary   71, 130
Hussein, Saddam   xiv, 8, 56, 73, 128, 146, 149, 151, 154, 171, 178; *see also timeline*, 3

Interior Ministry   21, 166
Iny, Frank   179, 187
Iranian Jews   91, 122, 123
Iraq-Iran War   201, 204
Israel Prize   73, 122
Israel Radio   49, 115
Israeli-Iraqi Friendship Committee   199, 205
Italy   86, 87, 149

Jaffa   50, 55
Japan   31, 63, 80, 81, 129, 141, 214
Jerusalem   xiii; *see also timeline*, 2, 3
Jerusalem Ben-Zvi Institute   213, 214, 215

Kaddish   43, 144
Kadoorie, Eli   3, 4, 74
Kashi, Dhiaa Kasim   192, 199ff, 206, 210
Kazzaz, Nissim   213, 214, 215
Khalastchi   193, 196, 197
Khedouri Aboudi Zilkha   25, 33, 57, 61, 63
Khedouri, Sasson   113, 152, 161; *see also timeline*, 2
Kibbutz Genossar   101, 103, 110
King Faisal I   4, 5, 18, 61, 81, 162; *see also timeline*, 1
Kirkuk   4, 114, 193
Kojaman, Yehezkel   23, 73, 214
Kol Yisrael   140, 141
Koran   36, 47
Kurds   137, 157, 175
Kuwaity Brothers   14, 18, *see also* el-Kuwaity, Salah; Daoud
Kvutzat Kinneret   101, 103

Liberation Square   130, 131, 149, 203
Lod Airport   54, 86, 93

Mapai   70, 75
Marcus, Ilana   94ff
Marseilles   32, 88, 90
Masouda Shemtob Synagogue   118, 119
Mecca   2, 4, 93
Meir, Golda   94, 165
Menachem Daniel Primary School   169, 185
Mesopitamia   2, 26
Michael, Sami   63ff
Michaelberg   85, 86
Mizrachi Jews   70, 71, 94, 121, 198
Moreh, Shmuel   1ff, 213, 214, 215
Mossad   116, 122
Muhabarat   68, 200
Munich Conference   31, 32
Murad, Salima Pasha   16, 17, 22, 24, 74, 112
Muslim Shiite   6, 134

Nairn Brothers   27, 28
Nazi (Germany)   1, 13, 31, 64
Negev   54, 95

Obadiah, Abdullah   164, 165, 176ff, 185
Obadiah, Richard   176ff
Operation Babylon   94, 214
Operation Michaelberg   80, 84
Or Yehuda   57, 121
Ottoman Bank   26, 29
Ottoman/s   2, 4, 5, 27, 160

Pashas   162, 163
Persians   70, 157

Qassem, Abd Al-Karim/Qassem, Abdul Al-Karim   7, 8, 9, 121, 129, 135, 141, 146, 148, 163, 170, 185, 186, 203

Rabin, Yitzhak   94, 192
Rashid Street   138, 140
Refuge   72
Rofeh, Malka   105, 110
Rome   83, 86, 93
Rosh Hashana   56, 160
Russia (or Russian)   48, 70, 71, 88, 191

Sachar, Howard   122, 123, 215
Samra, Da'ud   159, 186
Sasson, Zuhair   146ff, 151
Sassoon, Salim   13, 33ff, 36
Sassoon, Shaul   148, 151
Saudi Arabia   15, 116
Scapegoat   196, 197, 207, 213
Schunat Hatikva   23, 55
The Scribe   214, 215
Second Temple   2, 94
Sehayek, Shlomo   79, 100ff, 110, 123
Sephardi/Sephardim   10, 71, 72, 215
Sereni, Enzo   105, 106, 107, 108
Shalom, Saleh Shalom   74, 119; see also *timeline*, 2
Shasha, Alfred   13, 57ff, 63
Shasha, Hanina   13, 33, 57ff
Shaul, Anwar   5, 6, 66
Shemesh, Shaul   108, 109
Shemtob, Yehezkel   91, 115, 146
Shiblak, Amos   10, 215
Shiite Muslim   69, 111, 184, 192, 199
Six Day War   ix, 8, 49, 127, 129, 134, 141, 146, 163, 164, 168, 181, 186, 192, 194, 197, 213; see also *timeline*, 3
Stillman, Norman   9, 215
Storm among the Palms   65
Sukkot   23, 53, 64
Sunnis   21, 59, 200

Ta'awan   37, 60
Talmud   123, 147; see also *Babylonian Talmud*
Tiberias   43, 84, 110
Tigris River   50, 65, 159
Tin Shacks   72, 214
Trans-Jordan   82, 106, 112
A Trumpet in the Wadi   72–73
Tudela, Benjamin of   9, 213

Umm Kulthum   17, 18
United Kingdom (UK)   5, 68, 167, 185, 207, 209, 210, 213; see also *timeline*, 2

Victoria   64, 73

Yasmin   194, 197
Yavniel   84, 85, 86

Yemen 93, 123
Yiddish 88, 122
Yishuv 64
Yom Kippur 53, 56, 138
Yom Kippur War 174, 186
Young Turks 3, 4
Youth Aliyah 82, 122, 196, 197, 198

Zelouf, Aida 128, 168ff, 187, 174
Zilkha, Ezra 25ff
Zilkha, Joseph 131, 134
Zionist xiii, 5, 6, 7–9, 46–47, 66–74, 79–83, 100, 107, 110, 119, 121, 148, 154, 156, 165, 174, 176, 186, 190, 192, 193, 194, 195, 196, 210

Timeline

1864 Alliance Israelite Universelle opens first modern elementary school in Baghdad.
1893 Alliance Israelite Universelle for girls opens in Baghdad.
1911 Laura Kadoorie School for Girls, part of the Alliance network, is built by Sir Elly Kadoorie and named for his wife.
1917 Baghdad, until then occupied by the Ottoman Empire, falls to British forces during World War I. The British government promulgates the Balfour Declaration, stating its support of a national Jewish homeland in Palestine.
1919 The League of Nations is created and Iraq is placed under the British mandate. The same year, a broadly supported revolt against the British breaks out in Iraq. The British grant Iraq authoritative power to form a self-governing kingdom under British advisory administration.
1920 The British High Commissioner sets up a temporary government consisting of eight members, one of whom is a Jew, Sassoon Heskel. He is entrusted with the finance portfolio and setting up the finance ministry from scratch. He serves as minister of finance for the next 13 years, and is responsible for insisting on payment in gold to Iraq by the British Petroleum Company for oil revenues, resulting in considerable additional revenue for Iraq.
1921 Faisal Bin Hussein (1883–1933) is enthroned in Baghdad as King Faisal I. Prime ministers during the kingdom are Jafar Pasha Al-Askari (1887–1936) and Nuri el-Said (1888–1958).
1925 First parliament opens. The Jews of Baghdad, Basra and Mosul get five out of the 33 seats.
1930 The Anglo-Iraqi Treaty sets out terms of Iraq's expected independence, giving the United Kingdom a host of commercial and military rights including rights to Iraqi oil, which was discovered in 1927, and free movement of British troops throughout Iraq.
1932 Iraq is admitted as member of the League of Nations. Also, German Ambassador Dr. Fritz Grobba arrives in Iraq and begins to disseminate Nazi propaganda.
1933 Hitler comes to power in Germany. King Faisal I dies and is succeeded by his far less tolerant son, Ghazi (1912–1939).
1936 Iraqi Broadcasting Authority Orchestra is established by Salah and Daoud el-Kuwaity at the request of King Ghazi. Entire orchestra is Jewish with the exception of one musician.

During the Arab revolt in Palestine, Nazi propaganda and anti-Semitism intensifies, with a bomb thrown into a crowded synagogue on Yom Kippur and three Jews assassinated in the streets. Seven additional murders and six more bombings of Jewish sites occur from 1936 through 1939, despite a condemnation of Zionism issued in 1938 by 33 Iraqi Jewish leaders to the League of Nations.

1937　The Palestinian leader and Mufti of Jerusalem, Hajj Amin al-Husseini (1895–1974), is expelled from Palestine by the British and settles in Iraq, where, together with other Palestinian leaders and German diplomats, he begins to promote anti-Jewish sentiment in Iraq.

1939　King Ghazi dies in a car accident, leaving his four-year-old son, Faisal II. Ghazi's brother, Abd Al-Ilah (1913–1958), is set up as regent of Iraq.

1941　Pro-Nazi Rashid Ali al-Gailani forms cabinet following a military coup on April 1. State of war begins with Britain on May 1. After British victory, during power vacuum on June 1–2, the Farhoud occurs, killing more than 170 Jews, wounding many more, and involving widespread looting.

1948　The State of Israel is established on May 14. The next day, Iraqi troops join the Arab War against the new state, starting the Israeli War of Independence. Palestinian refugees flood into Iraq. Martial law is imposed in Iraq. Shafiq Adas, chief agent for the Ford Motor Company in Iraq and the wealthiest man in Iraq (and Jewish), is sentenced to death and hanged publicly outside his home in Basra on September 27. Government issues edicts removing Jews from many aspects of public life.

1949　One hundred Jews are tried for alleged connections to Zionism, many of whom receive prison terms; persecution continues. Hundreds of Jewish Communists are also arrested. Chief Rabbi Sasson Khedouri resigns as community head and is replaced by Yeheskel Shemtob. (Khedouri takes over again following the mass exodus in 1952.) The Frank Iny School is built in Baghdad and eventually becomes the last Jewish school in Iraq.

1950　Law permitting Jews to revoke their Iraqi nationality and leave Iraq permanently is passed on March 1. In what became known as Operation Ezra and Nehemiah, roughly 124,000 of the 137,000 Iraqi Jews leave for Israel on more than 900 flights. Over the next two years, five bombs explode in Baghdad, mostly at Jewish sites.

1951　Iraqi government passes a law on March 10 stripping those Jews who revoked their citizenship of their property.

1952　Yosef Basri and Shalom Saleh Shalom, both Jews, are hanged after the government declares them guilty of involvement in the Baghdad bombings of 1950–1951.

1953　Faisal II turns 18 and is enthroned as King of Iraq; Abd al-Ilah becomes Crown Prince.

1956　Following Egypt's decision in July to nationalize the Suez Canal and to refuse the passage of Israeli shipping, Britain, France, and Israel attack Egypt on October 29 in what becomes known as the Suez Crisis.

1958　Abd al-Kareem Qassem (1914–1963), a Communist considered friendly to the Jews, becomes president of Iraq in a coup, and leads Iraq for the next five years. All regulations against minorities are eliminated during his reign.

1963　The Ba'ath Party under General Abd al Sallam Aref (1921–1966) stages a coup, killing Qassem. Anti-Jewish restrictions begin to resurface. Multiple leaders take the reigns over the next five years.

1967　Following a blockade of the straits of Tiran (Israel's sea route to Asia) by Egypt and Egypt's calls for united Arab action against Israel, Israel launches a preemptive attack on Egypt's air force on June 5, fearing an invasion by Egypt. Egypt, Jordan, and Syria attack Israel, and Iraq, Saudi Arabia, Kuwait, and Algeria contribute troops to the ensuing Six Day War. By its end, on June 10, Israel has captured the Sinai Peninsula, the Golan Heights, eastern Jerusalem, and the West Bank. Anti-Jewish persecution in Iraq begins in earnest.

1968 Hasan al-Bakr (1914–1982) takes over as president, backed by his nephew Saddam Hussein (1937–2006). Anti-Jewish legislation is formally enacted on March 3, forbidding Jews to sell or lease real estate or other properties, work in any trades, and travel more than three-fourth's mile from their homes. Their telephone lines are cut, savings accounts blocked, and business licenses revoked.

1969 Following public trials in which they are accused of spying for Israel, nine Jews are hanged on January 27. Dozens of Jews are thrown in jail on similar charges during the year, tortured, and in some cases hanged or otherwise assassinated by the government. Over the next three years, most of the remaining 2,500 Jews flee the country, either with passports or illegally via Iran.

2003 Coalition forces, led by the United States, invade Iraq, deposing Saddam Hussein and his Ba'athists. Israel airlifts several dozen remaining Jews out of Iraq.

2006 After a lengthy trial surrounding his human rights abuses over more than three decades, Saddam is hanged by the new Iraqi government. His treatment of Jews is never raised in the trial.

SPRINGER NATURE

GPSR Compliance

The European Union's (EU) General Product Safety Regulation (GPSR) is a set of rules that requires consumer products to be safe and our obligations to ensure this.

If you have any concerns about our products, you can contact us on ProductSafety@springernature.com

In case Publisher is established outside the EU, the EU authorized representative is:

Springer Nature Customer Service Center GmbH
Europaplatz 3
69115 Heidelberg, Germany

The manufacturer's authorised representative in the EU is Springer Nature Customer Service Centre GmbH, Europaplatz 3, 69115 Heidelberg, Germany. If you have any concerns regarding our products, please contact ProductSafety@springernature.com

Printed and bound by CPI Group (UK) Ltd, Croydon, CR0 4YY
23/03/2026
02076673-0019